How grateful I am to have read Ja[...]
Preaching with Word Pictures! I hav[...]
in my library, but only a few of th[...]
fresh and interesting. Hughes' book[...]
number. It is a veritable course in word painting. In illustrating [...]
material from the sermons of Thomas Watson, the author demonstrates
that he, himself, is more than capable of writing powerful picturesque
prose of the sort that he highlights in Watson. The reader cannot but
learn much from Hughes own writing, as well as from Watson and
the Scriptures (in which Hughes convincingly shows how biblical
writers used such word pictures). Any preacher who does not beg,
borrow or do everything short of stealing to obtain this book, should
be horsewhipped!

Jay E. Adams, Enoree, SC

In his study of word pictures, Jack Hughes sets up his easel at the
head of a long line of painters: our author is indebted to Adams, Adams
to Spurgeon, Spurgeon to the Puritans and the Puritans to Scripture—
in effect, all to Scripture. This succession of preachers with their
colorful sermon palettes stands as a reminder that, throughout history,
our Lord has equipped His illustration artists sufficiently to help His
people see the Truth in brilliant colors. But with a slight change of
word picture, God's messengers must not distort their message from
the Cosmic King with rhetoric that sounds like advertising ploys,
sensationalist journalism, or other tactics that obscure the truth. In
short, Jack reminds us that our content must come from God's Word
and our packaging must not cheapen or distort it. Sounds simple and
refreshing!

Dave Deuel
Pastor of Ministry Training,
Grace Bible Church, Brandon, Florida

Dr. Jack Hughes engagingly presents the colorful words of Thomas
Watson in the context of Biblical exposition. We twenty-first century
preachers are indebted to the author for this grand study of a notable,
historic herald. Thomas Watson compelled people to listen to him,
whether he was preaching or writing, by the vivid word pictures that
he painted, both at his desk and in the pulpit. This rich study should
be a treasure in every preacher's library. I highly recommend it.

Dr. Richard Mayhue
Sr. Vice President and Dean
The Master's Seminary

My passion is expository preaching, and that is the chief reason I am an admirer of the Puritans. The finest examples of Puritan exposition I know may be found in the sermons of Thomas Watson. Unbelievably rich, Watson's messages still communicate today with a power and clarity that is simply breathtaking. Jack Hughes has done a tremendous job of analyzing Watson's expository style, especially his use of potent word pictures. This book will be a valuable tool for any preacher seeking to improve his skill in handling and communicating the Word of God.

John MacArthur, Jr.
The Master's Seminary

The ministry of Thomas Watson has obviously inspired Jack Hughes and as a result he has provided a real eye opener for the contemporary church. Hughes shows us that biblical preaching must be illustrated with colourful word pictures. It is refreshing to read a book which takes the methodology of the Puritan era and applies it so clearly to contemporary society. The book also takes the veil from our eyes when it shows us how much of the Bible is written in word pictures and how this is clearly seen in the teaching of Jesus and all the other biblical communicators.

In a society dominated by multi-media presentations in full Technicolor Jack Hughes tells us that there is no hiding place for the lazy preacher who is contented to preach in monochrome. If we are to communicate effectively to our generation we must spare no effort in communicating ideas with word pictures.

David Meredith,
Smithton Free Church of Scotland,
Inverness

In our image-saturated society, effective preachers who fail to reach the imagination of their listeners will never touch their hearts and move their wills. With the sermons of Thomas Watson as Exhibit A, the author shows you how to use a sanctified imagination to bring meaningful "pictures" out of the text and into your sermons, without sacrificing biblical content or homiletical structure. The beginning preacher and the seasoned homiletician will both benefit from this unusual book.

Warren W. Wiersbe
Author and Conference Speaker

EXPOSITORY PREACHING WITH WORD PICTURES

illustrated from the sermons of

Thomas Watson

Jack Hughes

Christian Focus

Christian Focus Publications publishes biblically-accurate books for adults and children. The books in the adult range are published in three imprints.

Christian Heritage contains classic writings from the past.

Christian Focus contains popular works including biographies, commentaries, doctrine, and Christian living.

Mentor focuses on books written at a level suitable for Bible College and seminary students, pastors, and others; the imprint includes commentaries, doctrinal studies, examination of current issues, and church history.

For a free catalogue of all our titles, please write to
Christian Focus Publications,
Geanies House, Fearn,
Ross-shire, IV20 1TW, Great Britain

For details of our titles visit us on our web site
http://www.christianfocus.com

ISBN 1 85792 658 7

Published in 2001
by
Christian Focus Publications
Geanies House, Fearn, Ross-shire
IV20 1TW, Great Britain

Cover design by Alister Macinnes

Contents

To Grace Bible Church of Boise, Idaho
for holding still in the pews while I experimented on you
and
to faithful men of God who desire to preach 'every word
that proceeds out of the mouth of God'.

INTRODUCTION

The prophet Amos lived in a time when the people of Israel were committing great social injustices. God raised up Amos to confront the sin of his wayward people. In Amos 7-9, God promised five future judgments which would come as a result of his people's sin and rebellion. The worst judgment was a famine. Not a normal famine but a spiritual one. Amos writes:

> 'Behold, days are coming,' declares the LORD God, 'When I will send a famine on the land, not a famine for bread or a thirst for water, but rather for hearing the words of the Lord. People will stagger from sea to sea And from the north even to the east; They will go to and fro to seek the word of the LORD, But they will not find it' (8:11-12).

We are living in a day and age when many are staggering from sea to sea, trying to find spiritual nourishment from the Word of God, but cannot find it. While many symptoms of this famine could be discussed, the root of the problem is to be laid at the feet of those called to preach the Word (1 Tim. 4:1-2). While there is a lot of preaching going on, biblical exposition is at a premium. Moses first said it, and Jesus affirmed it to Satan, 'It is written, "Man shall not live on bread alone, but on every word that proceeds out of the mouth of God" ' (Deut. 8:10; Matt. 4:4). Expository preaching is the only kind of preaching that feeds people *every word* that proceeds out of the mouth of God. In light of the present crisis, it is tempting to be like Adam and Eve and blame someone else. 'It is the fault of those who are not doing expository preaching,' we might be tempted to say. I would agree that many churches are moving away from biblical exposition. The sermon hour is being absorbed by music, drama, and other forms of entertainment. In addition to that, many preachers have a style of preaching which might best be described as a self-help discourse with a verse attached to the beginning of the message.

Satan knows that biblical exposition is the guardian of the church. He knows that if he can keep the whole counsel of God's Word from being preached, sin, false doctrine, and deception will increase as the quality of preaching decreases. Without the preaching of the Word men do not understand what God is like, how to be saved, how to worship in spirit and truth, or what God wants them to do or not do. It is like having a steady diet of junk food. You can live off junk food for a while, but soon it begins to cause health problems. This is what we are seeing in many churches today. Christians are malnourished, resulting in spiritual health problems. Shoddy preaching has as its consequence increased sin in the body and intolerant attitudes towards sound doctrine and personal holiness. The church's immune system is compromised, spiritual discernment decreases, and worldly philosophies and gimmicks increase. Once a church contracts worldliness it will strongly oppose those who preach and teach against sin and who call sinners to repentance and a holy lifestyle. I am amazed at how many churches will readily accept false doctrine and worldly methodologies but viciously attack sound doctrine and biblical mandates. If the preacher is faithful to stand on the truth of God's Word in one of these malnourished churches, he is labeled as divisive, unloving, and forsaking unity. Many churches today could aptly be described like the church of Sardis, *'I know your deeds, that you have a name that you are alive, but you are dead.'*

Many pastors are struggling to keep their churches from becoming like the church of Sardis. They try biblical exposition, but something doesn't seem to be working right. They faithfully preach the word, but contrary to the promise of God in Isaiah 55:11, the word of God seems to come back void. Their church doesn't grow spiritually or numerically. People don't seem to be responding. As they struggle to maintain a good attitude and fight the good fight, they see the church that doesn't do expository preaching growing by leaps and bounds. Legions of cars pack the car park of the 'seeker sensitive church' Saturday night, Sunday morning, and Wednesday night because it is meeting 'felt needs'. The choir at that church is bigger than the entire congregation of the church doing biblical exposition! The people are so excited to go to the other church – that doesn't preach the Word. They have professionally paid musicians, a huge youth group with many fun youth activities, a large drama team, and ten to fifteen minute devotionals instead of sermons. They never preach on sin, judgment, or the wrath of God. They would never perform church discipline or preach doctrine, yet, they grow and flourish like a green tree in its native soil. It is disheartening – depressing, to see people enthusiastically crowd into a church which isn't preaching the whole counsel of God's Word and calling sinners to repentance.

It can make an expositor have second thoughts. 'Maybe biblical exposition is a cultural thing. Times have changed. Maybe expository preaching is out, and we should try something new.' Snap out of it! Don't even begin to entertain such thoughts. Satan is willing to trade solid biblical preaching for numerical growth. He would be glad to fill your car park if you will dump expository preaching. Satan skips with joy when expository preaching is substituted with anything else. He knows, if he can get rid of expository preaching, he can steer the church any way he wants. Satan knows that, when faithful preaching is set aside, the church will become vulnerable to his subtle deceptions and become ineffective.

The question rises to the surface, 'Why does this happen?' Why do some biblical expositors have struggling churches which never seem to take off? Why is it they never even seem to get out of the hanger? I believe the problem is not expository preaching but method of delivery. It is a homiletics problem. In seminary I was trained to be a biblical expositor. I had some exposure to the original languages, diagrammatical analysis, hermeneutics, exegesis, etc. I was taught how not to be ashamed by 'accurately handling the Word of truth'. As I preached and taught the Word, I soon realized that the method of delivery was also very important. I needed to learn how to deliver the Word in such a way that it held people's attention, gave them understanding, and helped them remember. I needed to preach to the heart. It was then that I began my quest for insight. I began to look at well-known expositors and asked myself, 'What is it about their preaching that makes them so effective?' Many of the expositors that I like have radically different styles of communication, yet all of them are effective. People love to hear them preach the Word. Their preaching is engaging, interesting, and memorable. They are able to hold people's attention, explain the text, and make it practical. I realized that delivery, not content, was the difference. They understood how to preach to the heart, and I did not. I am still on my quest to be a better preacher but have learned some very helpful things.

Homiletics, which addresses issues related to sermon delivery, is the science and art of preaching. It is the preacher's job not merely to preach the word, but to preach it in such a way that people hear, understand and remember. People need to *hear* the message, or it will not profit them. People must also be able to *understand* the message, or it will not profit them. People also must *remember* the message, or it will not profit them. It is to these three issues that this book is written. *How does the expository preacher gain the attention of his people, give them understanding and help them remember what he preaches from the word?*

I began to ask questions such as, 'What kinds of preaching do I like listening to the most?' and 'What expositors have remained popular and stood the test of time?' While in seminary I purchased the book *Heaven Taken by Storm* by a Puritan preacher named Thomas Watson. Every time I read from the book it was like volunteering for open-heart surgery.

The book was so practical and convicting that I could hardly read more than a couple of pages a day. My heart could not take any more. Watson had a way of getting into my head and heart, exposing my sin and hypocrisy. I began to read other Puritans but none of them affected me like Thomas Watson. I loved the way he presented the truths of God's word. His picturesque style made God's truth clear and tangible.

I enjoy giving Watson's books to people because his writings are like spiritual grenades with the pin pulled. A fellow pastor was going on a reading holiday. I dared him to see if he could read all of *Heaven Taken by Storm* during that week. When he returned a week later, he had not finished the book. A person can only handle so much spiritual surgery in a week! Another time I gave *The Godly Man's Picture* to seven friends for Christmas. Only two of them have made it through the book, and that was five years ago. Watson knew how to drive the sword of the Spirit in deep.

I thought to myself, 'Why merely read him and be convicted? Why not learn to preach like he did?' I determined in my heart to analyse Thomas Watson as I read his works. What was it about Thomas Watson that made him the great spiritual surgeon in the pulpit? Why did the dust jackets of his books describe him as the most lucid, understandable and practical of the Puritans? Before seminary I had never even heard of him, but now I was determined to find answers to my questions. I began to acquire and read all of his works.

I enrolled in the Doctorate of Ministry programme at Westminster Seminary in Escondido, California. Before I arrived I knew which doctoral project I wanted to do – a case study of Thomas Watson. I wanted to find out why he was such an effective expositor. This book is the fruit of my labors. And it is my prayer that it will be a blessing to you just as researching and writing it has already been a blessing to me.

The ministers of Christ should wait for all opportunities of soul-service, because the preaching of the Word meets so many adverse forces that hinder the progress and success of it. Never did a pilot meet with so many Euroclydons and cross winds in a voyage, as the spiritual pilots of God's Church do when they are transporting souls to heaven. Some hearers have bad memories (James 1:25). Their memories are like leaking vessels. All the precious wine of the holy doctrine that is poured in runs out immediately. Ministers cannot by study find a truth so fast as others can lose it. If the meat does not stay in the stomach it can never breed good blood. If a truth delivered does not stay in the memory, we can never be, as the apostle says, 'nourished up in the words of the faith' (I Timothy 4:6). How often does the devil, that fowl of the air, pick up the good seed that is sown! If people suffer at the hands of thieves, they tell everyone and make their complaint they have been robbed; but there is a worse thief they are not aware of! How many sermons has the devil stolen from them! How many truths have they been robbed of, which might have been so many death-bed cordials! Now if the word preached slides so fast out of the memory, ministers had need the oftener to go up the preaching mount, that at last some truth may abide and he has 'a nail fastened by the masters of assemblies' (Thomas Watson).

1

GENUINE OR COUNTERFEIT?

What is expository preaching?

A few years ago I was away on holiday and visited a church where I was told the pastor did 'expository preaching'. Fresh paint, nice dark asphalt in the car park and lack of wear and tear on the furnishings told me it was a new church building. Several friendly people greeted me and one of them gave me a bulletin.

As I sat waiting for the service to begin, I anticipated a helpful expository sermon that would be good for my soul. On the bulletin was the title of the sermon, but since the outline was missing, I flipped over one of the bulletin inserts and composed my own outline. I opened my Bible to the sermon text and did a quick diagram of the passage. I found a main verb and several phrases modifying it in the text. Immediately, it was apparent that the sermon title did not fit the subject of the text. But I have been guilty of giving such strange titles to my sermons that not even Sherlock Holmes could deduce their meaning.

Then the pastor delivered the message. As a communicator, he rated highly. He had some great illustrations, funny stories and taught some important biblical concepts. But he first tortured, then murdered the text. It was exegetically gruesome. The blood of misinterpretation was splattered everywhere. He took one word from one of the grammatical sub-points and brutalized it by stretching it far beyond its contextual limits. His sermon had nothing to do with the meaning of the text. In fact, it was alien to the context. As he preached, I cringed at each of his fabricated points which he foisted upon the Scriptures. Yet, as is often the case, everything he said was true. He was not promoting false doctrine. He was preaching biblical truth – but from the wrong text! One thing was clear, he was not doing 'expository preaching'.

A deep quagmire surrounds the definition of expository preaching. It has become stylish for preachers today to call themselves 'expository preachers'. After all, who would want to be 'just a Bible teacher' when you could be an 'expositor' like famous preacher so-and-so? Quite a lot of pressure exists in conservative church circles for preachers to be 'expository'.

But what does it mean to be an expository preacher? Does it mean preaching through a book by first reading a verse and then talking about whatever you want? Does it mean only preaching small portions of Scripture? Does it mean teaching verse by verse all the time? Does it mean never doing a topical sermon, a thematic sermon, or preaching a large section of narrative? Since this is a book on expository preaching, it is important to ascertain what expository preaching is before we develop the specific topic at hand.

Modern day expositors have defined expository preaching for us. Dr. Stephen Olford states:

> A sermon is the proclamation of the Word of God only if the text of the Word is accurately expounded and preached. So, in the strictest sense of the term, authentic preaching is expository preaching.[1]

Sidney Greidanus, when defining expository preaching, quotes Merrill Unger:

> Expository preaching, as its name implies, is to expose, to lay open, the meaning of the preaching text in its contexts. Merrill Unger has provided a fine description of expository preaching: handling the text 'in such a way that its real and essential

meaning as it existed in the mind of the particular Biblical writer
and as it exists in the light of the over-all context of Scripture is
made plain and applied to the present-day needs of the hearers'.[2]

Haddon Robinson has defined expository preaching in this
way:

> Expository preaching is the communication of a biblical
> concept, derived from and transmitted through a historical,
> grammatical, and literary study of a passage in its context,
> which the Holy Spirit first applies to the personality and
> experience of the preacher, then through him to his hearers.[3]

John MacArthur, in discussing the issue of inerrancy and
expository preaching, explains:

> The only logical response to inerrant Scripture, then, is to
> preach it expositionally. By expositionally, I mean preaching in
> such a way that the meaning of the Bible passage is presented
> entirely and exactly as it was intended by God. Expository
> preaching is the proclamation of the truth of God as mediated
> through the preacher.[4]

John R. W. Stott defines expository preaching saying:

> It is my contention that all true Christian preaching is expository
> preaching. Of course if by an 'expository' sermon is meant a
> verse-by-verse explanation of a lengthy passage of Scripture,
> then indeed it is only one possible way of preaching, but this
> would be a misuse of the word. Properly speaking, 'exposition'
> has a much broader meaning. It refers to the content of the
> sermon (biblical truth) rather than its style (a running
> commentary). To expound Scripture is to bring out of the text
> what is there and expose it to view. The expositor pries open
> what appears to be closed, makes plain what is obscure,
> unravels what is knotted and unfolds what is tightly packed. The
> opposite of exposition is 'imposition', which is to impose on the
> text what is not there. But the 'text' in question could be a verse,

or a sentence, or even a single word. It could equally be a paragraph, or a chapter, or a whole book. The size of the text is immaterial, so long as it is biblical. What matters is what we do with it. Whether it is long or short, our responsibility as expositors is to open it up in such a way that it speaks its message clearly, plainly, accurately, relevantly, without addition, subtraction or falsification. In expository preaching the biblical text is neither a conventional introduction to a sermon on a largely different theme, nor a convenient peg on which to hang a ragbag of miscellaneous thoughts, but a master which dictates and controls what is said.[5]

All of these definitions of expository preaching are somewhat different. Yet, if all of them were put into the smelter and alloyed, a definition with certain attributes would result. The *content* of expository preaching is the word of God. The *method* of deriving the sermon is the application of the historical, grammatical method of interpretation and exegesis. The *quality* of the sermon is accuracy to the text of God's word. The *goal* of expository preaching is to represent or expose to view or plainly reveal what God and the authors of Scripture meant by what they said, exactly and entirely. The *practical purpose* of expository preaching is to show how the text of Scripture is to be applied in the believer's life. The expository sermon must also be *personally applied* by the preacher and *delivered in the power of the Holy Spirit.* The *mode* of delivery is public preaching or proclamation. Expository preaching is 'Christian preaching', 'authentic preaching' and 'biblical preaching'.

I first learned what expository preaching was while attending The Master's Seminary in southern California.[6] Before seminary, I thought expository preaching was a 'style of sermon delivery'. I soon discovered that expository preaching is like an iceberg. The delivery of the sermon is the part of the iceberg that shows above the water, but more is hidden under the surface which is not seen in the pulpit. The unseen part is the necessary training that enables one to be an expository preacher. In order for a gifted man to become an expository preacher he must be taught or teach himself certain disciplines. Three specific disciplines come to mind. The knowledge and skill of these disciplines are the tools of the preacher's trade.

First, expository preaching is the product of sound *hermeneutics*. When I say sound hermeneutics, I mean a system of hermeneutics which is objective, not subjective, which is inductive, not deductive. Many hermeneutical principles or rules are used for interpreting the Bible. These principles are like tools in a carpenter's tool box. When a carpenter goes to work, he has a large assortment of tools. Some he uses on every job – like a tape measure, pencil and saw. These are like the principles of historical context, far context and near context which are used every time a text is studied. But some tools in the carpenter's box are only used for specialized applications, such as the draw knife, plumb bob, or router. These might be compared to specialized hermeneutical principles used when studying certain types of biblical genre like parables or prophecy. For instance, some texts don't mention any cultural customs; because of this a study of cultural customs is not applicable. So the 'tool' of cultural studies stays in the tool box until a cultural custom is encountered in another text. Without solid hermeneutical training the preacher is like a carpenter with only some of the tools needed to do carpentry. Some preachers are able and gifted preachers, but many do not have the tools to produce an expository sermon from every text they encounter.

Second, expository preaching is not only the possession of the right hermeneutical tools, it is the skilled application of those tools. This is *exegesis*, the application of hermeneutical principles. Exegesis is the process of extracting information from the text, as opposed to eisegesis, which is reading information into the text. Some carpenters are magnificent tool collectors but poor craftsmen. They have the equipment but not the gift of carpentry. They have a hard time figuring out when to use a specific tool. This is like a preacher who attends the finest seminaries in the world but is not gifted by the Holy Spirit to be a preacher. Therefore he struggles with the 'art' of expository preaching because he doesn't know what tools to use when he approaches a specific text.

> The man who has pulpit talent is able to soar once in a while; often he can run without growing weary; sometimes he can only plod along through sand or mud. But if there is in the pulpit any shivering mortal who never soars, or even runs, who must plod along like an ox hitched to the plough, he should ask himself whether or not he has found the task for which God girded him.[7]

The expository preacher must not only have the tools, he must also have the gifts and the abilities to apply the tools skillfully. The study of hermeneutics is more of an exact science but the application of hermeneutics, i.e., exegesis, is more of an art.

Thirdly and finally, the Bible expositor is an exposer of the meaning of the text he preaches. At an exhibition, different companies or people display or expose their products. The carpenter takes wood and builds furniture with it. He skillfully applies his tools until he has something to display in the front window of his carpentry shop: that is exposition. *Biblical exposition* is displaying the truths of Scripture within their various biblical, historical and literary contexts. It is to accurately display God's truth to the masses in an understandable and practical way. It is to 'show them' what God meant to say from the text of Scripture being exposed. It is not merely teaching Bible facts or proclaiming sound doctrine. A preacher who teaches sound doctrine, but does it from the wrong text, is failing to be an expository preacher. As an expository preacher preaches the word, his congregation should be able to see from the text of Scripture where he derived the truths put forth in his sermon. By example, the expository preacher teaches a congregation how to study their Bibles. Every sermon is an example of 'handling accurately the word of truth' (2 Tim. 2:15).

Many preachers who think they are expository preachers are not because they: (1) do not have the proper hermeneutical training to produce an expository sermon; (2) do not have the giftedness needed to be an expository preacher; or (3) do not expose the meaning of the text within its various contexts in an understandable way. The true expository preacher is able to show his people from the text of Scripture what God and the authors of Scripture meant, so that people understand what the biblical text means. The revival under the leadership of Ezra and Nehemiah started when 'they read from the book, from the law of God, translating to give the sense so that they understood the reading' (Neh. 8:8). Exposition fails if it does not impart the understanding of the text of Scripture.

I believe that expository preaching is biblical preaching. The reason I believe this is that preachers are *commanded* to 'preach the word' (2 Tim. 4:2). They are *commanded* to be 'approved to God' by 'handling accurately the word of truth' (2 Tim. 2:15). Any sermon which fails to communicate the word of God accurately from its biblical contexts has failed; the preacher has sinned grievously. By reading one's thoughts into the text, by preaching biblical truth but from the wrong text, by mishandling the text, by using the text for what one wants it to say, or by hammering away on the anvil of one's own pet peeve, preachers sin. It is a direct violation of the word of God.

Poor preaching teaches people faulty hermeneutics. They are looking at the text and seeing one thing, but they are hearing something else from the pulpit. This usually takes them to one of two tragic conclusions.

In the first place, it frustrates them because they conclude they are not smart enough or educated enough to get from the text of Scripture the truths they are hearing from the pulpit. They think to themselves, 'I guess you have to go to seminary and learn Hebrew and Greek to understand what the Bible says.' Instead of motivating them to study their Bibles, poor preaching makes them want to give it up all together.

A second and equally frightening outcome of failing to preach the word accurately is that it teaches by example a faulty system of hermeneutics. It leads people to conclude that they can come to a text, ignore the context, ignore the theme, ignore the grammar and syntax and make it say whatever they want. This leads to false doctrine which gives birth to carnality. We need to remember that teachers will incur a stricter judgment (Jas. 3:1). It is hard to swim with a millstone around your neck (Matt. 18:6).

This leaves the preacher with only one way of study (sound hermeneutics in exegesis), one body of truth (the Bible), and one method of delivery (expository preaching). The style of sermon delivery is not necessarily defined by expository preaching. Bible expositors have many different preaching styles. The common denominator is that they all apply sound hermeneutics and expose to view what God meant in the Scriptures. Expository preaching is not necessarily verse-by-verse exposition through a book. It does not mean that you cannot have a topical expository sermon. Expository preaching can be done in many ways, but in every way that it can be done it contains the three non-negotiable elements: sound hermeneutics manifested in exegesis, a biblical focus and exposing biblical truth from its scriptural context. Expository preaching is a verbal conveyor belt that digs gold from the Scriptures and transports the nuggets of God's word to the hearts and minds of people. How to deliver the gold most effectively is the field of homiletics.

Homiletics, like hermeneutics and exegesis, is both a science and an art. The various communication or homiletic techniques are more of a science, but the application of those techniques is an art. Examples of homiletic techniques are eye contact, gesture, voice tone, pace of speech, pause, rhetorical questions, illustration, and a host of other practices that can help make one a better communicator. Preachers must ever strive to be excellent communicators of the word of God.

Homiletics has as its goal the effective delivery of biblical truth. Because preaching is the highest profession on the face of the earth, we must practice good homiletics.

God has raised up many great Bible expositors in the course of history. These men were mighty weapons in the hands of God to deliver the 'foolishness of the message preached to save those who believe' and to 'equip the saints for the work of service' (1 Cor. 1:21; Eph. 4:12). Thomas Watson, an English Puritan, was an exceptional case in point. Of the many great preachers of his day Watson rises to the top like cream. His sermons, preserved in written form, teach us by example how we might better preach from the word. The next chapter introduces one of the greatest preachers of the seventeenth century, Thomas Watson.

St. Paul's preaching was not with enticing words of wisdom but in the demonstration of the Spirit and power (1 Cor. 2:4). Plainness is ever best in beating down sin. When a wound festers, it is fitter to lance it than to embroider it with silk or lay vermilion upon it (Thomas Watson).

2

WHO IS THOMAS WATSON?

In recent years, there has been increasing interest in the Puritans. The fluffy, spiritual junk food which fills the shelves of most Christian bookshops is leaving many Christians malnourished. People are craving the meat of the word and are finding it in the rich and nourishing writings of the Puritans. The Puritan preachers produced deeply spiritual and eminently practical works based on the solid exposition of the Scriptures. They are being used by God to motivate modern readers to pursue greater excellence in their walk with the Lord. While some Puritan writings are like those of the Apostle Paul, 'in which are some things hard to understand' (2 Pet. 3:16), many wrote with simple and profound clarity. Their works are well within the grasp of most readers, which is remarkable, considering they lived over three hundred years ago! Thomas Watson is one such individual. He is hailed as the most readable, understandable and lucid of all the Puritans.[8] His sermons, preserved in written form, are spiritual treasures rich in sound doctrine. He skilfully wielded the sword of the Spirit to excise cancerous sins from even the most pious believer's soul. All his known works have been reprinted and gladly received by those who love the spiritual depth of the Puritan Divines. It is my hope that as preachers, we will not just read and admire men like Thomas Watson, but learn from their example. Watson, like Abel, *though he is dead, still speaks* (Heb. 11:4).

Thomas Watson's early life is somewhat of an enigma. Virtually nothing is known of the date and place of his birth, his parents, or the circumstances of his conversion. One person aptly described him as a Puritan Melchizedek since he is 'without father, mother, or genealogy'.[9] The earliest information we have concerning Watson is from Kennet's 'Register and Chronicle' that lists Watson among other Puritans as educated at Emmanuel College, Cambridge.[10]

While at Emmanuel College, Watson earned a Bachelor of Arts degree in 1639 and his Masters in 1642.[11] Emmanuel College was an educational fountainhead of great Puritan ministers. It produced other notable individuals such as Thomas Brooks and Stephen Charnock. Many of them were Nonconformists who protested against the execution of Charles I and Cromwell's treatment of King Charles II.[12] While at Emmanuel College, Watson had the reputation of being a very diligent student.[13] His intellect is apparent in his writings. Watson's works expose a profound grasp of the English language, as well as a solid understanding of Hebrew, Greek and Latin. He quotes from the early church fathers as if they were the morning newspaper. His familiarity with the breadth of the scriptural canon is stunning. Cross-references from the entire biblical corpus are sprinkled throughout his sermons, revealing a deep understanding of many texts obscure to most modern day Bible students. A solid understanding of history, botany, medicine, physics, the classics, logic and various trades are revealed in his sermons. From the beginning of his ministry in London, he was recognized as a man of great learning.[14] Today he is revered as one of the great pastor-theologians of the Puritan era.[15]

Watson's ministry had a great impact. He was first called to the pastorate at St Stephen's, Walbrook, in 1646. He continued to minister there until imprisoned in 1651 by the Cromwellian Army. He was confined to the Tower, along with several other dissenters, but was released and reinstated in 1652 after he petitioned for mercy and promised submission to the government.

His ministry at St Stephen's, located in the heart of London, was profound. C. H. Spurgeon describes his ministry with these telling words:

Watson became rector of St Stephen's, Walbrook, where in the very heart of London he executed for nearly sixteen years the office of a faithful pastor with great diligence and assiduity. Happy were the citizens who regularly attended so instructive and spiritual a ministry. The Church was constantly filled, for the fame and popularity of the preacher were deservedly great. Going in and out among his flock, fired with holy zeal for their eternal welfare, his years rolled on pleasantly enough amid the growing respect of all who knew him.[16]

After Watson had ministered at St Stephen's for sixteen years, in 1662 he was ejected from his pulpit by the Act of Uniformity, along with some two thousand other ministers because their consciences would not allow them to submit wholeheartedly to standardized worship.[17] Other Acts affected the Puritans, such as the Conventicle Act, which made it illegal for more than five non-family members to meet together in one place for worship. The Five Mile Act made it illegal for Nonconformist ministers to come within five miles of a city or corporate town except when travelling. These acts were feeble attempts to silence godly men, who understood they were commissioned by God to preach the word. Watson continued to preach the gospel, believing that it was better to obey God than men.[18] Watson, along with many other ejected Puritans, began ministering to obscure groups, in obscure places, always under the threat of being fined or imprisoned.[19]

In 1672, after the Declaration of Indulgence, Watson obtained a licence to hold worship services at Crosby Hall, since the London fire of 1666 had destroyed many of the churches. Three years later, in 1675, Watson was joined by the notable theologian and Puritan pastor Stephen Charnock.[20] One can only imagine the immense spiritual blessing of having two of the great Puritan Divines shepherding the same flock! Charnock ministered side by side with Watson until 1680. Charnock died while delivering his classic series of sermons on the existence and attributes of

God. Watson continued at Crosby Hall until his health began to give way, and he retired to Barnston in Essex.

As far as we can tell from his written sermons and a few select historical accounts, Thomas Watson was a master of the pulpit. His expositions of the word are eminently practical. Frequent and lucid analogies, word pictures and striking parallelisms are found throughout his sermons. He had an exceptional but plain elocution which he used to drive the truths of the Scriptures deep into the hearts of his hearers.[21] His mastery of the Scriptures, the sciences and the English language, coupled with great Spirit-filled giftedness, made him one of the clearest communicators of the Puritan era. On the back cover of one of his recently reprinted works the publisher says of Watson:

> ... a master of a terse, vigorous style and of a beauty of expression he could speak not only to win men's understanding but also to secure a place for the truth in their memories. More than most of his generation he sought to follow the example of Christ's teaching by employing all manner of illustrative material from common life, and with simplicity and charm he spoke words not easy to forget. Two hundred years after Thomas Watson's death William Jay of Bath said that he could go to any one of his books and 'find it ever fresh, pointed and instructive.'[22]

Watson was also a man of fervent prayer. Hamilton Smith relates a telling story of Watson's ability to pray:

> Calamy, in his 'Abridgements', relates that on a certain day when Mr. Watson was in the pulpit, 'among other hearers, there came in that Reverend and learned Prelate, Bishop Richardson, who was so well pleased with his sermon, but especially with his prayer after it that he followed him home, to give him thanks; and earnestly desired a copy of his prayer. "Alas!" said Mr. Watson, "that is what I cannot give; for I do not pen my prayers; it was no studied thing, but uttered as God enabled me from the

abundance of my heart and affections, *pro re nata*." Upon which the good Bishop went away wondering that any man could pray in that manner, *ex tempore*.'[23]

Many days of meditating on God's Word and much time in prayer equipped Watson to shepherd his flock with passion and conviction. His convictions concerning prayer are sprinkled throughout his works, especially in his sermons on the Lord's Prayer which he gave as part of his exposition of the Westminster Shorter Catechism. In another of his books, *The Godly Man's Picture*, Watson writes:

> Prayer is the soul's traffic with heaven. God comes down to us by his Spirit, and we go up to him by prayer.... A godly man cannot live without prayer. A man cannot live unless he takes his breath, nor can the soul, unless it breathes forth its desires to God. As soon as the babe of grace is born, it cries; no sooner was Paul converted than 'behold, he prayed' (Acts 9:11).... A godly man is on the mount of prayer every day; he begins the day with prayer; before he opens his shop, he opens his heart to God. We burn sweet perfumes in our houses; a godly man's house is 'a house of perfume'; he airs it with the incense of prayer; he engages in no business without seeking God.[24]

Watson's health grew worse while at Barnston. He eventually died, while praying to the Saviour he had served so faithfully for many years. He was buried at the grave site of his father-in-law, John Beadle, on July 28, 1686.[25]

Though Watson is absent from the body and present with the Lord, his works are a legacy that has continued to be a blessing to those who love sound, heart-searching exposition of the Scriptures. He was a master preacher who has something to teach us about preaching if we will take time to sit at his feet. I have attempted to read everything Thomas Watson has written. I can assure you of this, if you have read any of his works, you will not be spared the sword of the Spirit. Thomas Watson *never* takes captives.

In the law, the lips of the leper were to be covered; that minister who is by office an angel, but by his life a leper, ought to have his lips covered, he deserves silencing. A good preacher but a bad liver is like a physician that has the plague; though his advise and receipts which he gives may be good, yet his plague infects the patient: so though ministers may have good words, and give good receipts in the pulpit, yet the plague of their lives infects their people. If you find Hophni and Phinehas among the sons of Levi, whose unholy carriage make the offering of God to be abhorred, you will save God a labor in ejecting them.

Zeal in a minister is as proper as fire on the altar. Some are afraid to reprove, like the swordfish which has a sword in his head but is without a heart. So they carry the sword of the Spirit about them, but have no heart to draw it out in reproof against sin. How many have sown pillows under their people (Ezek. 13:18), making them sleep so securely that they never woke till they were in hell! (Thomas Watson).

3

MODEL OR DEAD PURITAN?

Why Thomas Watson?

This work attempts to set Thomas Watson before you as 'a model' of a specific aspect of homiletics. He is not being set before you as the best of expositors or even the best example of every area of homiletics. He is set before you as one who achieved mastery in one particular area of homiletics that has been sadly neglected by many expository preachers today.

If you were in need of a car, and someone were to ask you which car you preferred above all others; if they were to purchase that car for you and give it to you as a gift; would it not be considered a waste if you never drove it? Would it not be bad stewardship to talk about its wonderful attributes but never put it to its intended use? Yet how often have we done this with great expositors of the past? Someone has taken pains to record their sermons for us, yet all we do is talk about how wonderful their preaching was and treat them like historical decorations. It is my contention that we should put them to full use. We should not merely enjoy them and learn the Bible from them, but also let them teach us how to be better preachers. That is why I am setting Thomas Watson before you. I wish to put him to full use and have him teach you about an important area of homiletics in which he was especially gifted.

In order to learn from Thomas Watson and his preaching style we must ask a fundamental question, 'What made Thomas Watson an extraordinary preacher?' One answer is that Watson was a great word artist.

What set his preaching and teaching above the average

herald of his day was his ability to communicate biblical truth
in a vivid and picturesque manner. He avoided falling into the
pit of abstraction, which many have fallen into, never to
return. The communication of abstract exegetical data, lexical
facts, or theological terms, without connecting them to
persons, places, or things, is difficult for people to follow,
understand, and remember. The dictionary defines 'abstract'
as 'to draw away from, to disassociate from any specific
instance, difficult to understand, abstruse, expressing a
quality apart from an object, having only intrinsic form with
little or no attempt at pictorial representation'.[26]

The mind has great difficulty grasping abstract theological
concepts. Unfortunately, expository preachers are often the
champions of abstract truth. In their desire to be accurate to
the text of Scripture they can be dry and transcendent. They
are trained at seminaries that use the classical, abstract, Greek
approach to education, yet they are sent out to preach to
people who learn better by seeing. Haddon Robinson has
made this observation:

> Theologians and ministers too seem to keep themselves in jobs
> by resorting to language that bewilders ordinary mortals.
> Beware of jargon. Specialized vocabulary helps professionals
> within a discipline to communicate, but it becomes jargon when
> used unnecessarily. While it takes three years to get through
> seminary, it can take ten years to get over it.[27]

Watson was not lacking higher education, but he didn't use
his erudition to bewilder people. Like most Puritans, he was
thoroughly marinated in the Scriptures. Having had a classical
education he was quite versed in the Greek classics. Yet, when
preaching, Watson was a mental artist. He preached to be
understood by the common man. Watson understood that the
common man learned by *seeing*. He communicated his
exegetical nuggets so that people could *see* God's truth with
their mind's eye. Watson used a wide assortment of readily

perceived words, phrases, and illustrations that I have chosen to call *word pictures*. Because of his extensive use of word pictures, Watson rises out of history as one of the greatest Puritan preachers.[28] His ability to communicate the word of God in a clear and understandable way makes him a worthy model for expository preachers today.

What is a word picture?

But what is a word picture? We often think of word pictures as stories of some length which illustrate a truth. This is true, they can be lengthy. Yet, sometimes they may be a single word, as in 'That man is a *beast*.' The word beast conjures up a graphic image, a picture in our minds. It will probably conjure up something different in each person's mind, but it will conjure up something beast-like nonetheless. Men can be like beasts, animal-like, savage and untamed. Several single-word word pictures can be used together like a battering ram to drive a truth home; for example, 'The unrepentant sinner, when *stabbed* with the gospel, is a *cornered* and *wounded beast*.' People can *see* and *relate* to the graphic words used in that statement. Most people know what it means to be stabbed and can relate to the discomfort of being cornered. It is universally understood that a wounded animal can be dangerous and often savage. The sentence above uses four graphic words (word pictures) to describe the possible reaction of a person who loves darkness and how that person might respond when forcefully confronted with the sword of the Spirit. People can 'see' the possible reaction because the words used are clear and give them a vision of what is being said. Thus, word pictures are helpers which come in many configurations and dimensions. Like many great preachers of the past, Watson used a wide assortment of word pictures, *most of them being one word long*. When he preached, he chose to use concrete terms, nouns instead of adjectives. Robert McCraken has observed: 'A return to biblical preaching has always been marked by a return to the use of illustrations. The Puritans, who are the most scriptural of preachers, are also the preachers whose sermons are the richest in imagery.'[29]

In my study of word pictures, I discovered that different authors include word pictures under different categories. They might be discussed under the heading of illustration, imagination, eloquence, imagery, vivacity of language, attention, retention, comprehension, tropes, or sense appeal. Whatever title you give them, Thomas Watson's preaching was saturated with word pictures. Most of his word pictures might easily be defined or categorized as 'illustration'. All word pictures help illustrate or shed light on the truth. Yet, to facilitate discussion I would like to use the term 'word picture' as a more encompassing expression. Even though a word picture might be thought of as a sub-category of illustration, it will be used in this book to describe all types of concrete language, figures of speech and graphic language.

We will also include in the term 'word picture' references to historical events. Historical events are stories which engage the imagination and create pictures in the mind; therefore, they qualify as word pictures.

Scriptural cross-reference will also fit into our definition. Several reasons for this should be considered. First, many Scriptures contain figures of speech. By quoting a text of Scripture that contains graphic language, we are using word pictures. Secondly, the Scriptures are usually quoted because the hearers are familiar with their content and/or authority. To most of the people sitting in churches with expository preaching, the Bible is concrete, tangible, familiar and authoritative. When a preacher gives a cross-reference in a sermon, its purpose is to clarify truth. Preachers quote from the Bible, because they know that most Christians have read, heard, studied and/or meditated on the Bible. The Bible is not abstract to them but very concrete, objective and real. The effective use of cross-reference helps people *see* and *understand* what the preacher is saying. For this reason cross-references will also be included into our definition of word picture. Our working definition of a word picture will be *any word, phrase, story, analogy, illustration, metaphor, figure of speech, trope, allegory, graphic quotation, historical reference, cross-reference, or comparison used to help the listener, see, imagine, experience, sense, understand, remember and/or relate to abstract facts*.

From this point on, remember that the term 'word picture' will be used as a general overarching term to describe the many ways words can be used to communicate abstract truth in a picturable, understandable, and memorable way. Below are three quotations taken from Watson's work, *The Godly Man's Picture*. Notice how Watson used word pictures to paint truth for the mind's eye:

> There is a great deal of difference between a stake in the hedge and a tree in the garden. A stake rots and moulders, but a tree, having life in it, abides and flourishes. When godliness has taken root in the soul, it abides to eternity; 'His seed remaineth in him' (*1 John 3:9*). Godliness being engraved in the heart by the Holy Ghost, as with the point of a diamond, can never be erased.

> The hypocrite thinks of nothing but self-interest; the sails of his mill move only when the wind of promotion blows. He never dives into the waters of the sanctuary except to fetch up a piece of gold from the bottom.

> An impatient man is like a troubled sea that cannot rest *(Isa. 57:20)*. He tortures himself upon the rack of his own griefs and passions, whereas patience calms the heart, as Christ did the sea, when it was rough.[30]

Did you 'see' what Watson was saying? Oh, how many of us have tortured ourselves on the rack of our own griefs! We have probably never seen anyone being tortured on a rack, except possibly in a film or we may have read about it in a book, but most people know what a rack is and can relate to what it might feel like to be tortured on one. People can see in their mind a troubled sea, a rotten stake, a root, a diamond engraver, sails, a mill, a blowing wind, or someone picking up gold. The judicious use of word pictures is one of the factors that made Watson a great preacher. C. H. Spurgeon, a lover and collector of Puritan works and an admirer of Thomas Watson, said:

> Watson was one of the most concise, racy, illustrative, and suggestive of those eminent divines who made the Puritan age the Augustan period of evangelical literature. There is a happy union of sound doctrine, heart-searching experience and practical wisdom throughout all his works.[31]

As mentioned previously, word pictures come in many shapes and sizes. I want to give you a better idea of what word pictures are by looking at some of the larger subcategories of word pictures. This list is not exhaustive by any means, but it should give you a large enough sample to get you thinking on the right track. The first subcategory of what we will look at is 'sense appeal'.

Sense appeal
At Christmas time, I like to play the same old Christmas songs that my parents played when I was little. Playing those old familiar tunes brings back a flood of memories and happy moments spent with my family. One of the many songs that floods my mind with memories is 'chestnuts roasting on an open fire, Jack Frost nipping at your nose.' I can just see myself sitting by a warm fire, smelling the chestnuts roasting by the crackling fire, giving off their unique fragrance. Outside the snow is falling and the cold is nipping at my nose. The words to that song are very *sensuous*; not *sensual* but *sensuous*. The two terms are radically different. Sensuous means 'to be perceived by or affecting the senses'.[32] Sensual,

on the other hand, means 'arousing or preoccupied with gratification of the senses or appetites; carnal; lacking moral restraint; worldly'.[33] Obviously we do not want to be sensual in our preaching, but we do want to be sensuous. 'Sensuous words are words that are close to the five senses, suggesting pictures the mind can see, sounds it can hear, things it can touch, taste, smell.'[34] We want to appeal to the senses in our presentation of truth.

Does that scare you? It shouldn't. The Scriptures are full of sensuous terms and phrases, as we shall further consider later on. Many words, phrases, sentences and stories in the Bible are understandable because we have experienced or 'sensed' the same things or similar things in our own lives. This is what Dr. Jay Adams calls *sense appeal*. He says, 'By sense appeal I refer to the preacher's audio-visual appeal to the five senses.'[35] We are not talking here about the person who senses that God is telling him to divorce his wife. Nor are we talking about mysticism. I am talking about seeing, feeling, tasting, touching, hearing and smelling. Some words 'trigger' or 'stimulate' our minds because they remind us of things we have sensed with our five senses. That is 'sense appeal'. Adams, speaking of sense appeal in expository preaching, says:

> The immediate purpose of using sense appeal in preaching is to add the dimension of reality to truth by helping listeners to sense (experience) what you are teaching from the Scriptures. Sense stimulation in preaching enables listeners to 'live' or 'relive' an event or experience. There is a great difference between merely thinking about something and experiencing it.

Adams goes on to say:

> To experience an event in preaching is to enter into that event so fully that the emotions appropriate to that event are felt, just as if one were actually going through it. When a preacher says what he relates in such a way that he stimulates one or more of

the five senses, thus triggering emotion, then the listener may be said to 'experience' the event. In that way, the event will become 'real' to him, which means it has become concretized (or personalized), memorable, and in the fullest sense of the word, understandable.[36]

There was a large grove of eucalyptus trees behind the house where I grew up. Whenever I think of eucalyptus trees, I can smell them. Whenever I smell eucalyptus, I can see the eucalyptus trees behind my house. I can see their pointed leaves, their strips of shedding bark, and can feel their pointy little acorns under my bare feet. That is sense appeal: words that trigger experiences previously sensed.

Thomas Watson used word pictures that contained sense appeal. He related truth to things experienced or sensed by the average person. Below I have listed three quotations from Thomas Watson. As you read them, ask yourself, 'Have I ever sensed or experienced any of the word pictures he uses?'

Gain is the golden bait with which Satan fishes for souls: 'the sweet smell of money.' This was the last temptation he used with Christ: 'All these things will I give thee' *(Matt. 4:9)*. But Christ saw the hook under the bait. Many who have escaped gross sins are still caught in a golden net.

Do we think walking with God can do us any hurt? Did we ever hear any cry out on their deathbed that they have been too holy, that they have prayed too much, or walked with God too much? No, that which has cut them to the heart has been this, that they have not walked more closely with God; they have wrung their hand and torn their hair to think that they have been so bewitched with the pleasures of the world. Close walking with God will make our enemy (death) be at peace with us.

The time of childhood is the fittest time to be sowing seed of religion in our children. *'Whom shall he make to understand doctrine? Them that are weaned from the milk, and drawn from the breasts' (Isa. 28:9)*. The wax, while it is soft and tender, will take any impression. Children, while they are young, will fear a reproof; when they are old, they will hate it.[37]

I do not know about you, but I have had many experiences fooling fish with bait. I have also smelled crisp, freshly minted currency. I have seen gold and have seen fish caught with nets. I have been cut. I have wrung my hands and have had my hair pulled out. I have sown seeds in the garden. I have felt hot wax and played with warm wax. I have experienced all of these things; how about you? Most of the people in your congregations have either seen, read about, watched on television, or experienced all of these things also.

Now, it is interesting to note that Watson wrote over three hundred years ago, and the people sitting in the pews of his church experienced these things as well. That amazes me. It teaches me an important lesson. It helps me understand what *kind* of experiences I should appeal to in my presentation of the truth. I should appeal to things that are so common that three hundred and fifty years from now, in the year 2350, people could listen to one of my sermons, or read one of them in print, and still be able to relate to most of the sense type word pictures I use.

Later we will see that Jesus was a master of this also. Even though Jesus preached 2000 years ago, we can still relate to what he said. Not only this, we can go back to the earlier books of the biblical canon and still relate to the sense appeal that they used 3500 years ago! As Solomon so aptly put it, 'there is nothing new under the sun.'

If you appeal to common experiences in your preaching of God's word, you do your people a great favour because you help your people pay attention, comprehend, and understand what you are saying. If you want people to understand the word of God and remember it, you want to be able to relate the not-so-known truth of the Scriptures to things very familiar.

That, I believe, was Thomas Watson's great homiletical technique. Later, we will discover why word pictures work, why they are so helpful and where to find them. But for now, let us look at a few more kinds or types of word pictures.

Metaphor

Word pictures can also come in the form of metaphor. A metaphor is an *unexpressed comparison*. Metaphor does not use the words 'like' or 'as' to let you know a comparison is being made. For instance, Jesus said, 'I am the door,' 'I am the bread of life,' 'You are the light of the world.' It is obvious that Jesus did not intend these phrases to be taken literally. In fact, he often does not even explain himself when using these metaphors. Why is this?

God created man with the ability to 'figure out' metaphorical comparisons instantly. Warren Wiersbe says, 'Preachers of the Word especially need to focus on mastering metaphor, for that's the way language is made, the way people think, and the way the Bible was written.'[38] When Jesus used metaphor he made comparisons between familiar things (things previously experienced or sensed by his listeners) and abstract theological truths. Jesus, being the only way to heaven, is a door. He is the person you must 'go through' if you are going to get to heaven. If you do not go through the door (Jesus) you cannot get to heaven (e.g. John 10:7; 14:6; Acts 4:12). Jesus is also the 'bread of life'. Just as we need food to sustain us physically, so we need Jesus to sustain us spiritually. If we do not receive the bread of life (Jesus) we will die (John 6:35ff). Believers are also lights shining in a dark world. When we live in obedience to God, our lives will 'shine' in contrast to the deeds of those living in 'darkness'. Since metaphor is found all through the Bible, expository preachers should not be afraid to use it. It is a very effective and engaging way to confront people with truth. One of my favorite metaphors in the book of Acts is when Paul rebuked Ananias, the high priest, saying, 'God is going to strike you, you whitewashed wall!' (Acts 23:3). Ananias got the picture.

When metaphors are strung together in a running

relationship, an allegory is created. An allegory is an extended chain of metaphors or one metaphor linked to another to form a 'picturesque' story. Unlike parables, allegories do not have to be true to life. Also, while parables have some spiritual parallels, virtually every part of an allegory has some form of secondary meaning.[39] Biblical examples would be: Daniel's allegorical vision of the tree in Daniel 4:11-27; Paul's allegorical usage of Sarah and Hagar in Galatians 4:21–5:1; or John's vision of the beast in Revelation 13:1-4; 17:7-18.

One of the classic allegories of all time, *The Pilgrim's Progress,* was written by John Bunyan (another Puritan) to describe the pilgrimage of every believer's life. Bunyan effectively used allegory to teach biblical doctrine. 'Bunyan,' as someone has said, 'saw principles like men walking in the street.'[40] *The Pilgrim's Progress* has undergone countless printings and revisions. Why do you think it is still a favourite all over the world? Why is it still being printed? Why do people like to read about Christian and his pilgrimage to the celestial city? Because it 'pictures' the struggles, trials, failures and joys that *every* believer experiences in their Christian walk. Bunyan was able to relate to people where their experiences had already taken them. Bunyan was not an ear-tickling manpleaser, nor did he dilute sound doctrine. He merely took biblical truth and made it understandable through comparison. It was John Owen who said that he would give up all his learning to be able to preach 'like that shoe cobbler'. Donald Demaray said this of Bunyan: 'What made Bunyan the communication genius that he was? Bible mastery, an experience with God, a sure sense of divine call and guidance, extraordinary insight into human nature, and his narrative ability in depicting spiritual conflict and vigorous faith in word pictures.'[41]

Cranking out allegories, whether short or long, for every sermon is not practical. Most of us have neither the time nor talent to weave allegories into our sermons. But metaphor is well within the reach of every Bible expositor. Remember, allegory is a chain of metaphors linked together. In fact, you probably use metaphor in your sermons and may not even realize it. We might say, 'this person is a real *pillar* of the church,' or 'that person is an *angel,*' or 'I can really *grasp* what your saying'. We all use metaphor, but some use it more effectively than others. Metaphor in preaching helps hold people's attention. It can give our people a better understanding of the truth and fix it to their minds. This is why we should use metaphorical word pictures in expository preaching. Here are three more quotations from Watson. Look for metaphors and note how effective they are at communicating truth:

> The world is but a great inn where we are to stay a night or two and be gone. What madness it is so to set our heart upon our inn as to forget our home!

> Patience is a flower of God's planting. Pray that it may grow in your heart, and send forth its sweet perfume. Prayer is a holy charm, to charm down the evil spirit. Prayer composes the heart and puts it in tune, when impatience has broken the strings and put everything into confusion. Oh, go to God. Prayer delights God's ear; it melts his heart; it opens his hand.

> An idle person is the devil's tennis ball, which he bandies up and down with temptation till at last the ball goes out of play.[42]

Metaphor works! As Dr. Stan Toussaint would say, 'Those dogs will hunt!' Who wants to live in a hotel all their life when they have a mansion to go home to? Not me! Who longs to have God plant the flower of patience in their heart and send forth its sweet perfume? I do! We have known and grieved over the devil's tennis balls that he has knocked out of play by temptation. People can 'see' and relate to metaphor. This is why we must take the truth so carefully mined by exegesis and metaphorize it for our people. We need to be like Watson and make our people see what the Bible is saying. Some may say,

'Resorting to that kind of falderal is ear tickling,' but when you think about it, just the opposite is true. The preacher who is the best communicator, who clearly imparts the understanding of the text, who makes people face the truth of the text is not the 'ear tickler'; rather, he is the one who calls down fire from heaven. Obscurity is not a blessing, it is a curse. A great difference exists between imparting under-standing and diluting truth. Metaphor used correctly will *always* be more effective in communicating truth than abstract concepts.

A close cousin to metaphor also needs to be considered and that is 'simile'.

Simile

The class of word pictures which fit the criteria of simile constitutes a large army. A simile is an *expressed comparison* and uses the words 'like' or 'as' to indicate that a comparison is being made. The purpose of a simile is to direct the mind of the listener to something the listener is familiar with so that he can understand something unfamiliar. Simile welds what is abstract and not known to what is concrete and well known. Simile does everything metaphor does, but is flagged by the words 'like' or 'as' so that your mind knows that a comparison is coming.

We are familiar with the many disputes that Jesus had with the Pharisees. They were an obnoxious, hypocritical bunch of self-righteous legalists. It is obvious that Jesus never read Dale Carnegie's book, *How to Win Friends and Influence People.* Notice how Jesus used simile to hew down the Pharisees: 'Woe to you, scribes and Pharisees, hypocrites! For you are *like* whitewashed tombs which on the outside appear beautiful, but inside they are full of dead men's bones and all uncleanness' (Matt. 23:27). 'Woe' is right! Do you ever speak to religious hypocrites that way? Jesus did! Jesus used simile very effectively to communicate truth. He was obviously not ear tickling or entertaining the scribes and the

Pharisees. Jesus could have said to the Pharisees: 'Your outward appearance does not match your inward thoughts and attitudes.' Both this statement and the one found in Matthew 23:27 communicate the same basic truth, but Jesus' simile does it better. A statement like the second one would have bounced off them 'like' a rubber ball off a Sherman tank. It would have been 'like' hitting them with a grain of sand. But telling people they are 'like' whitewashed tombs full of dead men's bones is 'like' hitting someone with a sledgehammer. Simile is a very effective form of communication. I don't know about you, but when I preach, I don't want merely to irritate people with a spray of sand, I want to hit them with a sledgehammer. I want them to be struck with the truth of God's word in a forceful way. I want people to leave with God's word burned on their heart. That is why Thomas Watson used simile in his preaching and why we need to use simile in our preaching.

Simile is sprinkled throughout the Bible. If you have a computer and Bible software you might want to try an experiment. Do a search for any verses containing 'like' or 'as'. The NASB contains 5,235 occurrences of these two words. Not all of them are used to indicate that a comparison is being made, but many of them are. It is eye opening to see what comparisons are being made in the text. We will look at some of these later but the sheer volume of simile illustrates a point that I think expository preachers need to learn: *Simile is effective for communicating the word of God.*

Imagine being in prison on the lonely island of Patmos and receiving a glorious vision of the resurrected and exalted Lord. How could you narrate a scene like that? What could you do to describe the indescribable? How could you relate to mere mortals 'things which eye has not seen, and ear has not heard, and which has not entered into the heart of man?' I know how John did it, he used many similes:

and in the middle of the lampstands one *like* a son of man, clothed in a robe reaching to the feet, and girded across His breast with a golden girdle. And His head and His hair were white *like* white wool, *like* snow; and His eyes were *like* a flame of fire; and His feet were *like* burnished bronze, when it has been caused to glow in a furnace, and His voice was *like* the sound of many waters. And in His right hand He held seven stars; and out of His mouth came a sharp two-edged sword; and His face was *like* the sun shining in its strength (Rev. 1:13-16, emphasis mine).

The more complicated the truth or doctrine being taught, the more simile and metaphor we should use. John saw something no one else had ever seen. He knew that the best way to explain his vision of the exalted Christ was to use many word pictures. Even though we did not see the vision ourselves, we know the component parts: the Son of Man has hair white as wool or snow, eyes like a flame of fire, feet like hot, polished bronze, a voice like the sound of many waters, and is radiant like the brightness of the sun shining in its strength. Because John used these similes we know by experience something of what he saw in his vision. It is not that we saw the vision ourselves, but since we have seen a collection of comparable things we can understand the vision. Comparison is the power of simile. Read the quotations below by Watson and look for the words 'like' and 'as'. Notice the frequency and effectiveness of Watson's metaphors and similes:

Many love the Word preached only for its eloquence and notion. They come to a sermon as to a music lecture *(Ezek. 33:31-32)* or as to a garden to pick flowers, but not to have their lusts subdued or their hearts bettered. These are like a foolish woman who paints her face but neglects her health.

The besetting sin is of all others most dangerous. As Samson's strength lay in his hair, so the strength of sin lies in this beloved sin. This is like a poison striking the heart, which brings death. A godly man will lay the axe of repentance to this sin and hew it down. He sets this sin, like Uriah, in the forefront of battle, so that it may be slain. He will sacrifice this Isaac, he will pluck out this right eye, so that he may see better to go to heaven.

Walking in the ways of sin is like walking on the banks of a river. The sinner treads on the banks of the bottomless pit, and if death gives him a jog, he tumbles in.[43]

No doubt, Watson could have chosen not to use simile, but why would any preacher choose abstraction over clarity? Why put in opaque windows instead of transparent? Who would be brave enough to argue that the truths Watson taught in these quotations would have been helped or advanced by the removal of simile and metaphor? As expository preachers we need to be concerned not only with accuracy to the text of Scripture, but also with clarity of presentation. We want the people in the pews to understand and remember as much of our sermons as possible. We should not be content with firing over people's heads, but with aiming at their hearts. Simile is another reason why Thomas Watson was such a great preacher.

Before we examine why word pictures work, let us look at another close cousin of word picture – illustration.

Illustration

Word pictures might also be categorized under illustration because they are words that 'picture', and pictures illustrate. We often think of an illustration as some cute anecdote or story that rambles on for a while and then finally reaches a conclusion. Some are like that, but I want you to remember that illustrations can be one word long. The word 'illustrate' literally means to shine light upon, explain, clarify, or illuminate. It is the process of explaining what is not known by analogy or comparison with what is already known.

'Illustrations are the photographs or pictures that go along with abstract ideas.'[44] Sense appeal, metaphor, and simile can all be used to illustrate truth. Illustrations are verbal flashlights. The better the illustration, the higher the wattage, the more the truth is revealed. A good illustration will throw enough light on the truth you are trying to teach for the people to see clearly what the Bible is saying. In spite of this, some expository preachers have an aversion to illustration. One reason is that illustrations are often used inaccurately. I think this reason is captured well by Halford Luccock:

> The chief trouble with sermonic illustrations, which are indispensable to preaching that etches into the mind, is that they are too often falsely considered as a sort of thing apart by themselves rather than a quality of writing and thinking. They are hung on the body of a sermon as bright ornaments are hung on a Christmas tree. They did not grow there. The wire which ties them on is all too often visible. They are decorative rather than in any sense structural like an arch or a keystone. Then all too often the illustrations are treated as Pharaoh treated the Egyptian slaves – they are expected to make bricks without straw, to make sermons without coherent, consecutive thought.[45]

Illustrations are not to be used or perceived as sermonic ornament. They are helpers to 'coherent, consecutive thought'. We do not need to reject illustrations because many preachers have abused them, any more than we need to stop driving cars because people have misused them. We need to come to grips with the fact that 'a simple illustration is often more vivid and compelling than many exhortations'.[46] Most people love to hear a great illustration, but many expositors fail to use them.

Another reason for this is that they are just too much trouble. Usually a preacher is so pressed for time that he can barely get his exegesis done and flesh out a sermon in a coherent fashion before Sunday comes. Spending time searching for illustrations often comes low on the priority list.

I remember hearing a guest speaker in our seminary homiletics class tell us that he spent all his spare time speed reading through books, magazines and newspapers in search of illustrations for the next Sunday's sermon. He was there to help us but he only succeeded in exasperating me. I have always been a slow, methodical reader. The thought of spending every spare moment reading at breakneck speed to find illustrations is loathsome to my soul. For me, if a book is worth reading, it is worth reading carefully and methodically. Illustrations are bonuses in my reading but never the main goal. When I speed read, my retention is cut drastically, and I soon forget what I read. It just does not seem worth it. That does not mean that everyone is a slow reader like me or that speed reading will not work for others. I needed an easier method of finding illustrations that took less time but produced quality word pictures. So I tried other things.

One of those methods was to buy dictionaries and encyclopedias of quotations, anecdotes and illustrations. Usually they are topically and alphabetically arranged and most are easy to use. They can be helpful, but for me, most of the illustrations do not seem to have the 'zing' and 'zap' I am looking for. Some preachers say you should 'never' use them.[47] But we have probably all heard preachers use them very effectively. When you think about it, there is really no difference in finding an illustration from an illustration book or finding one in the morning paper or while reading a missionary biography.

Yet, if you are not careful, they can sound as if you got them out of the gutter. They can dribble out of your mouth instead of flash with fire. It is the preacher's fault when the illustration fails, not the source they are derived from. I know when I do a poor job giving an illustration. Nevertheless, I find it is usually easier to make home-grown illustrations work than store-bought ones.

Another danger when using illustration books is that you

run the risk of forgetting which ones you used in previous sermons and which ones you considered using but did not. Often you will read quite a few to find just the right one. Later, when you open the illustration book, you can't remember which one you used before and which one you only considered using.

I have used illustrations from books a few times in my preaching, but I have never used them on a regular basis. An exception would be books on biblical illustration or the Bible itself. Biblical illustrations or cross-references help you teach the Bible with the Bible.[48] David Burrell says, 'If the preacher wants a "Handbook of Illustrations" the Bible will serve his purpose.'[49] This is quite true. We often do not think of cross-references as illustrations, but they are. Their purpose is to shed light upon the text or the truth you are trying to teach.

So where can a preacher get an endless supply of good, home grown illustrative material? Inside and outside your head is a good place to look. They are everywhere. Your mind can be trained to think comparatively. You can learn to use sense appeal, metaphor and simile. You can learn the art of using historical references and cross-references to illustrate truth. As mentioned earlier, our definition of a word picture includes any quotation, comparison, or figure of speech. Your brain can be cultivated to grow a heavy crop of illustrations. We will look at this later, but I want you to take note in the following examples of how Watson was able to shed light on foundational Christian truths because his word pictures were 'illustrative':

The Word written is our pillar of fire to guide us. It shows us what rocks we are to avoid; it is the map by which we sail to the new Jerusalem.

Thus sinners walk according to the flesh. If a drunken or unclean lust calls, they gratify it. They brand as cowards all who dare not sin at the same rate as they do. These, instead of walking with

God, walk contrary to Him. Lust is the compass they sail by.
Satan is their pilot and hell the port they are bound for.

'He that believeth not, the wrath of God abideth on him' (John
3:36). Whoever lacks grace is like someone who lacks pardon;
every hour he is in fear of execution. How can a wicked man
rejoice? Over his head hangs the sword of God's justice and
under him hell-fire burns.[50]

Watson did not scrounge up his word pictures from
illustration encyclopedias. He grew them in the garden of his
mind and harvested them when needed. When I read his
works, I am amazed at the crop of word pictures he produced.
Our minds contain the necessary environment to produce a
bumper crop of word pictures as well. It is true that different
preachers will be able to produce different yields of word
pictures from their mind, but I believe every preacher will be
able to produce thirty, sixty, or one-hundredfold if they make
an effort. Everyone can learn to produce a never-ending
supply of illustrations. Watson sometimes goes on for pages
presenting a never-ending sequence of simile, metaphor,
sense appeal, quotation and illustration. Granted, he was
exceptionally good at it, but we can learn to be good at it too.
Later, I will give you some practical ways to increase your
word picture yield. For now I want to look at the reason why
word pictures work.

Imagination

Wait! Do not skip this section! I know what some of you are
thinking, 'What does "make-believe" have to do with
preaching the word of God?' I want to put your mind at ease,
I am not talking about 'make-believe'. Neither am I talking
about 'fancy', the mind's ability to think of things that do not
exist. Warren Wiersbe explains: 'There's a vast difference
between imagination and fancy. Imagination helps us
penetrate reality and better understand it, while fancy helps us
temporarily escape reality and better endure it.'[51]

Fancy or imaginary things are thoughts that only exist in

the mind. They are not real or true. Henry Ward Beecher put it this way:

> The imagination in its relations to art and beauty is one thing; and in its relations to moral truth it is another thing, of the most substantial character. Imagination of this kind is the true germ of faith; it is the power of conceiving as definite the things which are invisible to the senses – of giving them distinct shape.[52]

Imagination is the God-given ability which enables us to see with our mind ideas presented in words. Imagination is a word processor which converts graphic words into mental images. Our imaginations help us learn abstract truth. John Broadus, describing the necessity of imagination in preaching, says:

> It may be said that imagination is of indispensable value in the construction of discourse.... Piles of bricks and lumber and sand are as much a house as the mere piling up of thoughts will constitute a discourse. The builder, of palace or cabin, works by constructive imagination; and it is the same faculty that builds speech.[53]

We need to think of the imagination as a mental mechanism which compares metaphor, simile, word pictures, sense appeal and other picturesque language with things already experienced. By mental comparison of the known with the unknown, our imagination helps us to experience truth with the mind, which leads to understanding. Abstract truth starves the imagination, but word pictures feed it. Let us look at some other helpful definitions of imagination. Andrew Blackwood says:

> It is the God-given power which enables the minister to see what is hidden from others' eyes, and then share his experience with his friend in the pew. [54]

Henry Ward Beecher has a concise definition:

The imagination, then, is that power of the mind by which it conceives of invisible things, and is able to present them as though they were visible to others.[55]

Jay Adams explains it this way:

Imagery has to do with imaging, or imagining. Until a preacher can picture for himself what he is talking about, it is very doubtful that he himself adequately understands what he is trying to tell others. At any rate, it is almost certain that, apart from imagery, few, if any, of the members of his congregation will understand – even if he does. [56]

John Broadus again:

Imagination is the imaging function of the mind. It is thinking by seeing, as contrasted with reasoning.[57]

Finally, the dictionary definition is:

The action or faculty of forming mental images or concepts of what is not actually present to the senses.[58]

Imagination is the engine that makes word pictures useful and effective. When a person 'sees truth', he understands it and remembers it more readily. Imagination is a necessary component in almost all learning. John Broadus affirms this when he says, 'A preacher, without imagination, may be respected for his sound sense, may be loved for his homely goodness, but he will not move a congregation, he will not be a power in the community.'[59] At first, a statement like that seems hyperbolic. Yet, when the great preachers of the past are considered, it is the rare exception to find one who did not engage the imagination by the proficient implementation of a variety of word pictures. Also, if you use Jesus as the model preacher, that statement seems even less extreme. Thomas Watson's excellence as a preacher hinged on his ability to take abstract truth and run it through the imagination mill, so that it could be seen, experienced, and understood.

Let me try to illustrate how imagination works by telling you about something unknown to you. What I want to tell you about is a cuzzbot. Does that bring anything to mind? It had better not because it is an imaginary word I have just created. Right now that word means nothing to you because it is an abstract concept. But I know what it is because I can see it in my mind. Now as I explain to you a little more what a cuzzbot is, you will be able to see it in your mind also. It is something to play with. It is a round rubber ball, about the size of a football, soft and squishy, with rubber knobs that stick out about a half an inch and glow in the dark. Can you imagine what a cuzzbot might look like? With each descriptive piece of information you understand a little better what a cuzzbot is. Your imagination is the part of you that sees 'round', sees 'rubber', sees 'a football', remembers feeling something 'soft and squishy', sees 'knobs' and sees 'glow in the dark'. Your imagination assembles familiar data creating a cuzzbot even though you have never even seen one before. This is imagination and every preacher should use it in his sermon preparation and delivery. We must not forget that people learn with their imaginations. One person expressed the necessity of imagination with these words, 'It is by imagination that men have lived; and imagination rules all our lives. The human mind is not, as philosophers would have you think, a debating hall, but a picture gallery.'[60]

Now let us move from the hypothetical to reality. You are preaching about God's sovereign decree and how he guides history to its predestined conclusion by 'providence' and 'concurrence'. Now when those words pop out of your mouth, for many in your congregations, they sound like 'cuzzbot'. They mean nothing! Those who have studied the doctrines of providence and concurrence may have no problem following you, but the rest, the majority, will become hopelessly lost. Now most preachers attempt to define theological jargon, but they do it with abstract lexical or theological definitions. They say something like this: 'Providence is the supernatural working out of God's sovereign decree. It is the ability of God to bring to fruition all he has predestined to occur.' 'Concurrence is the simultaneity of first and second causes guided by providence for the working out of God's sovereign decree.' So you have defined these two terms for your people and now they 'know' what you are talking about?

Probably not. Most of them will not have the faintest idea of what you are talking about because they cannot 'see' what you are saying. The imagination does not have anything to process because it has not been fed any word pictures, only abstract concepts. The imagination of most people cannot see predestination, sovereignty, concurrence, simultaneity, or first and second causes unless those concepts are attached to word pictures, things they can see. Once you attach those abstract concepts to word pictures then comes 'understanding', and with understanding comes 'remembering'. Charles Brown has stated, 'The good sermon is not all roast beef medium and mashed potatoes. Solid argument walks on the ground until imagination gives it wings to reach the high places of moral appeal.'[61] Henry Ward Beecher was bold enough to describe it as 'the most important of all the factors which go to make the preacher'.[62] I believe that spiritual giftedness, accuracy to the text of God's word and personal holiness of the preacher are the most important factors – but beyond that Beecher has made a valid point.

Recently, I experimented on a friend with the same two doctrines mentioned above. I do this rather frequently. I like to use my congregation and friends as guinea pigs. I don't even get written consent. I rationalize this abuse because, after all, it is for their own benefit. It helps me to be a better preacher. Let us return to the experiment. I purposely directed our conversation to the doctrines of providence and concurrence. I defined them in several abstract ways. I could tell she was straining to grasp the truth but the abstract concepts were not getting through. I could tell by her furrowed brow and catatonic look that I had not given her 'understanding'. Then

I broke forth with two word pictures.

The first word picture was borrowed from none other than Thomas Watson. 'Providence and concurrence,' I explained, 'are like the gears of a clock which are different sizes, and move contrary to one another, but together they move the hands of the clock forward round the dial.' With the first word picture I could see relief on her face and the first words out of her mouth were 'I see.'

The second illustration I used was from the Bible. I explained how God had sent his Son into the world to die. Even though Jesus said, 'No one takes my life from me,' evil men crucified him. Yet it was all part of God's perfect plan. I quoted Acts 2:23: 'this Man, delivered up by the predetermined plan and foreknowledge of God, you nailed to a cross by the hands of godless men and put him to death.'

Now she had something to process with her imagination and she began to understand providence and concurrence. She could see how God was sovereignly working through evil men to bring about his predestined plan. The word pictures I used were processed by her imagination so she could understand abstract concepts.

Before we move on, consider how Watson uses word pictures to illustrate God's providence in the quotations below. Notice how he attempts to put flesh on the dry bones of an abstract theological concept.

> The wheels in a watch move cross one to another, but they all carry on the motion of the watch; so the wheels of Providence often move cross to our desires, but still they carry on God's unchangeable decree.

> The providence of God is 'the queen and governess of the world': it is the eye that sees, and the hand that turns all the wheels in the universe. God is not like an artificer that builds a house, and then leaves it, but like a pilot He steers the ship of the whole creation.

Suppose you were in a smith's shop, and should see there several sorts of tools, some crooked, some bowed, others hooked, would you condemn all these things, because they do not look handsome? The smith makes use of them all for doing his work. Thus it is with the providences of God; they seem to us to be very crooked and strange, yet they all carry on God's work.[63]

I know that expository preachers are a finicky group of individuals. They are preaching mavericks. While the majority of churches are swapping the sermon hour for drama, entertainment, upbeat music and cappuccino time, expositors stand firm against the raging torrent of truncated, superficial preaching and maintain their commitment to 'preach the word'. They are a fearless and noble crowd who are nauseated by the sad state of preaching in many churches. Their revulsion against baby formula sermons has caused their personal pendulum to swing to the opposite end of the preaching spectrum. Because of the many abuses and misuses in preaching today, they do not want to be named among the slick-talking orators who wow their people with worldly wisdom and sermons void of any spiritual nutrition.

But some expositors have thrown the baby out with the bath water when it comes to being *effective* communicators. They reason to themselves, 'It is my job to preach the word, and it is the Holy Spirit's job to take it from there.' But this can be like giving someone who needs shelter a pile of building materials and telling them to 'take it from there'. If someone needs bread, they don't need a sack of flour, an egg, a packet of yeast and a jug of water. They need bread. Some expositors are fearful of preaching interesting, engaging, attention-grabbing sermons, because they might fall into the chasms of pragmatism or entertainment. After all, we do not want to give people what they want, we want to give them what God says they need. But let us not give them uncooked exegetical data and expect them to feast on dry flour and raw eggs.

If people start complaining that they can't understand the sermon or they leave the church to be 'refreshed' at the First Church of Pragmatism, we often blame it on them. When people don't understand our sermons, 'it's their fault!' They should be more committed, study harder, get more sleep the night before, be more diligent at taking notes, concentrate harder and be more godly. Thus we feed them the raw ingredients, dry abstract truths, and tell them to be 'warm and filled'. But most people cannot stomach that kind of preaching. They need the truth of God's word, prepared and served in a way they can mentally digest it. Thomas Watson was a great preacher because he served up God's word in a digestible way. Notice how Watson describes the 'call of the believers' (do not forget to notice the word pictures):

God so calls as he allures; he does not force, but draws. The freedom of the will is not taken away, but the stubbornness of it is conquered. *'Thy people shall be willing in the day of thy power' (Ps. 110:3)....* As chastity distinguishes a virtuous woman from a harlot, so holiness distinguishes the godly from the wicked. It is a holy calling; *'For God hath not called us unto uncleanness, but unto holiness' (I Thess. 4:7).* Let not any man say he is called of God, that lives in sin. Has God called you to be a swearer, to be a drunkard? Nay, let not the merely moral person say he is effectually called. What is civility without sanctity? It is but a dead carcass strewed with flowers. The king's picture stamped upon brass will not go current for gold. The merely moral man looks as if he had the King of heaven's image stamped upon him; but he is not better than counterfeit metal, which will not pass for current with God.... When God calls a man by his grace, he cannot but come. You may resist the minister's call, but you cannot the Spirit's call. The finger of the blessed Spirit can write upon a heart of stone, as once He wrote His law upon tables of stone. God's words are creating words; when He says, 'Let there be light', there was light, and when He says, 'Let there be faith,' it shall be so. When God called Paul, he answered to the call. *'I was not disobedient to the heavenly vision' (Acts 26:19).* God rides forth conquering in the chariot of his gospel; he makes the blind eyes see, and the stony heart bleed. If God will call a man, nothing shall lie in the way to hinder; difficulties shall be untied, the powers of hell shall disband. *'Who hath resisted his will?' (Rom. 9:19).* God bends the iron sinew, and cuts asunder the gates of brass *(Ps. 107:6).* When the Lord touches a man's heart by his Spirit, all proud imaginations are brought down, and the fort-royal of the will yields to God.[64]

So we have learned that one of the reasons Thomas Watson was such an excellent preacher was his skill at using word pictures. We defined word pictures as *any word, phrase, story, analogy, illustration, metaphor, figure of speech, trope, allegory, graphic quotation, historical reference, cross-reference, or comparison used to help the listener, see, imagine, experience, sense, understand, remember and/or relate to abstract facts.* We have examined some of the larger categories of word pictures, namely, sense appeal, metaphor, simile and illustration. We have also discovered that word pictures work because they feed the imagination, allowing us to 'see' truth. In the next chapter we explore further why Thomas Watson's method of preaching with word pictures is needed today.

4

HURDLES TO LEAP OVER
AND GIANTS TO SLAY

Why we need to use word
pictures in expository preaching

When I was in Junior High, I used to mow the lawn of an elderly gentleman who lived several blocks away. One of the great pleasures of mowing his lawn, besides the five dollars I received, was being able to ride my bike down a long, steep street on the way home. As I coasted down the hill on my racing bike, the wind, like a poor man's air conditioner, cooled me off. One day, as I air conditioned myself, I failed to notice a small obstacle in the middle of the road. It was a rock about the size of a tennis ball. Because I was unaware of its presence, I made no effort to avoid it. The consequences were tragic. When the front tire of my bicycle hit the rock, the wheel turned perpendicular to my direction of travel, launching me into the air like a rock out of a catapult. Newton's Law proceeded to take over, and I eventually came down, grinding to a bloody halt on the hot asphalt. My bike flew over the top of me and battered its way to a stop further down the road. To make things worse, I had an audience. There was an elderly lady in her front garden watering her flowers. She saw the whole thing. There I was, lying in the middle of the street, bruised and bleeding; my beautiful bike crumpled up in a heap. Blood was dripping from my body like water from a sieve. The lady, lacking a good grasp of the obvious, spoke with profundity, 'Are you OK?' It was all I could take. Like Job, after being afflicted with boils, I wanted to die. Of course I wasn't OK!

Now you may be wondering, 'What does this story have to do with expository preaching?' I am glad you asked. It illustrates an important point. The expository preacher who is unaware of the obstacles between him and his congregation will invariably fail to avoid them. If he fails to avoid them, his sermons are bound to fall flat on their face in the presence of many witnesses.

Word pictures help overcome the obstacles which hinder your congregation from listening to, understanding and remembering God's word. People learn primarily by *seeing*, either with the eye or with the mind. Studies have revealed that 85 per cent of everything we learn is by sight, 10 per cent by hearing and the other 5 per cent by touch, smell and taste.[65] That is a handy piece of information considering that preaching is one-way verbal communication. It tells that an abstract sermon devoid of word pictures may only produce about 10 per cent absorption, apart from any supernatural intervention. That is unacceptable. Then if you take into consideration that people only use about 5–10 per cent of their brains, it becomes alarming. If you were moving from one house to another, and had a removal firm to move you, would you be content with only 10 per cent of your belongings reaching their final destination? In the same way, any preacher who has the word of God to deliver from his mouth to the hearts of his people should not be content with 10 per cent delivery. He should seek maximum delivery and storage. Of course, many obstacles stand between your sermon and the hearts of your people. These obstacles are like pillars of coral just under the surface of the water. If you do not know where they lie, it is likely that your sermon will suffer shipwreck. Thomas Watson learned to navigate around the coral reefs with word pictures.

As I have demonstrated, word pictures help people 'see' God's truth in their minds. When they see what you are saying, they understand what you are saying. Mental perception, understanding, and retention are vital in preaching. You need all three of them if truth is going to have maximum delivery and storage. Truth that is not understood is like seed sown by the side of the road: 'When anyone hears the word of the kingdom, *and does not understand it*, the evil one comes and snatches away what has been sown in his heart. This is the one on whom seed was sown beside the road' (Matt. 13:19). Understanding is critical. Paul understood that one of Satan's strategies is to promote 'mental blindness' in order to thwart understanding. Paul, speaking of Satan in 2 Corinthians 4:4, said of the unbelievers: 'in whose case the god of this world has *blinded the minds* of the unbelieving, that they *might not see* the light of the gospel of the glory of Christ, who is the image of God' (emphasis mine).

To 'see' the truth is also important. Satan knows that if he can keep people from 'seeing' the truth, he can keep them from understanding, remembering and being transformed by it. If you are thinking to yourself, 'It's the Holy Spirit's job to give people understanding!': be patient. In the next chapter we will look at the preacher's responsibility and the Holy Spirit's activity in relation to imparting understanding. The point I am driving at is this: your congregation cannot be transformed by truth they do not *hear, understand*, or *remember*.

It is obvious that we cannot call to mind a truth we have never heard. We also cannot live by what we do not understand or remember. In order for the truth of God's word to transform the lives of the people in your church, they have to listen, understand and remember. This is why the Psalmist says, 'Your word I have treasured in my heart, that I may not sin against You' (Ps. 119:11). If you do not lock God's word like a treasure in the vault of your heart, then, when you need it the most, it will not be there to help keep you from sinning. Therefore it is crucial that the expository preacher considers his task (imparting the truth of God's word), the target (the hearts and minds of his people) and the obstacles in between the task and the target. Speaking of the issue of obstacles in preaching Spurgeon writes:

Often mental mosquitoes sting the man while you are preaching to him, and he is thinking more of trifling distractions than of your discourse; is it so very wonderful that he does? You must drive the mosquitoes away, and secure your people's undistracted thoughts, turning them out of the channel in which they have been running six days into one suitable for the Sabbath. You must have sufficient leverage in your discourse and its subject to lift them right up from the earth to which they cleave, and to elevate them a little nearer heaven.[66]

Thomas Watson, speaking of this issue, writes:

[A minister must be] a plain preacher, suiting his matter and style to the capacity of his audience (1 Cor. 14:19). Some ministers, like eagles, love to soar aloft in abstruse metaphysical notions, thinking they are most admired when they are least understood. They who preach in the clouds, instead of hitting their people's conscience, shoot over their heads. [67]

The expository preacher tends to have more obstacles to overcome than the people-pleasing preacher. Because of his commitment to the word, his sermons will usually contain more abstract doctrinal 'data'. Therefore, he must learn to overcome the barriers if he is ever going to deliver a high percentage of truth to the hearts of his people. Ear ticklers do not need to worry much about abstract truth because their sermons are void of theological substance. The content of the text does not compel them; being well liked by their people is the target they fire at. For the expositor, word pictures will act like levers to move the boulders aside so that the interest of his hearers can be focused on the truth. Daniel Kidder, addressing the necessity of getting the people's attention, comments:

Its essential importance is seen in the fact that no mind can be profited unless its attention is both arrested and occupied. Memory is also dependent upon the fact and the degree of attention; while there is little hope of the heart being affected by any discourse in which the mind does not become deeply interested.[68]

Consider some of these obstacles. Everything in our society is shifting towards what is visual. There is a reason for this. The mind easily accepts and remembers what is visual, graphic and concrete. This is why marketing companies spend billions of dollars putting visual images in front of people. Every year it amazes me when I learn how many millions of dollars companies spend to advertise during the Super Bowl. Companies spend multiple millions of dollars for a fifteen to thirty second commercial spot. Why do they do this? They know if they can get people all over the United States to *see* their product or the name of their company, the commercials will more than pay for themselves! I am not saying that we should abandon preaching in favour of films in church. Preaching is a mandate that cannot be set aside for 'film time'. It is not that people have recently become visually orientated either, they have always been that way. It is just that the media and advertising industries are capitalizing on this characteristic of mankind. Most people cannot mentally digest an abstract sermon. Halford Luccock has noted: 'The seminaries give four-fifths of their attention to training men to preach to one-fifth of their audience, that is, to the one-fifth of the congregation which can follow an abstract train of reasoning.'[69] David Burrell states:

> It is rumoured that dull preachers are to be found in some parts of the world. Charles Lamb came upon one of them of whom he said, 'He is so dry that if you were to prick a hole in him nothing would come out but sawdust.'... No man likes to travel over a flat country; better a steep climb occasionally than a monotonous stretch of prairie. It is not enough for a preacher to declare the truth. God makes raw meat, but the cook must create an appetite by furnishing the feast aright. No man can hold an audience by the bald presentation of abstract facts.[70]

Think with me for a moment. How many magazines on the racks of your local supermarket or newsagents are like theological journals, devoid of pictures? Would you rather read *Biblical Archeology Review* with or without pictures? Think about it. You and I may have no problem reading theological journals without pictures, but how many people in your congregation subscribe to 'pictureless' technical journals? A very small number of people in the world subscribe to magazines or journals with no pictures. Most people can't handle loads of technical abstract data. Geoffrey Thomas has said:

> One of the great perils that face preachers of the Reformed Faith is the problem of a hyper-intellectualism, that is, the constant danger of lapsing into a purely cerebral form of proclamation, which falls exclusively upon the intellect. Men become obsessed with doctrine and end up as brain-oriented preachers. There is consequently a fearful impoverishment in their hearers emotionally, devotionally, and practically. Such men are men of books and not men of people; they know the doctrines, but they know nothing of the emotional side of religion.[71]

If you want to see what it is like for your congregation to hear an abstract sermon, go to your public library and find a technical journal in a field you have not studied and read it. Make sure it does not have any pictures. Read it for as long as you normally preach on Sunday. You will then know how most people feel when they have endured an abstract sermon with few or no word pictures. You will know why some fall asleep during the message. Consider how many people would rather *listen* to their favourite TV show or movie instead of *watching* it. This is a huge boulder in the way. We need to acknowledge that a boulder exists and take steps either to move it or to go round it. Again, I am not saying we should resort to entertainment, slide shows, or drama. But technology has caused our society to be addicted to visual learning. People want to see it!

Think of all the visual gadgets and gizmos on the market today. We have digital cameras, wide screen TVs, plasma TVs, video players, camcorders, DVD and virtual reality

computer games that incorporate sight, sound, and vibrations
in the controls. New cinemas are springing up all over the
place with wall to wall, ceiling to floor screens, digital
surround sound, and computer enhanced pictures. Special
effects crews work for months and spend millions of dollars to
produce scenes that last seconds! People no longer go to the
cinema to watch a story, they go to have an experience! Every
scene is cut up into small, rapidly changing, pieces. Camera
angles are constantly changing, zooming in and out. Music,
usually unnoticed, constantly plays in the background, rising
and falling in synchronization with what is happening on the
screen. Sound bombards you from every direction.
Subwoofers, with amplifiers so powerful they could tear the
panelling off the walls, rock you in your seat. The next
morning those same cinema goers drag themselves out of bed
to come and hear you preach. It can be frightening to think
about, but we need to do it anyway.

Preaching is a challenge in this day and age. This is why
many churches are reducing the preaching hour to the
devotional minute. They have tried preaching abstract
sermons, but people don't respond. So they replace preaching
with music, drama and slide shows because people are more
willing to sit still for an hour of 'entertainment'. But the
expositor cannot do this. We have the biblical mandate to
'preach the word; be ready in season and out of season;
reprove, rebuke, exhort, with great patience and instruction'
(2 Tim. 4:2). Preaching is 'the method' God has chosen. Even
though some churches have forsaken this mandate, the
expository preacher cannot. He must not! He does not care
what the mega-church is doing to fill its pews. He is not going
to capitulate and sin against God by neglecting the
confrontive preaching of the word. He is not primarily
concerned with pleasing the people in his congregation. He
wants to please God. He knows that *God was well-pleased
through the foolishness of the message preached to save those
who believe* (1 Cor. 1:21). Biblical mandates constrain him.

They compel him. He is driven to *preach* the whole counsel of God's word. He must preach!

The expository preacher then has to decide what to do with boulders standing in the way. Some have 'dealt' with the obstacles by practising denial. These preachers are those who keep on preaching abstract truth to left-brained sheep. When people come to visit their churches they leave saying, 'I couldn't understand a thing he was saying, but he certainly sounded well educated,' or 'That preacher really knew his Bible, but I just couldn't follow him. Let us try the church down the road next Sunday.' This is a tragedy, especially when the church down the road is neglecting to preach the word. In essence we have encouraged them to eat junk food.

When the abstract expositor hears through the grapevine these kinds of responses to his sermons, he immediately blames the sheep. He is like an alcoholic in denial who blames everyone else, but never himself. Such expositors pile the blame on those 'uncommitted', 'undisciplined', 'worldly', 'professing' Christians. He thinks to himself, 'If they were really saved, they would love my solid biblical (left-brained) exposition of the word and would not be so fickle (right-brained), wanting to have their ears tickled (things explained with word pictures).' So he plays the martyr and keeps on delivering sermons that are dry as dust, but 'full of nutrition'. Sydney Smith says, 'The sin of the pulpit against the Holy Ghost is dullness.'[72] Haddon Robinson rightly states, 'For the preacher clarity is a moral matter.'[73] Paul Bull writes:

> So the preacher's first duty is to be sure that the Word he is to proclaim is with God, and is drawn from the heart of Deity ; and his second duty is to see that the Word becomes flesh and dwells amongst us. In other words, he has no right to present his hearers with naked abstract thoughts. It is his duty to translate the abstract thoughts into the concrete terms of human life and to clothe them with the warm flesh and blood of human passion and emotion.[74]

I worked for a while installing grain tempering systems for cattle feedlots. Tempering is the process of adding moisture to the grain so that it can be crushed or rolled flat. It is crushed or rolled flat so that cattle can get most of the nutrition out of the grain, which causes them to gain weight faster. If grain is left whole, very little nutrition can be absorbed by the cattle. It is important to consider that both tempered and untempered grain have the same essence, the same nutrition, and are the same thing – grain: the only difference is the 'form'. This is exactly what we are talking about with regard to sermons. Abstract sermons are like untempered grain: they have all the intrinsic nutrition, but the 'cattle' are unable to absorb the nutrients. An expositor who learns to communicate with word pictures will make more of the nutrition of God's word available to his people. Spurgeon, speaking of this, said, 'Right royal truths should ride in a chariot of gold. Bring forth the noblest of your milk-white steeds, and let the music sound forth melodiously from the silver trumpets, as truth rides through the streets.'[75]

As with a drunkard, your first step to recovery is to admit that you have an 'abstract problem' that needs to be dealt with. Warren Wiersbe rightly says, 'Exegesis and analysis are launching pads, not parking lots, and it's imagination that fuels the rocket.'[76] God has commanded you to *preach the word* ; but the command, *'Be thou difficult to understand,'* does not exist. 'Expository preaching' and 'obscurity' are not synonyms, though in some churches you would think they were. Your goal in preaching is to permanently fix the truth of God's word in the minds and hearts of your listeners. Your effectiveness as a herald is not determined by your ability to know what *you* are saying, but your ability to *get the people to whom you are preaching to know and understand* what you are saying. If you are going to do this you must overcome the obstacles standing between you and your people. You must achieve three things: (1) you must hold people's attention; (2) you must give them understanding; and (3) you must help them remember. Preaching with word pictures helps to accomplish all three goals. Let us consider each of them separately.

You must hold people's attention
The first and most basic task of the one proclaiming God's word is to maintain the attention of his hearers. The preacher needs someone to *listen to him*. This is such an obvious truth that it is rarely considered by many expository preachers. Most homiletics books do not even discuss 'attention' as it relates to preaching. Spurgeon said, 'I suppose the homiletical *savans* consider that their entire volumes are seasoned with this subject, and that they need not give it to us in lumps.'[77] I believe the reason attention is overlooked by most expositors is they assume if people are present and sitting in the pews they are listening. Yet what about that man in the back row who has his head tilted back, mouth gaping open, who is carefully examining the backs of his eyelids? Is he listening? What about the lady in the front row who is looking right at you, but her mind is on the pot roast she has cooking at home? What about the young man with a catatonic look on his face, that man stuck in a mental mud-hole because you threw out the word 'eschatology' and failed to define it? These people are present *but not listening*. We deceive ourselves if we think that the presence of warm bodies means that people are listening. People are easily distracted. If a sermon has a dry or abstract stretch, people will mentally opt out. When they are *out*, the word is not going *in*. The gate of their mind is shut, and the living word is outside but not flowing into their hearts. This is one of the reasons why we need to use word pictures in our preaching. Large or small, word pictures are attention grabbers. W. B. Riley, speaking of this, said:

> The average audience, if it grows a bit listless under the sound
> of a sermon, is quickened in interest the moment an illustration
> is introduced; and, since there is no possibility of producing

results in the minds and hearts of men apart from interest, the employment of the illustration is a prime element of success.

As fox hunters thrill to the voice of hounds when by their louder and more rapid barking they indicate that the trail has become fresher and hotter, so an audience responds to a vivid illustration of truth with awakened interest. Its use, therefore, is not only in clarifying thought but in engaging attention.[78]

Next time you look out from behind the pulpit at that sea of faces remember that the people are present, but their minds may be playing with Alice in Wonderland. We must come to grips with the fact that those we preach to are distracted from the sermon by legions of ideas floating around in their heads, by Satan and by their environment. Like Martha, they are distracted with all their preparations. People will often respond to an abstract sermon as dead fish packed in ice will respond to a lure. Too much abstract information will sever the artery of attention. Everyone has, at some time or another, caught themselves looking at the person in front of them, the ceiling tiles, the wall decorations, or a snag in the carpet during a dry stretch of a sermon. It is the preacher's job to wake people out of their mental slumber and to hold their attention on the truth of God's word. If people aren't listening to you, you are boxing the air. David Burrell has commented:

Happy is the man who can preach two sermons every week in the same parish, year in and year out, on a single system of truth, and always keep the eyes of his auditors open and their ears pricked up. In order to do this the preacher must obviously do something more than say solemn things in a commonplace way. He must command a hearing by making his old message stand forth in changing lights and guises ever new.[79]

Later, Burrell quotes Spurgeon as saying:

I have often seen some poor fellow standing at the aisle in the Tabernacle. Why, he looks just like a sparrow that has got into a church and cannot get out again. He cannot make out what sort of service it is; he begins to count how many people are sitting in the front row in the gallery, and all kinds of ideas pass through his mind. Now I want to attract his attention; how shall I do it? If I quote a text of Scripture, he may not know what it means and may not be interested in it. Shall I put a bit of Latin into the sermon, or quote the original Hebrew or Greek of my text? That will not do for such a man. What shall I do? Ah! I know a story that will, I believe, just fit him. Out it comes, and the man does not look up at the gallery any more; but he is wondering whatever the preacher is at.[80]

Ideally, a preacher should attempt to capture and retain the minds of his congregation for the duration of the sermon. As one of my homiletics professors in seminary stated, 'If the people in your church aren't listening to your sermon – it's your fault!'[81] Spurgeon said basically the same thing: 'It may be their duty to attend, but it is far more your duty to make them do so. You must attract fish to your hook, and if they do not come, you should blame the fisherman and not the fish.'[82] If you are preaching the word, you have something worth hearing; so say it in a way that will be interesting. If we love our sheep, we help them pay attention to God's truth.

Word pictures will help you maintain the attention of the people you are preaching to. You must have listeners! We will look at how to use word pictures to help gain attention in the chapter entitled 'Do it yourself word pictures', but for now we move on to the role of understanding and how that relates to expository preaching.

You must give people understanding

It is the preacher's task to help people to *understand* what the Bible means by what it says. Abstraction not only discourages attention, it is also an obstacle that stands in the way of understanding. Word pictures greatly increase a person's ability to understand. Imparting understanding is what biblical exposition is all about, to expose and bring understanding to the truths latent in the text of God's word.

This is how the revival of Ezra's time began: 'And they read from the book, from the law of God, *translating to give the sense* so that they *understood the reading*' (Neh. 8:8). It is the preacher's job to explain the text of Scripture in such a way that people understand what God is saying to them. Exegetical precision, without understanding, profits nothing. The goal of preaching is not the dissection of a passage but the communication of the meaning of the passage. You can take the body of a dead man and weigh him, measure him, take x-rays, and do blood tests; you can describe his looks and take pictures of him; but that does not mean you know the person – you only know facts about him. Exegetical data needs to be understood before it becomes 'knowledge' and before it can be turned into 'wisdom'. Exegesis provides the framework which bears the load of our sermon, but it does not make a suitable house to dwell in. It is not the finished product of preaching. Sometimes expository preachers can give their people exegetical data and fail utterly to give them understanding. When the truth is not clearly explained the result is a failure to understand.

If you have been preaching for any length of time, you have probably taught the doctrines of justification, grace, and sanctification. Let us say you were to hire some hit-men (hypothetically speaking) to stand at the door of your church and shoot every person in your church who could not define justification, grace, and sanctification. How many people in your congregation would make it home alive? Just because you know what those terms mean, that does not mean that everyone in your congregation does. Just because you defined those terms from a theological lexicon six months ago, that does not mean that they now remember what you quoted from the lexicon.

Think of the kinds of 'theological definitions' that people remember. For 'justification' they are more likely to remember 'just as if I had never sinned', than 'a forensic declaration of innocence based on the vicarious atonement of

Christ'. People have an easier time understanding things they can relate to, things they can see, things that are concrete, ideas broken down and rolled out into their basic parts. Yet, many preachers do not hesitate to use abstract words ending in '-tion' or '-ence' and never define them in an engaging and understandable way.[83] In doing this you rob your people of spiritual nutrition. Nuts must be cracked open before eating. Cows need to be killed, butchered, cut up, cooked, cut up into smaller pieces, then dipped in steak sauce, chewed and swallowed before they deliver nutrition. We must avoid serving up theological terms 'on the hoof'. If we fail to give our people understanding, we fail to nourish them with God's word. The preacher must make the truth of God's word vivid, concrete, and understandable. Word pictures help impart understanding.

You must help people to remember
Finally, it is the preacher's task to help people to remember what the Bible says. Word pictures are effective at supergluing truth to people's minds. Abstract truth does not stick very well to the brain and doesn't maintain attention well either. It is also much harder to understand. But if we associate abstract thoughts with picturesque words, phrases and illustrations, then abstract truths are much easier to retain. Think of the things that you clearly remember from sermons you heard years ago.

I remember one instance twelve years ago as if it was yesterday. I was in seminary, and Albert Martin, a very capable expository preacher, preached in chapel on the subject of personal purity in the life of a minister. He was waxing eloquent on the hypocrisy and vileness of unconfessed sin in the life of any preacher. Then in a deep, forceful tone he said, 'Gentlemen! When you go to the grocery store and stare at the half-dressed women on the front covers of those magazines while you wait in line to purchase your groceries; when you lust after them and then look the other way with a pious look on your face. [Volume increases by many decibels] Gentlemen!!!! That sin will lie in the *cavern* of your heart and will arise a great *monster* that will consume you and your ministry!' Everyone of us felt like running for cover! We were ready to drop down on our knees and start confessing. We knew exactly what he was saying. He so clearly and effectively communicated to us the danger of unconfessed sin that every time I go into a grocery store and 'run the temptation gauntlet' through the magazine racks to get to the cash register, I remember what he said. Pastor Martin not only held my attention, he not only gave me understanding, he helped me remember for ever the seriousness of unconfessed sin in my life and what it will do to my ministry.

How did he accomplish this? Primarily with word pictures. I could see and relate to countless times when I was tempted to stare at the front covers of the magazines while waiting in line at the grocery store. I could relate to times when I did stare at them for a moment and then look away with a 'pious look on my face'. I knew that many times I went away with unconfessed sin lying in my heart. I knew what a cavern was, what a monster was, and I did not want my ministry gobbled up by the monster of unconfessed sin. I am so thankful for preaching like that, which presents truth in an easy to remember format. William Evans says, 'Indeed, many an entire sermon, which otherwise would have been forgotten, has been recalled in its entirety by means of recalling an illustration used in a sermon.'[84] I want to help people to remember God's word, not just to preach at them. We must never forget that *any truth worth preaching is a truth worth remembering*. Andrew Blackwood says that when a person remembers, 'He can take it home, share it with his loved ones, and live in its light until traveling days on earth are done.'[85] It is true that some people have failing hard drives, but this is no excuse for boring our congregations with the treasures of God's word by cloaking them in abstract terminology. Alford Garvie writes:

It is surely a matter of common observation that many sermons, which at the time of delivery made an impression, are very soon forgotten. There is a vague sense of pleasure or profit which survives, but no distinct recollections. If a preacher believes (and if he does not, why does he preach?) that his message has a permanent value for the Christian life of his hearers, he must desire that his sermon should not be forgotten almost as soon as it is heard. Desiring this, he should make it his aim to throw his material into such a shape that it will be easily remembered.[86]

Watson has written:

The word is a jewel; it adorns the hidden man, and shall we not remember it? If the word stays not in the memory, it cannot profit. Some can better remember a piece of news than a line of Scripture; their memories are like those ponds, where the frogs live, but the fish die.[87]

Watson's quotation makes me ask the question, 'What can we do to keep the fish from dying?' What can we do to help people to remember what we preach? If we can get people to pay attention and understand our sermons we are going to help them to remember them too. If we use word pictures correctly, we should be able to keep people focused on and interested in the word. Interest is a key ingredient in memory. If people are not interested in what we are saying, it probably will not reside in their memories for very long.

Consider how many men can easily spout off endless lines of statistics related to their favourite hobbies. Think of all the recipes, conversations and birth statistics which the average housewife can readily call to mind. The statistics themselves are as abstract as they can be, but they are remembered because they are associated with something that the person is interested in, something very concrete and real. If the preacher can hold people's attention, give them understanding by relating biblical truth to what is interesting or familiar, people will better remember what is preached.

Now I am not talking about feeding people's lusts from the pulpit. People are interested in many carnal things, and we should not feed their sinful passions. What I am talking about are interests such as, How can I keep from sinning?, How can I raise my children?, How can I handle my finances?, How can I keep from worrying? and so on. This is why the Bible expositor needs to know not only *what* the Bible says but *how* it applies to people today. This is why it is common practice for many expositors to start a sermon with an illustration that shows people that they have a practical need to know what God's word says in the passage being preached on. Once people see that they have a need to know something, then they get interested. Yet even if they are interested, we can hide the truth from them if we communicate in abstract language. That is why we must help them to see how the truth applies to their need. When word pictures are used to present what people are interested in, they listen better and remember more.

One of the great compliments any preacher can receive is to have someone remember a sermon preached a week, a month, or even a year earlier. When someone says to me, 'You know that sermon you preached a while back on such and such? Well, that really helped me,' I like to ask them, 'Why do you think you remembered that particular sermon?' Invariably they will respond, 'I remember that sermon because at that time in my life I was really struggling with....' They remember the sermon because it addressed a personal need or struggle that they were interested in overcoming. But interest alone is not enough. Truth must be understandable. Word pictures help flesh out the dry bones of theological data, giving them substance and making them interesting, thus aiding memory retention. One person describes word pictures: 'They are like pictures to the eye which rivet attention, and help to fasten the truth in the memory.'[88]

Before moving on let me summarize what we have discussed up to this point. First, I introduced you to an exceptional

Puritan preacher named Thomas Watson. We learned that
Watson used an extensive variety of illustrative devices
which we have decided to call word pictures. These include
many kinds of illustrative devices such as sense appeal,
metaphor, simile, quotation, cross-reference and historical
reference. In this chapter we have looked at some of the
hurdles and obstacles which stand between the preacher's
sermon and the hearts of his people. We have noted three
primary goals one must attempt to achieve when preaching
the word: one must get people to listen to God's word; one
must help them to understand God's word; and one must help
them to remember God's word. I have attempted to argue that
word pictures help achieve these three essential goals. Before
we look at the Scriptures to see how God uses word pictures
in his word, I want to address some of the *objections* I have
collected concerning homiletical techniques in general and
the use of word pictures in particular.

5

HEY! YOU CAN'T DO THAT!

Objections to using word pictures in preaching

If you were to teach homiletics, you would eventually run into a certain class of diligent Bible students who scoff at what they see as superfluous, extraneous, homiletic gimmicks. I know, I used to be one. I also have friends who are of that persuasion. This is interesting to me because everyone who preaches practises homiletics. Speaking, using hand gestures, raising and lowering your voice, are all homiletical gimmicks. Preaching is applied homiletics. The aversion some have to homiletics, I have discovered, is only a symptom of a bigger issue. The basis of their aversion is that they are convinced that the *content* of the sermon is far more important than the *method* of delivery. For some it is all important – so important that it does not matter how the content comes out of their mouth as long as it gets out and within earshot of their people.

I would have to agree that they have a legitimate point. Who would dare argue that it matters not what you preach as long as it is interesting, engaging and entertaining? The *content is* far more important than the *method* of delivery. Content is the reason for expository preaching. We must preach the word of God. Biblical truth must be our content. But is it true that content is 'all important?' Does it matter that you speak in the same language as those to whom you preach? Does it matter that you speak loud enough for people to hear you? Yes, these and other homiletical techniques matter. Content is primary, but it is not all that matters.

Paul, when addressing the proper use of tongues in the church, said, 'For one who speaks in a tongue does not speak to men, but to God; for no one understands, but in his spirit he speaks mysteries' (1 Cor. 14:2). A few verses later he said:

> Now I wish that you all spoke in tongues, but even more that you would prophesy; and greater is one who prophesies than one who speaks in tongues, unless he interprets, so that the church may receive edifying. But now, brethren, if I come to you speaking in tongues, what shall I profit you, unless I speak to you either by way of revelation or of knowledge or of prophecy or of teaching? Yet even lifeless things, either flute or harp, in producing a sound, if they do not produce a distinction in the tones, how will it be known what is played on the flute or on the harp? For if the bugle produces an indistinct sound, who will prepare himself for battle? So also you, unless you utter by the tongue speech that is clear, how will it be known what is spoken? For you will be speaking into the air (1 Cor. 14:5-9).

Paul's point is that all spiritual gifts should be used to edify and profit the body (see 1 Corinthians 14:3, 4, 6, 12, 26). If the church cannot understand what the tongue-speaker is saying, he has misappropriated that spiritual gift; he has failed to edify. The word 'edification' literally means to be built up or to be strengthened spiritually.[89] Believers are not edified when understanding is not imparted. In the same way when a preacher speaks over the heads of his people, he is not profiting the church; he is 'speaking into the air'. The preacher who fails to *communicate* is like a madman or barbarian (1 Cor. 14:11, 23).

When I use the word 'communicate', I am not talking about speaking, heralding, or proclaiming. I am talking about the verbal exchange of information. You can speak, herald, or proclaim the truth to a brick wall, but you are not communicating. The preacher must *communicate* God's word to the people. A communicator is 'one who imparts knowledge'.[90] Communication is 'the imparting or interchange of thoughts, opinions, or information by speech, writing, or signs'.[91] If knowledge is not imparted, communication has not taken place. This is why we must not only pay attention to our sermon *content* but also to the *method* of our sermon delivery. It is a false inference to conclude that solid content excludes effective methodology. The two are not mutually exclusive, they are complimentary.

Some preachers protest that content must be sacrificed when word pictures are employed. That is not the case. It is true that you cannot give people as much exegetical data during the sermon if you are having to stop and make it understandable. Yet why preach sixty minutes of exegetical data if your audience cannot understand most of what you are saying? It would be better to give them half as much exegetical data but make it clearly understood and remembered. If you fail to impart knowledge and understanding, you fail as a preacher because you have failed to *communicate* the word of God. Listen to Solomon recounting David's advice to him:

> Then he taught me and said to me, 'Let your heart hold fast my words; Keep my commandments and live; Acquire wisdom! Acquire understanding! Do not forget, nor turn away from the words of my mouth. Do not forsake her, and she will guard you; Love her, and she will watch over you. The beginning of wisdom is: Acquire wisdom; And with all your acquiring, get understanding (Prov. 4:4-7).

Notice the advice Solomon received from David was to *hold fast my words, keep my commandments, acquire wisdom* (twice), *acquire understanding* (twice), and *do not forget*. This is what we should aim for in our preaching. We want to help people to hold fast the word and not forget it. We want them to acquire wisdom by being able to put their knowledge into practice. We also want to give them understanding. The preacher who succeeds in doing these things has succeeded as a preacher of the word.

Consider the story I once heard about a farmer. He went to court because he had a disagreement with the insurance company over medical expenses incurred after an accident. The insurance company claimed that, at the time of the accident, the farmer had said he was fine but later had changed his story. When it was the farmer's turn to testify, the lawyer for the insurance company asked him one question: 'Did you not say to the officer at the scene of the accident that you were fine? Yes or no?' The farmer hesitated for a moment and said, 'Your Honour, mind if I explain a couple of things real quick before I answer that question?' The judge said, 'Go ahead.' The farmer then began to explain what had happened. 'I was hauling my mule Betsy across the road in the back of my Ford pickup truck.' At this point the lawyer for the insurance company became visibly agitated and objected with theatrical sighs and groans, but the judge let the farmer continue. 'As I was saying, I was hauling my mule across the road when this here crazy person come barrelin' down the highway and crashed right into us. I went flyin' one way and Betsy when flyin' the other. I was hurtin' pretty bad. Soon the sheriff arrived at the scene and found Betsy all broken up and sufferin'. He did the only humane thing a person could do. He drew his pistol and shot Betsy right between the eyes to put her out of her misery. Then he came over to me, gun still drawn and barrel still smokin' and said, "Are you OK?" The only thing I could think to say was, "I'm just fine." ' That is the difference between giving someone the facts and giving them understanding. It is true that the farmer had said he was 'just fine'. Those were the facts. But until the facts were understood, justice could not be served.

In the same way, preachers who only deliver facts are frequently not understood. That is why we need to use word pictures. Now let us look at some of the objections expositors have when it comes to using certain homiletical techniques.

Objection 1 – Paul said that we should not use them. 1 Corinthians 1:17; 2:1, 4-5

Some of the best missiles launched at the use of homiletical techniques, such as word pictures, come from Paul's first letter to the Corinthians. In the first two chapters of that letter, Paul takes time to explain his methodology for communicating the gospel to the lost. He makes several statements which at first glance seem to rule out anything but raw, exegetical, abstract preaching. Paul, writing under the inspiration of the Holy Spirit, said this:

> For Christ did not send me to baptize, but to preach the gospel, *not in cleverness of speech*, that the cross of Christ should not be made void (1 Cor. 1:17, emphasis mine).

and

> And when I came to you, brethren, *I did not come with superiority of speech or of wisdom*, proclaiming to you the testimony of God.... And my message and my preaching *were not in persuasive words of wisdom*, but in demonstration of the Spirit and of power, that your faith should not rest on the wisdom of men, but on the power of God (1 Cor. 2:1, 4-5, emphasis mine).

One might conclude from reading those verses that Paul did not care about communication techniques or homiletical gimmicks. After all, who would want to *make void* the cross of Christ? But when one studies what Paul was up against at that time in the Greek culture of Corinth, things become much clearer. The Greeks prized debate and rhetoric. In fact, it was a form of entertainment.[92] That is what Paul is addressing in these texts. Paul was not going to play the game of the Greek philosophers and rhetoricians when he preached the word. He did not come to entertain people, to draw attention to himself, or spread worldly wisdom. He came to clearly deliver to the lost people of Corinth the message of *Jesus Christ and him crucified*, in the power of the Holy Spirit. He did not come in *cleverness of speech* to debate the truthfulness of God's word, and he did not come in *persuasive words of wisdom*, i.e., worldly wisdom, the wisdom of men (see 1:19-24; 2:5-8).

Paul, when preaching to the lost, presupposed that God existed and that the Scriptures were true. God's word was not up for debate. If Paul had added worldly wisdom to the word of God, or if he had preached to entertain or attract attention to himself, he would have been sinning. He would have run the risk of making void the very message God had sent him to proclaim. It was Paul's goal to preach the gospel, but it was not his goal to ignore effective communication techniques. Many reasons to believe this become apparent upon closer examination. Let us look at them now.

First, Paul was not against using word pictures and other homiletical devices to communicate the gospel clearly. Paul asked the Colossians, in Colossians 4:4, to pray *that I may make it clear in the way I ought to speak.* In verse 3 Paul says he is praying that God might *open up to us a door for the word* (notice the word picture), so that he *may speak forth the mystery of Christ.* Then in verse 4 he prays for clarity of presentation in *the way I ought to speak.* Paul was concerned with homiletics. He wanted to speak forth the mystery of Christ with 'clarity'. Paul did not want the faith of the Corinthians resting on sands of human wisdom (1 Cor. 2:5). He wanted their faith resting on the word of God. Paul knew that he was not an especially gifted communicator (see 2 Cor. 10:10; 11:6), so he asked people to pray for him in that area (Col. 4:4). The Greek word φανερόω (*phaneroō*), according to one lexicon, means,

> to cause something to be fully known by revealing clearly and in some detail – to make known, to make plain, to reveal, to bring to the light, or to disclose.... All of these meanings involve a shift from the sensory domain of seeing, causing to see or giving light to, to the cognitive domain of making something fully known, evident, and clear.[93]

That is exactly what word pictures help to accomplish.

Secondly, some might conclude that when Paul says, *not in*

persuasive words of wisdom (1 Cor. 2:4), he meant that preachers should never try to persuade people with a graphic presentation of the gospel. But this could not be what Paul had in mind. Paul said in 2 Corinthians 5:11, *Therefore knowing the fear of the Lord, we persuade men.* In Acts 26:28-29 Paul pressed King Agrippa so forcefully with the truth of the gospel that Agrippa replied, 'In a short time you will persuade me to become a Christian.' And Paul said, 'I would to God, that whether in a short or long time, not only you, but also all who hear me this day, might become such as I am, except for these chains.' Paul was not against persuading people with the truth; he was against persuading people with worldly wisdom and error. John MacArthur, speaking of expository preaching, said, 'Biblical preaching is articulating theology in a powerful, convincing, persuasive way.'[94] It is a losing battle to argue that abstract preaching is more powerful, convincing, or persuasive than well-illustrated truth. That is why Paul used many word pictures in his preaching. The bulk of his testimony to Agrippa was the *story* of his conversion and the 'story' of Jesus' death, burial and resurrection. Everything he said was concrete, graphic and illustrative.

Thirdly, I do not believe that Paul was opposed to using word pictures because his letters are liberally seasoned with them. Paul uses metaphor, simile and illustration extensively. Now if Paul was against effective communication techniques, you would think that by the end of his life he would have perfected his method as much as possible. If he was against using metaphor, simile and sense appeal, you would think the last epistle he ever wrote, his second epistle to Timothy, would be a polished example of straightforward, abstract communication. Yet we find just the opposite is true. I began to count the number of word pictures in 2 Timothy and stopped in chapter two after I had recorded forty-five of them! Notice the sense appeal, metaphor, simile, the graphic and concrete language that Paul used:

beloved son; clear conscience; the way my forefathers did; as I recall your tears; filled with joy; kindle afresh the gift of God; He is able to guard; Retain the standard of sound words; Guard ... the treasure; not ashamed of my chains; as a good soldier; no soldier in active service entangles himself in the affairs of everyday life, so that he may please the one who enlisted him as a soldier; if anyone competes as an athlete, he does not win the prize unless he competes according to the rules; the hard working farmer ought to be the first to receive his share of the crops; as a criminal; the word of God is not imprisoned; not to wrangle about words; as a workman who does not need to be ashamed; avoid worldly and empty chatter; their talk will spread like gangrene; now in a large house there are not only gold and silver vessels, but also vessels of wood, and earthenware, and some to honor and some to dishonor. Therefore if any man cleanses himself from these things, he will be a vessel for honor; flee from youthful lusts; pursue righteousness; the Lord's bond servant; they may come to their senses and escape from the snare of the devil, having been held captive by him to do his will.[95]

It is beyond dispute that Paul used many word pictures. Because of this, we need to ask ourselves some questions. Why did Paul use so many word pictures in every inspired letter he wrote to the churches? Did he do it to 'make void the cross of Christ'? Was he trying to have his readers place their faith in the 'wisdom of men'? Did he want to hide the truth of the gospel? Was he using *cleverness of speech, superiority of speech,* or *persuasive words of wisdom*? At the end of his life, did he change his methodology for preaching and teaching the truth? Was he sinning under the inspiration of the Holy Spirit? We can answer these questions with a definitive NO! He was communicating the word of God! He did it effectively by using words which helped his readers to *see, feel,* and *experience* the truth of the gospel. It is conclusive that Paul did not have word pictures in mind when he was speaking of 'superiority of speech' or 'worldly wisdom'. He was not against using word pictures.

A fourth rebuttal is that Paul also used *historical reference* word pictures extensively in his sermons and defences recorded in the book of Acts.[96] We have already mentioned that Paul tried to persuade Agrippa with the truth of the gospel preached using word pictures. Most of Paul's defences consisted of one historical reference or story after another. Consider Paul's sermon in Pisidian Antioch (Acts 13:16-41) as a test case. Paul begins his sermon with sense appeal by appealing to the Israelites' 'fear of God' (v. 16), by restating the story of the Exodus (vv. 17-19), by reminding them of the time of the judges and Samuel (v. 20), by reminding them of the reign of Saul (v. 21), by telling them of David (v. 22), by reminding them of the promised descendant of David (v. 23), by telling John the Baptist's story (vv. 24-25), by appealing to their fear of God again (v. 26), by telling them the story of Jesus' death, burial, and resurrection (vv. 27-31), by appealing to their hope that God would send the Messiah (vv. 32-33), by showing how Jesus was the fulfilment of two different Psalms (vv. 33-35), by graphically pointing out that David *fell asleep*, and *was laid among his fathers* (vv. 36-37), by talking about being *freed* from sin and how the law could not *free* them from sins (vv. 38-39), by telling them to take heed so that the words of the prophets will not *come upon* them (v. 40), and finally by illustrating their unbelief by quoting Habakkuk 1:5, which promises judgment to those who would not believe (v. 41). Paul uses word pictures in the form of historical references, familiar stories, metaphor and cross-reference. He preached with a never-ending string of word pictures in this sermon. Everything he said was attached to something familiar and concrete.

That does not mean that he did that every time, but he did it at Pisidian Antioch in that particular sermon. If you look at his other sermons in the book of Acts, you find a similar style of sermon delivery. That is why I say with confidence that Paul did not neglect homiletics and especially word pictures. I do not believe that his story telling was extraneous 'filler' or that it hindered the gospel. It was *the most effective way* to share the gospel in that setting.

It might be argued that if Paul taught that word pictures obscured, made void, or nullified the truth, then all the writers of Scripture are guilty of this grievous sin. Every author of Scripture uses word pictures to communicate the Word of God. We will look at this in more detail later, but for now you will have to trust me until we get to the next chapter where we will discover that the Scriptures are an encyclopedia of word pictures.

Fifthly, if Paul was teaching us in 1 Corinthians that using word pictures was a carnal means of preaching truth, then every great preacher who has ever lived has repeatedly engaged in 'making void the cross of Christ'. Augustine, Chrysostom, Luther, Calvin, Spurgeon, Edwards, Meyers, Jowett, Moody, Morgan, Campbell, Guthrie, Magee, Swindoll, MacArthur, Jeremiah, Robinson, Hendricks, Stott, and the like, all used – or presently use – word pictures in their preaching. God has used every one of these men in great ways because they preached Jesus Christ and him crucified and did it well by employing word pictures in their sermons.

The sixth and final argument for why Paul could not have been rejecting homiletics in general or word pictures in particular, is that every godly preacher in the Bible, including the greatest man ever born of women (John the Baptist, Matt. 11:11) and the Lord Jesus Christ, used word pictures in never-ending succession in their sermons. If Paul was condemning the use of word pictures, then he was condemning himself and every preacher and prophet in the pages of Scripture. Therefore, it is clear that Paul was not against effective communication techniques. He was not against using many word pictures. What Paul was opposed to in 1 Corinthians 1:17 and 2:1, 4-5 was debating the word of God, preaching to entertain people, preaching error, and the worldly wisdom of men.

Objection 2 – the Holy Spirit can use raw exegetical data to hold people's attention, give them comprehension and help them not to forget

This argument is a straw man. It begs the question. The Holy Spirit can do anything. Nothing is impossible with God! If he wanted to, he could give mouths to starfish, enable them to fly through the air and proclaim the gospel. He could make rocks cry out, 'Hosanna in the highest.' He made Balaam's donkey speak! No problem! That does not give us licence to be mediocre communicators. Spurgeon rebukes preachers who fail to employ effective homiletical techniques, saying:

> If men's minds are wandering far away they cannot receive the truth, and it is much the same if they are inactive. Sin cannot be taken out of men, as Eve was taken out of the side of Adam, while they are fast asleep. They must awake, understanding what we are saying, and feeling its force, or else we may as well go to sleep too. There are preachers who care very little whether they are attended to or not; so long as they can hold on through the allotted time it is of very small importance to them whether their people hear for eternity, or hear in vain: the sooner such ministers sleep in the churchyard and preach by the verse on their gravestones the better.[97]

I am glad he said that and not me, but I agree. The Holy Spirit has inspired the finest sermons, prose and poetry ever written, and has chosen to saturate the word of God with picturesque language. Why? Because God gave men imaginations. He knows that our imaginations process word pictures. God knows that word pictures grab our attention and feed our understanding. He also knows that when we are interested and have understanding it helps fasten truth to our hearts and minds. Yes, the Holy Spirit can do anything he wants. He can even use a dry abstract preacher to lead a worldwide revival. But he has called us to preach the word, to preach it clearly, to preach it accurately and to preach to *communicate* the content of the gospel. He has shown us by example in the word of God, and it has been verified in the lives of godly men, that word pictures greatly facilitate communication.

Objection 3 – we cannot make men accept the gospel or give them understanding; that is the job of the Holy Spirit

That is true – in a specific context. The Scriptures teach that God grants people the ability to understand his word through the illuminating work of the Holy Spirit. Jesus taught that the truth of the kingdom had to be revealed by a divine fiat:

> At that time Jesus answered and said, 'I praise You, O Father, Lord of heaven and earth, that *You have hidden these things from the wise and intelligent and have revealed them to babes.* Yes, Father, for this way was well-pleasing in Your sight. All things have been handed over to Me by My Father; and no one knows the Son, except the Father; nor does anyone know the Father except the Son, and anyone to *whom the Son wills to reveal Him* (Matt. 11:25-27, emphasis mine).

Jesus also told the disciples in Matthew 13:11: '*To you it has been granted to know the mysteries of the kingdom of heaven, but to them it has not been granted.*' Paul later explained in more detail that believers can know the Scriptures because the Holy Spirit gives them understanding:

> For to us *God revealed them through the Spirit*; for the Spirit searches all things, even the depths of God.... Now *we have received*, not the spirit of the world, but *the Spirit* who is from God, *that we might know the things freely given to us by God,* which things we also speak, not in words taught by human wisdom, but in *those taught by the Spirit*, combining spiritual thoughts with spiritual words (1 Cor. 2:10, 12-13, emphasis mine).

Immediately following those verses Paul explains why the unbeliever cannot understand God's word: 'But a natural man does not *accept* the things of the Spirit of God; for they are foolishness to him, and he cannot *understand* them, because they are spiritually appraised' (1 Cor. 2:14, emphasis mine). Paul says men can neither *accept* nor *understand* God's truth apart from the illuminating work of the Holy Spirit. Thomas Watson acknowledges this when he says (with word pictures of course):

> The motions of the Spirit are always consonant with the Word. The Word is the chariot in which the Spirit of God rides; whichever way the tide of the Word runs, that way the wind of the Spirit blows.

and,

> The ship of ordinances will not carry us to heaven, though an angel is pilot, unless the wind of God's Spirit blows. The Spirit is the soul of the Word without which it is but a dead letter. Ministers may prescribe medicine, but it is God's Spirit who must make it work.[98]

We must remember that in 1 Corinthians 1 and 2 Paul was speaking of his methodology for preaching the gospel to *the lost*, that is, to those who did not know Christ and who were not indwelt by the Holy Spirit. When preaching to believers, the Holy Spirit would be permanently abiding and giving understanding. Most expository preaching today is done in churches to those who profess to know Christ. But whoever the audience may be, preaching is not exclusively an act of the Holy Spirit. Three parties are involved: a preacher, his listeners and the Holy Spirit. Paul mentions the first two parties in Romans 10:14 when he says, 'How then shall they call upon Him in whom they have not believed? And how shall they believe in Him whom they have not heard? And how shall they hear without a preacher?' The implied answers to Paul's rhetorical triad are: (1) people cannot call upon

Christ if they have not believed in him; (2) people cannot believe in Christ if they have never heard him; and (3) people cannot hear Christ without a preacher.

The third party needed in expository preaching is the Holy Spirit. The preaching of the Word needs to be escorted and empowered by the Spirit of God (as noted above). Preaching is our responsibility, while illumination, conversion and transformation are the Holy Spirit's responsibility. The effectiveness of preaching is a multifaceted process. The Holy Spirit, the preacher, the Word of God, demonic opposition and listeners with sin-cursed hearts must be considered. The expository preacher preaches the Word, in the power of the Spirit, to the listeners. The preacher does not tell the Spirit what to do, nor is he able to do the works of illumination, conversion, or regeneration. He is not in control of the Holy Spirit nor is he responsible for making sure the Holy Spirit does his work correctly. The preacher is responsible for preaching God's truth, preaching it clearly and preaching it to people who are willing to listen. The preacher is responsible for doing his task right. But what about giving people understanding? Whose task is that, the preacher's or the Holy Spirit's? This is a point of confusion.

Actually, that was a trick question. It is not a case of either/or but a case of both/and, and I will show you why. First, we must consider what *kind of understanding* the Holy Spirit is responsible for giving to men as opposed to what *kind of understanding* the preacher is responsible for giving. Paul said in 1 Corinthians 2:14: 'But a natural man *does not accept* the things of the Spirit of God; for they are foolishness to him, and *he cannot understand them*, because they are spiritually appraised' (emphasis mine). He uses two words to describe what the natural man, on his own, unaided by the Holy Spirit, cannot do with the gospel message. Paul says he cannot *accept* or *understand*. What he cannot accept or understand are 'the things of the Spirit of God', described in the preceding context as 'the word of the cross' (1:18); 'the foolishness of the message preached' (1:21); 'Christ crucified' (1:23); 'the testimony of God' (2:1); 'Jesus Christ and him crucified' (2:2); and 'God's wisdom in a mystery' (2:7). Again, he is speaking of the unbeliever, a person dead in trespasses and sins (Eph. 2:1-3).

The word translated *accept* is the Greek word δέχεται (*dechetai*), the present middle indicative of δέχομαι (*dechomai*). The word means 'to readily accept or receive' and is a synonym for faith in this context.[99] Paul is saying that the natural man or unbeliever is presently unwilling to *accept* or place his faith in the truth of the gospel. Clearly, it is *not* the task of the preacher to grant repentance, to make people accept the truth, or to impart faith. Faith is a gift of God (Eph. 2:8; Phil. 1:29; Heb. 12:2).

Paul also says the natural man *cannot understand* the things of the Spirit of God. This is a translation of the Greek words οὐ δύναται γνῶναι (*ou dunatai gnōnai*) which could be translated 'does not have the power to know or understand'. The unbeliever does not have the ability or mental muscle to know or understand the gospel. But, the general definition of γινώσκω (*ginōskō*), 'to know, perceive, or understand', cannot apply here. Paul has a specific *kind* of understanding in mind when he uses this word. It is a kind of understanding that only the Holy Spirit can impart. To discover what this is, let us first take a moment to look at what the unbeliever *can* understand apart from the Holy Spirit.

The unbeliever has the ability to know the facts of the gospel story. He can understand intellectually the content of the Bible, its original languages, its grammar, syntax and even be an unbelieving Bible scholar. He can *understand* the facts and content of the Bible without the assistance of the Holy Spirit. That is the kind of understanding that the preacher is responsible to impart, the content and facts of the Word of God. But what the unbeliever does not have the ability to do is to allow his sin-cursed heart, mind, and will to *accept, receive* and *trust* in the gospel message. He cannot 'experience' the truth of the gospel because he does not have a personal relationship with Christ. He does not *want* to turn from his sin, and to love Christ, and to obey the Saviour. He cannot, as Paul said to the Ephesian believers, 'know the love of Christ which surpasses knowledge' (Eph. 3:19). Unbelievers are held captive by the devil to do his will (2 Tim. 2:26). Only the Holy Spirit can grant people repentance leading to salvation. He causes the unbeliever to have a 'change of mind' resulting in a 'change of direction' (Acts 5:31; 11:18; 2 Tim. 2:24-26).

The preacher is not responsible for, and is unable to give, this *kind* of understanding. Clearly, the turning of a sinner's heart away from sin and to God is not the preacher's task but a supernatural work of God. Because of this, the preacher does not need to concern himself with either of these divine works of imparting the ability to *accept* the truth of the gospel or *imparting understanding* so that they see that God's way is the right way to follow. No one ever turns to Christ unless the Father draws him (John 6:44). There are none who *seek* after God or *understand* that God's ways are right on their own, no, not even one (Rom. 3:10ff). Turning a soul to God is the work of the Holy Spirit. Paul is saying in 1 Corinthians 2:14 that the natural man does not have it in himself to turn from sin and to accept the gospel of Jesus Christ. He cannot bring himself to love light rather than darkness on his own (John 3:19-21). The turning of the will away from sin to God and the conversion of a sinner, which brings him to the place where he not only accepts the facts of the gospel as true but understands that he must trust in them, is *not* the work of the preacher, but of the Holy Spirit.

So what *kind of understanding* is the preacher responsible for imparting? As already mentioned, it is the preacher's responsibility to preach the word so that people can hear it, to preach it clearly so that people can understand the facts, and to preach it in its entirety. It is the preacher's task to get the content of the word etched on the minds and hearts of his hearers. He is responsible for imparting the gospel story to unbelievers and sound doctrine to believers. It is his job to explain the text of the Scripture so that his listeners receive and remember the 'data' of the gospel. The preacher communicates what the text of the Bible says, what it means, and how it applies. That is the preacher's responsibility, and he must do it with excellence. The rest is up to the Holy Spirit.

Objection 4 – we do not need to be concerned about being effective communicators because God is able to use poor or inexperienced communicators like Moses and Jeremiah

In Exodus 4:10 we read: 'Then Moses said to the LORD, "Please, Lord, I have never been eloquent, neither recently nor in time past, nor since You have spoken to Your servant; for I am slow of speech and slow of tongue." ' This verse is encouraging to me because I feel like Moses when I preach. But it is obvious from the books of Moses and especially from his recorded songs (e.g. Exod. 15:1ff; Deut. 32:1ff; Rev. 15:3-4) that God made him into a great communicator. Moses could have been making an excuse, but if he was not, this tells me that sometimes God gives us gifts but we have to do our part to develop them. God is always faithful to do his part even when we are unfaithful to do ours (Phil. 1:6; 2 Tim. 2:13). God calls us to be excellent, the best we can be, and he will take care of the rest. The New Testament's commentary on Moses' ability to communicate is found in Acts 7:22: 'And Moses was educated in all the learning of the Egyptians, and he was a man of power in words and deeds.'

The prophet Jeremiah is another encouraging example of what God can do with a person who is an inexperienced preacher. In Jeremiah 1:6f., Jeremiah writes, 'Then I said, "Alas, Lord GOD! Behold, I do not know how to speak, because I am a youth." But the LORD said to me, "Do not say, 'I am a youth,' because everywhere I send you, you shall go, and all that I command you, you shall speak."' It is clear from the books of Jeremiah and Lamentations that Jeremiah became a very skilled communicator, employing many kinds of word pictures in his preaching and teaching ministry.

These two examples of Moses and Jeremiah merely strengthen the argument that we are presenting. They teach us that insecure or inexperienced preachers can be transformed by God into mighty proclaimers of the word.

Objection 5 – we cannot model our preaching after the writers of Scripture or Jesus because they were inspired and we are not

This argument has some teeth. It is interesting because Jesus did some things that we cannot model our lives upon. I believe that the Charismatic and Pentecostal churches err in this area. They try to model their ministries on the supernatural works of God. Their logic is simple: we are to follow Jesus and the Apostles and be like them. Jesus did miracles, the Apostles did miracles, therefore we should all do miracles too.

Another example which follows a similar type of logic is what is called 'apostolic hermeneutics'. Apostolic hermeneutics basically says that we should interpret the Scriptures in the way that Jesus and the Apostles did. In some instances Jesus and the Apostles seemed to spiritualize or 'read Christ into' certain Old Testament Scriptures. The logic goes something like this: Jesus read himself into some Old Testament passages; the Apostles read Jesus into some Old Testament passages; therefore I can read Christ into Old Testament passages too.

I disagree with both of those examples. Without taking a long detour from our discussion of word pictures, let me briefly explain why. First, miracles were never the norm in history but always the exception. Only in a few periods did God perform miracles through individuals. He performed miracles through Moses; several hundred years later through Elijah and Elisha; then several hundred years after that through Jesus and the Apostles. Those were the only three periods in biblical history when miracles happened with any sort of regularity through individuals. Signs and wonders have always been performed by a select group of individuals, in isolated areas, accompanied by proclamation of the word of God. The miracles were undeniable, obviously supernatural, and ceased after their appointed time.

We also need to consider the nature of those miracles. Jesus and the Apostles healed *all* manner of disease. They even raised the dead![100] What is passed off as 'miraculous gifts today' in some circles does not even come close to resembling what Jesus and the Apostles did. If God was still giving those gifts to men, they would manifest themselves in the *same way* and for the *same purpose.*

These are some strong objections against those who want to follow Jesus and the Apostles by making signs and wonders the norm for today.

Concerning apostolic hermeneutics, there are several reasons why I do not feel comfortable with that hermeneutical approach.

First, I do not believe the Scriptures give us any mandates concerning *how* to interpret the Bible. General instructions such as 'accurately handling the word of truth' (2 Tim. 2:15) can be found; but no specific 'how to do it' statements.

Second, I do not see Jesus and the Apostles interpreting the Scriptures in any one specific way. Usually they take a literal approach when interpreting the Old Testament. At other times they use the Old Testament in an illustrative way and sometimes in an allegorical way. Even if it was only interpreted literally 25 per cent of the time, who decides which method is 'the method'? A good exercise is to go through the book of Acts. Every time an Old Testament Scripture is quoted, ask yourself, 'Was this Scripture literally fulfilled or not?' You will discover a variety of ways are used in the book of Acts.

Third, the Scriptures make it clear that the Bible is a product of inspiration, for 'men, moved by the Holy Spirit spoke from God' (2 Pet. 1:20-21). Some of the things New Testament authors saw in Old Testament texts could not be derived by a study of the syntax and grammar of that text within its original context. That tells us that they were either using the text for illustrative purposes or that God gave them *additional* information that could not be derived from the text. As interpreters we are not inspired and hence do not have that 'additional information'. When I depart from exegesis (reading from the text) and begin to do eisegesis (reading into the text) I am heading for deep trouble. Some would argue that the context is 'the entire Bible'. That is true in some respects, but an interpretation that cannot be derived from the near context is an interpretation which does not come from the text. It has to be imported from somewhere else – which is eisegesis. Once we begin to read things into the text, which the original authors could not have had in mind, all objectivity is lost. Interpretation becomes a free-for-all. Finally, if the text means something new or different in the New Testament from what it did in the Old Testament, which interpretation is *the single meaning* of the text? If the interpretation of the Old Testament is the new meaning assigned to it by the New Testament, this means that its original audience could not have understand the meaning of the text within its original context.

Those are just some of the problems I have with canonizing one specific way Jesus and the Apostles interpreted or dealt with the Old Testament.

So, then, why is it legitimate to say that we can follow the authors of Scripture, Jesus and the Apostles in the area of communication techniques?

First, I would argue that signs, wonders and inspired interpretations are supernatural works of God, but communication is not. Communication is a natural, not a supernatural process. This is what I believe is the primary difference. God created man to communicate without supernatural intervention.

Secondly, I believe that the ability to communicate has been the norm for all times, places and cultures. Even after the tower of Babel, the various language groups could communicate among themselves. Man's ability to communicate already existed. God inspired his word to accommodate the process of communication which he had already given man.

Also, I believe that, since God is perfect, his methods of communication cannot be improved upon. The Bible contains some of the finest prose and poetry ever written.

It is true that inspiration is not merely dictation. God superintended the authors of Scripture so that their personalities, experiences and writing styles were still theirs, yet God perfectly communicated what he wanted to say through them. God wanted his word to be understood (the concept of the perspicuity of Scripture). He moved the authors of Scripture to use the clearest and best means of communication. In Jesus' case, his teaching and preaching were perfect. Charles Bridges has written, 'Our Lord's discourses – without any of the artificial pomp of oratory, and with a profusion of imagery – are a perfect model of simplicity.'[101]

That is why I believe that word pictures are so important in preaching. The authors of Scripture and Jesus used them extensively. Spurgeon observes:

> Our Saviour, who is the light of the world, took care to fill his speech with similitudes, so that the common people heard him gladly: his example stamps with high authority the practice of illuminating heavenly instruction with comparisons and similes.[102]

We do not have to be inspired to use metaphor, simile, analogy, or sense appeal. Paul tells us to follow him as he follows Christ, and to model our lives and ministries after the good examples found in God's word (Rom. 15:4; Phil. 3:17;

2 Thess. 3:7, 9; 1 Tim. 1:16; 2 Tim. 3:16). This includes, among other things, effective communication techniques. One would have difficulty arguing against the Scriptures, claiming that Jesus and the authors of Scripture communicated inadequately. Also, if we are to ignore the Scriptures, and not learn effective preaching techniques from them, where then do we turn? If we turn to other great preachers and teachers of the last two millennia, we discover that they employed word pictures as did Jesus and the Apostles. If we turn to the world, we 'make void the cross of Christ'. We need to ask ourselves, 'Was Jesus the greatest preacher who ever walked the face of the earth or not? Shall we not learn from the greatest communicators found in the word of God?' I believe that we should not only learn from them, but model our preaching and teaching after them.

Objection 6 – just because other preachers used word pictures extensively and effectively does not mean that we should too

This follows on the heels of the objection above. It may be argued that the Scriptures do not specifically tell us to model our preaching after other preachers. Yet, it does not mean that we should not either. I realize that Thomas Watson is not 'the model', nor is any other great expositor. I believe Jesus is 'the model' and all other great preachers are just 'models' to the degree that they obey what the Bible mandates for preachers. I have chosen Thomas Watson because he was an exceptional preacher. The fact that his sermons, preserved in written form, still effectively communicate to people in our day and age, three hundred and fifty years after he first preached them, is significant. As already stated, any effective preacher can be a model if he follows the biblical mandates God has given to preachers. When looking to men such as Thomas Watson, we must ask ourselves:
    (1) Did they preach the word (2 Tim. 4:2)?
    (2) Did they rightly divide the word of truth (2 Tim. 2:15)?

(3) Did they live a holy life before God (2 Tim. 2:21)?
(4) Did they help people to understand, apply and remember the truth of God's word (Acts 20:17-35; 1 Thess. 1:2-10)?

If we can say 'yes' to these questions, then we can follow them, because they are preaching in obedience to the word of God. Of course, we must remember that they are all sinful, fallible individuals. We can learn from godly preachers only to the degree that they submit to the word of God.

Objection 7 – some preachers are effective communicators even though they do not use many word pictures.

I would strongly disagree with this objection. My studies have taught me that many popular preachers today excel at only a few of the many homiletical techniques available. One may be master of voice tone and fluctuation, while another has mastered the art of pause and rhetorical questions. Yet I have not listened to a single effective preacher today who did not employ graphic terms and vivid word pictures.

I will use John MacArthur, pastor-teacher of Grace Community Church in Sun Valley, California, and popular radio programme host of 'Grace to You', as a case in point. I have heard John MacArthur state on several occasions that he does not put much energy into generating illustrations for his sermons. Yet his sermons are full of word pictures. I believe there are several reasons for this.

First, I believe that God has gifted John MacArthur to be an effective communicator.

Secondly, John is the product of several generations of preachers. I believe he learned from his father and grandfather how to be an effective communicator. I also believe he has learned from the example of others.

Thirdly, I believe he has learned by trial and error in the pulpit. When you are preaching, you know when people are following you and when they are not. I believe that John has learned to speak in graphic concrete terms without even thinking about it. Often his sermons begin with an 'opener' illustration and are sprinkled from stem to stern with both biblical and extra-biblical quotations, figures of speech and illustrations. I experimented with John's sermon on 2 Timothy 4:3-5,[103] where Paul warns Timothy about the inevitability of 'ear tickling' preachers. I figured that if there ever was a sermon that John would avoid 'worldly' communication techniques it would be when preaching from that text. Below I have tried to break down the various types or kinds of word pictures that John used in that one particular sermon and how many of each category were used. This is what I discovered:

type of word picture	number used
Scripture cross-references	about 65
Quotations containing graphic language from various sources	about 25
Personal examples appealing to his personal experiences	about 5
Hypothetical examples which appeal to the listeners experiences	about 5
Comparative definition of success vs. excellence	comparisons about 20
Graphic concrete terms	well over 100
Number of word pictures used	*about 220*

John MacArthur is not a flowery, ear-tickling preacher. Yet, in this one sermon alone, he used well over 200 word pictures! Some of them were only one word long, but nevertheless he used many of them to communicate the truth. Granted, the sermon examined above may not be representative of the majority of his sermons, but by itself, it was an engaging, convicting and thought-provoking message on preaching.

I believe people prefer sermons which are amply

illustrated because they are more interesting, better understood and more easily remembered. No preacher can excel at every point of homiletics, but I believe that no preacher should neglect the use of word pictures.

Objection 8 – Jonathan Edwards read his sermon from a manuscript in a monotone voice, and God used his preaching as the primary catalyst in the Great Awakening

It has been my experience that as soon as you start speaking to those who dismiss the value of homiletical techniques, they eventually mention Jonathan Edwards. They are quick to point out, 'You know Jonathan Edwards read his sermons from a manuscript in a monotone voice and look how God used him!' In response, I would first mention the advice given by D. Martyn Lloyd-Jones, 'You do not make rules out of exceptions.'[104] In addition to that I would say that this argument seems impressive, only *if* you have never read any of Edwards' sermons. The first thing I ask people who hold up Edwards as 'the model' is, 'Do you preach in a monotone voice and read your sermons from a manuscript?' I have not found one who said yes to that question. Interesting isn't it? I do get some pleasure from pointing out to those who use this objection that Jonathan Edwards just happens to be the quintessential exhibit 'A,' and supreme commander of word pictures!

The facts are clear. God used the preaching of Jonathan Edwards to launch the Great Awakening in America. It is also true that Edwards was concerned about not manipulating people into thinking they received Christ, so he read his sermons in a monotone voice from his manuscripts.[105] No gestures, no arm flailing, no sweeping motions of the hands and arms. He did not raise his voice to a squeaky pitch, then bring it down to a low rumble, nor did he talk slowly and then faster to hold people's attention. He did not make much eye contact with his congregation or insert long deafening pauses to move people to listen harder. No, he seems to have read his sermons in a monotone voice. One person speaking of Edwards said, 'Mr Edwards in preaching used no gestures, but looked straight forward,' and another said, 'He looked on the bell rope until he looked it off.'[106] Personally I think Edwards could have improved his preaching by using other homiletical techniques. I admire him for not wanting to manipulate people from the pulpit. It is tragic when people trust in an emotional response to the gospel rather than a rational, volitional commitment to Christ.

The greatest error I see in this objection is to point to Edwards' weaknesses and imply that they were his strengths. Reading sermons in a monotone voice and looking straight ahead was not Edwards' strength; word pictures were his strength. I do not recommend that you try this, but if a preacher were to adopt Edwards' monotone method of reading and not use many word pictures, I believe that soon he would be looking for another line of work.

Anyone who has read any of Edwards' sermons will realize that his word pictures carried the day. John Piper has written: 'Edwards strained to make the glories of heaven look irresistibly beautiful and the torments of hell look intolerably horrible.'[107] I believe that God used Edwards not because he lacked so many good communication techniques, but because he excelled in one – word pictures. Edwards probably would have failed the average seminary homiletics class because of his lack of gestures, voice tone, word speed, eye contact, and so on, but he more than compensated for these insufficiencies by mastering the art of communicating with word pictures. His word pictures were like Elijah's fiery chariot which carried him to heaven. Those who heard Edwards' sermons could 'see' what he was saying.

R. C. Sproul illustrates Edwards' ability to communicate with word pictures by pointing to his most famous sermon, *Sinners in the Hands of an Angry God*. Sproul lays before us a dry, dusty, abstract sentence of his own, and then compares it with a juicy, concrete sentence by Edwards. You decide which one communicates best. And don't forget to notice the word pictures.

> The supreme being is given to a proclivity of indignation in the general direction of fallen humanity. [*Sproul uses one word picture, i.e., fallen.*]

or

> O sinner, you hang over the pit of hell by a slender thread, like a spider over a burning fire; the flames of divine wrath thrashing about it ready to singe it at any moment and drop you in the pit.[108] [*Edwards uses eleven word pictures.*]

I do not believe that Edwards was effective as a preacher because the Holy Spirit prefers or requires that we preach monotone sermons, but that the Holy Spirit used Edwards' ability to communicate the truth graphically. God created men to respond to that kind of teaching. What Edwards lacked in nearly every other area of homiletics, he made up for in his excellent and extensive use of word pictures. That, I believe, provides us with a solid brick to add to the foundation of our argument that word pictures may be the single most important communication technique for the preacher. Even if nearly every other homiletical technique is neglected, Edwards' sermons argue that the Spirit is still willing to work mightily to convert sinners and equip the saints, through a preaching ministry that focuses on the effective use of word pictures to the neglect of nearly all other homiletical practices.

Now that we have looked at some of the more common objections to using word pictures in expository preaching, we will move on to greener pastures – pastures that we have all grazed in before but possibly never stopped in long enough to smell the flowers that grew there. The greatest encyclopedia of word pictures available is the Bible itself.

The Word preached is the engine God uses to effect repentance. It is compared to a hammer and to a fire (Jer. 23:29), the one to break, the other to melt the heart. How great a blessing it is to have the Word, which is of such virtue, dispensed! And how hard they who put out the lights of heaven will find it to escape hell.

The Word written is a repository in which God has laid up sovereign oils and balsams to recover sick souls; and the Word preached is the pouring out of these oils, and applying them to the sick patient (Thomas Watson).

6

AN ENCYCLOPEDIA OF WORD PICTURES

Scripture uses word pictures extensively

Entire books have been written on different kinds of word pictures in the Bible, and a good deal more could be written, because the word of God is an encyclopedia of word pictures. It is not my purpose in this chapter to list exhaustively or discuss comprehensively the nature of word pictures found in God's word. I have my sights on three smaller targets: first, I hope to convince you that the Bible is indeed an encyclopedia of word pictures; second, it is my desire to give you 'samplings' of word pictures found in different biblical genres; third, it is my hope that this chapter will help you to pay attention to and learn from the treasury of word pictures found in the word of God.

Use of word pictures in narrative portions of Scripture
Bible scholars will often categorize the first five books of the Bible as 'the law of Moses', 'the Pentateuch', or 'the Torah'. That is understandable since those books contain the laws that God gave to the nation of Israel. Yet within the books of Moses, major portions of narrative can be found: for example, the book of Genesis, Exodus 1–18 and Numbers 11–36 are mostly narrative in nature. Even within the sections dealing with the Law small narratives are inserted, such as the graphic account of Nadab and Abihu in Leviticus 10. I mention this so that you will know that I am not only speaking about the books from Samuel to Esther, and the Gospels and Acts, but any narrative portion of the Bible.

At first glance, when we read through narrative portions of

the Bible, word pictures seem to be relatively scarce. That is
a problem when trying to persuade people that word pictures
are one of the most effective means of communication. A
simple explanation for this is that narratives *are* word
pictures. When I first began to study the subject of word
pictures in the Bible, I was so intent on finding 'small' word
pictures that I could not see the forest for the trees. Then I
realized that narratives, because they are concrete, vivid and
graphic stories, are big word pictures! It is important to ask
ourselves, 'What is all of that narrative doing in the word of
God?' That question is interesting given that the Bible is
primarily a book of theology, written to tell us about God and
his purposes. God's use of narrative to reveal himself is not
accidental. As I have attempted to show, people learn best
when truth is presented in word pictures. That is especially so
when one is trying to teach abstract concepts. How does God,
being an infinite, transcendent Spirit, explain himself to finite
men? He uses word pictures.

In the narrative portions of the Bible we 'see' what God is
like. Look in any systematic theology and notice how they
define God. For example, the Westminster Shorter Catechism
says that 'God is a Spirit, infinite, eternal, and unchangeable,
in his being, wisdom, power, holiness, justice, goodness, and
truth'.[109] That is a good, technical, abstract definition of God,
but nowhere is that definition found in the pages of the Bible.
We can find each part of that definition in different portions of
the Bible, but nowhere do we find those words framed
together. Instead we begin to learn from the beginning of
Genesis that God is the powerful creator and sustainer of the
universe. We learn that he is generous as he creates a perfect
environment for Adam and Eve; we learn that he is a God of
order as we see him give regulations to Adam and Eve; we see
he is just as he deals out the consequences of sin after the fall.
That continues through the pages of Scripture. God is
revealed through stories found in narrative. He lets us 'see'
him through the eyes of word pictures. When Jesus came on

the scene he was a three-dimensional, interactive, dramatic representation of the Father, 'he who has seen me has seen the Father' (John 14:9; cf. 1:1, 14; Heb. 1:1-2). God uses word pictures because he created us to learn by comparison, simile, metaphor and analogy.

Then I began to ponder how the New Testament authors often summarized the *stories* of the Old Testament to make application in the New. We have already seen this in the sermon Paul preached at Pisidian Antioch in Acts 13:16-41. Paul summarized certain Old Testament events, pointing to the person and work of Christ. Another example of how narrative might be used in expository preaching is to consider Stephen's sermon in Acts 7. Stephen's sermon consisted of a continual string of micronarratives strung together and climaxing in the Jews' execution of their own Messiah. Stephen started with Abraham and ended with Solomon, tracing the historical redemptive plan of God through the Old Testament up until the time of the divided kingdom. Most of the prophets were sent after the time of the divided kingdom. Stephen's audience would have been following him and would have expected him to continue with the times of the prophets. Their minds were primed and flowing through the Old Testament. Every Jew knew that one of the bleakest spiritual wastelands in the history of Israel occurred after the time of Solomon. Except for a few godly kings in the southern kingdom of Judah, the Jews were continually bogged down in sin and idolatry. They persecuted, tortured, mocked and killed God's messengers, the prophets. Stephen knew that they did not need to be reminded of that bleak period of their history. It was a sore spot in the bosom of every Jew.

Stephen, knowing that they would be following him, stopped after Solomon, then hit them with the first uppercut to the jaw:

You men who are stiff-necked and uncircumcised in heart and
ears are always resisting the Holy Spirit; you are doing just as
your fathers did. Which one of the prophets did your fathers not
persecute? And they killed those who had previously
announced the coming of the Righteous One, whose betrayers
and murderers you have now become; you who received the law
as ordained by angels, and yet did not keep it (Acts 7:51-53).

This was an extremely effective approach. They were
following Stephen's word pictures and were probably
thinking 'Amen!' all the way until he finished with Solomon.
They were ready to hear about the next phase of Jewish
history, but instead they were instantly compared to their
wicked ancestors. Stephen then knocked them off balance by
using graphic word pictures borrowed from the Old
Testament: 'You ... stiff-necked', 'uncircumcised in heart',
'ears ... resisting' and 'just as your fathers did' men of Israel!
Then came the knockout punch, 'which one of the prophets
did your fathers not persecute?' What could they say? He had
them lined up like bowling pins and was knocking them all
down! He hit them so hard with a graphic presentation of the
truth that verse 54 says, 'Now when they heard this, they were
cut to the quick, and they began gnashing their teeth at him.'
I like how Luke uses two graphic word pictures to describe
their response: 'cut to the quick' and 'gnashing their teeth at
him'. Unfortunately, that was Stephen's last sermon, but at
least it was an extremely effective one. What a way to go!

Thomas Watson must have realized this because he
frequently alludes to familiar stories found in narrative
sections of the Bible as teaching aids. In the quotations below,
notice how Watson uses episodes out of King David's life to
illustrate biblical truth.

Those iniquities which men hide in their hearts shall be written
one day on their foreheads as with the point of a diamond. They
who will not confess their sin as David did, that they may be
pardoned, shall confess their sins as Achan did, that they may be

stoned. It is dangerous to keep the devil's counsel; 'He that covers his sins shall not prosper' (Prov. 28:13).[110]

Let us be like Christ in mildness and sweetness. Let us pray for our enemies, and conquer them by love. David's kindness melted Saul's heart (1 Sam. 24:16). A frozen heart will be thawed with the fire of love.[111]

We glorify God, when we sacrifice the praise and glory of all to God. 'I laboured more abundantly than they all' (1 Cor. 15:10), a speech, one would think, savoured of pride; but the apostle pulls the crown from his own head, and sets it upon the head of free grace: 'yet not I, but the grace of God which was with me.' As Joab, when he fought against Rabbah, sent for King David, that he might carry away the crown of the victory (2 Sam. 12:28), so a Christian, when he has gotten power over any corruption or temptation, sends for Christ, that he may carry away the crown of the victory. As the silkworm, when she weaves her curious work, hides herself under the silk, and is not seen; so when we have done anything praiseworthy, we must hide ourselves under the veil of humility, and transfer the glory of all we have done to God. As Constantine used to write the name of Christ over his door, so should we write the name of Christ over our duties. Let him wear the garland of praise.[112]

We should remember that people love stories, and the narrative portions of Scripture are just that. I have done certain experiments when preaching and encourage you to try this out for yourself. Purposely preach abstract truth for about five minutes or so and watch people slowly wilt as they begin to drift off into 'dreamland'. Then say something like, 'Let me tell you a story,' and watch their faces. There will be immediate signs of perkiness. One person said, 'Reason assaults the fortress walls of the mind, but stories slip gently through the back door into the heart – and begin to change us.'[113] William Evans writes, 'The pictorial and picturesque preacher will always get a hearing. The ability of any public speaker to turn the ears of his audience into eyes constitutes an essential element in his success.'[114]

It does not matter what kind of story it is, people *love* stories. You can tell them about someone else, about yourself, about a story you read in the newspaper, or allude to a familiar story from the pages of Scripture. It matters not. People pay attention to stories. It makes you realize why Jesus told so many. That is why the narrative portions of Scripture are such a great word picture resource. You can illustrate the Bible with the Bible, hold people's attention and teach them biblical truth with other biblical truth. Donald Demaray affirms this when he says, 'A literary characteristic of the Bible is its pictorial quality. This accounts in no small measure for its capacity to communicate in any age to any people.'[115]

There is a danger of 'ear tickling' when you are teaching narrative or using narrative to teach some other type of biblical genre. We will discuss some of the pitfalls of using word pictures in the chapter entitled 'Burmese Tiger Traps', but you should never preach to entertain. You should make sure that your word pictures lift up, clarify, or explain the text you are preaching on, not obscure it. We should never tell stories for story's sake but for truth's sake. If we can learn to use word pictures like Stephen did, everyone will be pierced through by the sword of the Spirit, and we may get stoned to death!

As you begin reading the narrative of creation found in Genesis, the first word pictures you come to are found in Genesis 1:2: 'And the earth was formless and void, and darkness was over the surface of the deep; and the Spirit of God was moving over the surface of the waters.' Genesis is the beginning of a long line of word pictures which stretches to Revelation chapter 22.

As I mentioned earlier, narrative portions of Scripture are word pictures. Yet even inside these larger word pictures we discover smaller ones. I have observed high concentrations of simile and metaphor in certain sections of narrative that record dialogues between individuals. For instance, after Cain kills Abel, God has a talk with Cain. Notice the word pictures:

Then the LORD said to Cain, 'Where is Abel your brother?' And he said, 'I do not know. Am I my *brother's keeper*?' And he said, 'What have you done? The *voice of your brother's blood is crying to me from the ground.* And now you are cursed from the ground, which has *opened its mouth to receive your brother's blood from your hand.* When you cultivate the ground, it shall no longer *yield its strength to you*; you shall be *a vagrant and a wanderer on the earth.*' And Cain said to the LORD, 'My punishment is too great to *bear*! Behold, You have *driven me this day from the face of the ground*; and from *Your face I shall be hidden,* and I shall be a *vagrant and a wanderer on the earth,* and it will come about that whoever finds me will kill me (Gen. 4:9-14; emphasis mine).

Notice how both God and Cain communicated with word pictures. Their dialogue is permeated with them. That is a common phenomenon in many of the dialogues found in the narrative portions of Scripture. The examples that one could point to are many. Make an effort to notice them as you read your Bible and you will see what I mean. Let me give you one more example.

Have you ever noticed the word pictures Jacob uses when blessing his sons in Genesis 49:3-27? They are really creative and very graphic. He does a superb job of communicating the character of his sons and what the future holds for them. I encourage you to read the entire section in Genesis 49 sometime, but let me point out a few of my favourite word pictures in that section. Reuben is described as 'uncontrolled as water'. Judah is described with these words: 'Your hand shall be on the neck of your enemies; your father's sons shall bow down to you. Judah is a lion's whelp; from the prey, my son, you have gone up. He couches, he lies down as a lion, and as a lion, who dares rouse him up? The scepter shall not depart from Judah, nor the ruler's staff from between his feet ... he ties his foal to the vine, and his donkey's colt to the choice vine; he washes his garments in wine, and his robes in the blood of grapes. His eyes are dull from wine, and his teeth white from milk.' You can see what the future holds for Judah clear as day.

Dan is portrayed with these striking words: 'Dan shall be a serpent in the way, a horned snake in the path, that bites the horse's heels, so that his rider falls backward.'

Every son is described with word pictures but my favourite word pictures are used for Benjamin: 'Benjamin is a ravenous wolf; in the morning he devours the prey, and in the evening he divides the spoil.'

Why did Jacob use all these word pictures? He didn't do it because he wanted to hide what he was trying to say or to be more verbose. He used a battalion of word pictures so that his sons would *never forget* his words. When your dad says to you, 'You are a mean person,' you might soon forget that, but if he calls you a 'ravenous wolf' that is harder to forget. John Piper has said, 'Experience and Scripture teach that the heart is most powerfully touched, not when the mind is entertaining abstract ideas, but when it is filled with vivid images of amazing reality.'[116] That is what makes word pictures so effective. That is why I believe Thomas Watson used them and why I think we should use them in our preaching too.

Use of word pictures in the Law of Moses
In the first five books of the Old Testament, the Law of Moses, we encounter sections of Scripture that are very legal in nature. They have a high concentration of law. The larger sections of law are found in Exodus 20–40, the book of Leviticus, the first ten chapters of Numbers, and the book of Deuteronomy. Although these portions of the Pentateuch contain sections of narrative too, they present us with a different class of literature, a class that contains a specific kind or subcategory of word pictures. We might call them 'example' or 'application' word pictures.

In Exodus we have the condensed version of the law followed by the blueprints for building the tabernacle. In Leviticus and the first ten chapters of Numbers, we have the operations manual for the tabernacle and the ceremonial regulations. As Israel moved from place to place, the tabernacle had to be disassembled and then assembled again upon arriving at their new location. The book of Deuteronomy was the amplified version of the law with practical application examples.

These sections of the Bible contain few simile and metaphor word pictures. That is understandable because the language used in these portions is 'fat' with concrete, tangible language: 'And you shall take all the fat that covers the entrails and the lobe of the liver, and the two kidneys and the fat that is on them, and offer them up in smoke on the altar' (Exod. 29:13). God does not just tell them to offer up sacrifices and he does not tell them merely to offer up fat. He gives them specific examples of what *kind* of fat is to be offered. God is very concretely describing exactly what he wants them to do. The instructions for building the tabernacle, operating it, offering sacrifices, taking it down, transporting it and setting it up are plain and explicit. There was no need to employ a variety of metaphors and similes because the language and concepts were not abstract. That is why certain kinds of word picture are scarcer in these sections.

Still, you can find a good number of them as you read through the law sections of the Bible. For instance, you find thirty-seven occurrences of sense appeal as sacrifices are described as a 'soothing aroma' to the Lord.[117]

The sections of law teach us something important that we can apply to our preaching. Even when God was giving abstract rules and regulations he did it with concrete examples. This can be seen throughout the law. We need to do this too when we preach the word. Instead of telling our congregations, 'Read your Bibles!,' we need to give them some examples of how to do so. We need to hold their hand a bit and say, 'Try using a "read through the Bible in a year" schedule;' or 'Look at the date and read that chapter in Proverbs;' or 'Read five Psalms a day, and you will finish the book of Psalms in a month;' or 'Read thirty minutes a day alternating between the books of the Old and New Testaments.' I know I have been guilty of not giving my hearers specific examples of how to apply the truth I exhort them to obey. Exhortation, without implementation, can soon become a verbal beating. We need to help them to obey. The Puritans were very practical preachers. After interpreting the text or giving what they called 'the doctrine', they then gave 'uses' or practical ways to apply the doctrine.

Notice how Thomas Watson gives concrete examples of how to apply the text:

> Let me tell you, all you who are yet in your natural estate, your souls are mortgaged. If your land were mortgaged, you would endeavor to redeem it. Your souls are mortgaged: sin has mortgaged them, and has laid your souls to pawn, and where do you think your souls are? The pawn is in the devil's hand, therefore a man in the state of nature is said to be 'under the power of Satan' (Acts 26:18). Now there are but two ways to fetch home the pawn, and both are set down in Acts 20:21; 'Repentance towards God, and faith towards our Lord Jesus Christ.' Unravel all your works of sin by repentance, honor Christ's merits by believing: divines call it saving faith, because upon this wing the soul flies to the ark Christ, and is secured from danger.[118]

> Walk with them that are holy. 'He that walketh with the wise shall be wise' (Prov. 13:20). Be among the spices and you will smell of them. Association begets assimilation. Nothing has a greater power and energy to effect holiness than the communion of saints.[119]

> The husband should show his love to his wife by covering infirmities; by avoiding occasions of strife; by sweet, endearing expressions; by pious counsel; by love tokens; by encouraging what he sees amiable and virtuous in her; by mutual prayer; by associating with her, unless detained by urgency of business. The pilot who leaves his ship and abandons it entirely to the

merciless waves, declares that he does not value it or reckon there is any treasure in it.[120]

Preachers are not to be flame-throwers but caring shepherds. We must do everything we can to help our people obey God. The way we can do this is by giving them examples of *how* to obey. If we exhort our congregations, 'Do not to be anxious,' then send them home thoroughly convicted, but uncertain as to how they might go about obeying the exhortation, we do them a disfavor. It would be much more beneficial to explain to them why anxiety is a sin and how to overcome anxiety in their life. That is what preaching is all about.

Our people need God's word explained and illustrated. That is what God does in the law sections of the Old Testament; he gives examples. Notice how the more abstract of the Ten Commandments are illustrated:

You shall have no other gods before Me.
Motivation – I am the Lord your God, who brought you out of the land of Egypt, out of the house of slavery.

[This command is illustrated in all the commands that follow. We show that God is first in our lives as we obey all His commandments.]

You shall make no idols:
Five illustrations: You shall not make for yourself an idol, or any likeness of what is in heaven above or on the earth beneath or in the water under the earth. You shall not worship them or serve them;

Motivation: for I, the LORD your God, am a jealous God, visiting the iniquity of the fathers on the children, on the third and the fourth generations of those who hate me, but showing lovingkindness to thousands, to those who love me and keep my commandments.

Remember the Sabbath
Illustration of how to remember the Sabbath to keep it holy: Six days you shall labor and do all your work, but the seventh

day is a Sabbath of the Lord your God; in it you shall not do any work,

specifics of 'who' must keep the Sabbath: you or your son or your daughter, your male or your female servant or your cattle or your sojourner who stays with you.

Illustration of how to remember the Sabbath: For in six days the LORD made the heavens and the earth, the sea and all that is in them, and rested on the seventh day;

Why we need to remember the Sabbath: therefore the LORD blessed the Sabbath day and made it holy.

You shall not covet:

Eight illustrations of how not to covet: You shall not covet your neighbor's house; you shall not covet your neighbor's wife or his male servant or his female servant or his ox or his donkey or anything that belongs to your neighbor.

Exhortation, without explanation, leads to exasperation. If you want to exasperate a child, all you need to do is ask him to do something he does not know how to do. That is why God gave Israel so many examples of how to apply the Ten Commandments in the rest of the law.

It is the preacher's task to give his people specific ways and means to avoid the sins they are convicted about. The goal of preaching is to communicate the word of God in such a way that people know how to obey it. In order for preaching to be effective, God's truth must be presented in an understandable way and practical application must be given. The law shows us that word pictures in the form of concrete examples help people to obey. Each example clarifies the command because it illustrates how that command is to be obeyed. As you read the law, remember that all of those commands can be categorized under the two great commandments – love God and love your neighbour as yourself. Everything we are told to do or not do in the Bible is an example of how to obey those two commands.

Use of word pictures in poetic portions of Scripture
The wisdom literature contains the largest yields of metaphor and simile found anywhere in the Bible. Because of that I will not take the time to develop the point. Check it out for yourself. Open the books of Job, Psalms, Proverbs, Song of Solomon, or Ecclesiastes and start reading. You will immediately discover that the lines of poetic Scripture which do not have metaphor, simile, or sense appeal are the exception. God put all of those figures of speech in the Bible because he created humans to learn by analogy and comparison, by word pictures. Consider the many word pictures found in Psalm 1:

> How blessed is the man *who does not walk in the counsel of the wicked,*
> Nor *stand in the path of sinners,*
> Nor *sit in the seat of scoffers!*
> But his *delight is in the law of the* LORD,
> And in His law *he meditates day and night.*
> And *he will be like a tree firmly planted by streams of water,*
> *Which yields its fruit in its season,*
> *And its leaf does not wither;*
> And in whatever he does, he prospers.
> The wicked are not so,
> But *they are like chaff which the wind drives away.*
> Therefore *the wicked will not stand in the judgment,*
> Nor sinners *in the assembly of the righteous.*
> For the LORD knows *the way* of the righteous,
> But *the way of the wicked will perish* (Psalm 1, emphasis mine).

God could have said, 'He who obeys me will be blessed and he who does not obey me will be judged,' and left it there. But he did not. Instead he talks about walking, standing, sitting, delighting, meditating, trees firmly planted by the water yielding their fruit in season, leaves not withering and chaff driven away by the wind. That is how God teaches theology and doctrine in the wisdom literature. Expository preachers need to learn that lesson!

Thomas Watson learned that lesson and models for us how we can communicate theology and doctrine with word pictures and not compromise content. If you need some instructions on how to apply metaphor or simile, the wisdom literature is the place to look for examples. Proverbs 26:1-11, for instance, contains an abundance of simile (emphasis mine):

> *Like* snow in summer and *like* rain in harvest,
> So honor is not fitting for a fool.
> *Like* a sparrow in its flitting, *like* a swallow in its flying,
> So a curse without cause does not alight.
> A whip is for the horse, a bridle for the donkey,
> And a rod for the back of fools.
> Do not answer a fool according to his folly,
> Lest you also be like him.
> Answer a fool as his folly deserves,
> Lest he be wise in his own eyes.
> He cuts off his own feet, and drinks violence,
> Who sends a message by the hand of a fool.
> *Like* the legs which hang down from the lame,
> So is a proverb in the mouth of fools.
> *Like* one who binds a stone in a sling,
> So is he who gives honor to a fool.
> *Like* a thorn which falls into the hand of a drunkard,
> So is a proverb in the mouth of fools.
> *Like* an archer who wounds everyone,
> So is he who hires a fool or who hires those who pass by.
> *Like* a dog that returns to its vomit
> Is a fool who repeats his folly.

I have loved reading the wisdom literature of the Old Testament from the time I was a new Christian, but I did not know why. Now I know! The wisdom literature shows me the foolishness of sin. It paints pictures for me so I can see the blessings of obedience. It lets me see how to love God and keep his commandments. Although I do not recommend that people only read one fourth of their Bibles, I think the popularity and existence of 'New Testaments with Psalms and Proverbs' teaches us something. Wisdom literature is engaging. It is engaging because it opens our eyes to God and his will for us.

Contemplate the last line quoted above, Proverbs 26:11: 'Like a dog that returns to its vomit, is a fool who repeats his folly.' That proverb strikes oil! For anyone who has ever owned or spent time around a dog, they 'experience' the meaning of that proverb when they read it. If we stop to meditate on what that proverb is saying, our response will be one of repulsion. That is the 'experience' that God wants us to feel, think, or relate to when we repeat the same sin.

Word pictures help maintain attention, they give us a deeper understanding and they help us remember.

Use of word pictures in prophetic sections of Scripture
I am confident by now that even those with severe doubts have to admit that the Bible is indeed an encyclopedia of word pictures. The prophetic writings are no exception. From Isaiah chapter one to John's apocalypse of Jesus Christ, God has chosen to use very strong word pictures. It is my observation that God chose to use the most gruesome and graphic word pictures for the people with the hardest hearts. The harder the rock, the harder it must be hit in order to break it. God had the prophets hit hard with word pictures.

It has always been God's desire that we have broken spirits and contrite hearts (Ps. 51:17); but the heart of the natural man is hard. Zechariah comments on the heart condition of unrepentant Israel with these picturesque words: 'And they made their hearts like flint so that they could not hear the law and the words which the LORD of hosts had sent by His Spirit through the former prophets; therefore great wrath came from the LORD of hosts' (Zech. 7:12). The prophets were up against some very 'flinty' hearts. It is interesting to note that the prophets responded to this problem with heartbreaking word pictures. They did not just tell Israel to repent but *showed them* why they needed to repent with frightening word pictures. Of course, God could have used an abstract message, but he did not. Notice the unchained vividness of God's words spoken through Jeremiah (Jer. 13:23-27, emphasis mine):

> 'Can the Ethiopian change his skin,
> Or the leopard his spots?*
> Then you also can do good,
> Who are accustomed to do evil.
> Therefore *I will scatter them like drifting straw,*
> *To the desert wind.*
> This is *your lot, the portion measured to you,*
> From Me,' declares the LORD, 'Because you have forgotten Me,
> And trusted in falsehood.
> So I Myself have also *stripped your skirts off over your face,*
> That your shame may be seen.
> As for your adulteries and *your lustful neighings,*
> The *lewdness of your prostitution,*
> *On the hills in the field,*
> I have seen your abominations.
> Woe to you, O Jerusalem! How long will you remain *unclean?'*

Consider the frightening words of Joel:

> *Blow a trumpet* in Zion,
> And *sound an alarm* on My holy mountain!
> Let all the inhabitants of the land tremble,
> For the day of the LORD is coming;
> Surely it is near,
> A day of *darkness and gloom,*
> *A day of clouds and thick darkness.*
> *As the dawn is spread over the mountains,*
> So there is a great and mighty people;
> There has never been anything like it,
> Nor will there be again after it
> To the years of many generations.

A fire consumes before them,
And behind them a flame burns.
The land is like the garden of Eden before them,
But a desolate wilderness behind them,
And nothing at all escapes them.
Their appearance is like the appearance of horses;
And like war horses, so they run.
With a noise as of chariots
They leap on the tops of the mountains,
Like the crackling of a flame of fire consuming the stubble,
Like a mighty people arranged for battle.
Before them the people are in anguish;
All faces turn pale (Joel 2:1-6, italics added).

Nahum takes a verse or two to get warmed up but then presents the coming wrath of God with such clarity that it would cause the average man to faint with terror:

A jealous and avenging God is the Lord;
The Lord is avenging and wrathful.
The Lord takes vengeance on His adversaries,
And He reserves wrath for His enemies.
The Lord is slow to anger and great in power,
And the Lord will by no means leave the guilty unpunished.
In whirlwind and storm is His way,
And clouds are the dust beneath His feet.
He rebukes the sea and makes it dry;
He dries up all the rivers.
Bashan and Carmel wither;
The blossoms of Lebanon wither.
Mountains quake because of Him,
And the hills dissolve;
Indeed the earth is upheaved by His presence,
The world and all the inhabitants in it.
Who can stand before His indignation?
Who can endure *the burning of His anger*?
His wrath is *poured out like fire,*
And *the rocks are broken up by Him.*

The Lord is good,
A stronghold in the day of trouble,
And He knows those *who take refuge in Him.*
But with *an overflowing flood*
He will make a complete end of its site,
And will pursue *His enemies into darkness.*
Whatever you devise against the LORD,
He will make a complete end of it.
Distress will not rise up twice.
Like tangled thorns,
And like those who are drunken with their drink,
They are consumed,
As stubble completely withered (Nah. 1:2-10, italics added).

These are only three examples, but others can be readily found. The prophetic portions of the Bible are full of this kind of language. God consistently chose to address hard-hearted sinners with horrific word pictures. He pillaged their minds with the cold hard facts of a 'certain terrifying expectation of judgment, and a fury of a fire which will consume the adversary' (Heb. 10:27). This is the same technique used by Thomas Watson. Below Watson discusses the eternal character of God and the ramifications which God's eternal nature has on the judgment of sinners:

Eternity is a sea without bottom and banks. After millions of years, there is not one minute in eternity wasted; and the damned must be ever burning, but never consuming, always dying, but never dead (Rev. 9:6). 'They shall seek death, but shall not find it.' The fire of hell is such, as multitudes of tears will not quench it, length of time will not finish it; the vial of God's wrath will be always dropping upon a sinner. As long as God is eternal, he lives to be avenged upon the wicked. Oh eternity! eternity! who can fathom it? Mariners have their plummets to measure the depths of the sea; but what line or plummet shall we use to fathom the depth of eternity? The breath of the Lord kindles the infernal lake (Isa. 30:33), and where shall we have engines or buckets to quench that fire? Oh eternity! If all the body of earth and sea were turned into sand, and all the air up to the starry heaven were nothing but sand, and a little bird should come every thousand years, and fetch away in her bill but the tenth part of a grain of all that heap of sand, what numberless years would be spent before that vast heap of sand would be fetched away! Yet, if at the end of that time, the sinner might come out of hell, there would be some hope; but that word 'Ever' breaks the heart. 'The smoke of their torment ascendeth up for ever and ever.' What a terror this is to the wicked, enough to put them into a cold sweat, to think, as long as God is eternal, he lives for ever to be avenged upon them![121]

Watson, like the prophets, was able to communicate with striking clarity. For men with hard hearts, that seems to be the preferred approach by God. As Broadus points out, 'a picture of reality is often more convincing than an argument.'[122] Word pictures cannot bring a man to repentance, but they can help engrave the truth of God's word upon his calcified heart. Once the truth is etched on the heart, the Spirit can move at any moment to give the sinner a heart of flesh. Arthur Hoyt says, 'Vividness is an element of strength. The strongest words in the language are the pictorial words. They touch the sensibilities. We can feel strongly only as we see vividly.'[123]

The preacher may wield the sword to inform, but only the Spirit of God can do heart surgery and grant repentance. 'The word of God,' we are reminded by the author of Hebrews, 'is sharper than any two-edged sword.' God encouraged Jeremiah as he struggled with his ministry by reminding him of the power God invests in his Word, 'Is not My word like fire?' declares the LORD, 'and like a hammer which shatters a rock?' (Jer. 23:29). Thus the prophetic portions of Scripture often use brutal word pictures to spin people round so they will face the truth.

While today's seeker-sensitive movement is trying to coddle sinners into the kingdom, it might serve the ministry of the word well if we would remember that God used 'uglier' word pictures when dealing with the hardest hearts. Jesus said, 'Do not think that I came to bring peace on the earth; I did not come to bring peace, but a sword' (Matt. 10:34). The truth of God's word is our only offensive weapon (Eph. 6:17), and we must learn to wield it effectively. We need to be like the prophets and preach repentance and coming judgment with word pictures. That is a lesson that we learn from the prophets, and which was modelled by Thomas Watson.

Now we move on to Jesus, to see how God incarnate used word pictures.

Jesus preached and taught with many word pictures
Most are willing to admit that Jesus was 'the greatest preacher who ever walked the face of the earth', yet many do not ask and answer the fundamental question, 'Why?' We can reason in our hearts: Jesus was God; God is perfect; therefore Jesus' sermons were perfect. That is logical reasoning. But we err when we continue to reason: God is perfect, but we are not perfect, therefore we should not try to follow Jesus' preaching and teaching techniques. Just because we will never attain to the perfection of Christ's preaching does not mean that we should not try to learn from him. It would be the same thing as reasoning: Jesus is God; God is perfectly holy; and Jesus never sinned; then conclude: we are sinners; we are not holy like God; therefore we should not try to avoid sinning. Most would cry out, 'That is demonic reasoning!' Jesus is our example in all areas of the Christian life, including preaching. It is true that we cannot model our lives after the supernatural works of Jesus or the incommunicable attributes of God. But we should strive to be Christlike in our conduct, prayer life, sacrificial service to God, love for others, compassion and, yes, even in our preaching. Granted, most of us will never come close to preaching like Jesus, just as we will not come close to being perfectly holy as he was, but that does not mean we shouldn't try.

As one reads through the Gospels it becomes apparent that Jesus used large quantities of word pictures. In fact, Jesus used so many word pictures during certain times in his ministry that Matthew wrote, 'He did not speak to them without a parable' (Matt. 13:34). Mark said in his Gospel: 'And with many such parables He was speaking the word to them as they were able to hear it; and He did not speak to them without a parable; but He was explaining everything privately to His own disciples' (Mark 4:33-34). One person's study concluded that 75 per cent of Christ's teaching, recorded in the Gospels, was in word picture form.[124]

Jesus used word pictures both to conceal and to reveal truth. As a casual reading of any red letter Bible will quickly reveal, Jesus not only used parables but all forms of word pictures in his teaching, preaching, rebuking and casual conversations. He said things like 'feed my sheep,' 'For which one of you, when he wants to build a tower, does not first sit down and calculate the cost,' 'I send you out as sheep among wolves.' Again, it is not my purpose to do an exhaustive survey of Jesus' word pictures, but I will establish the fact from a selection of the available evidence.

First, consider Jesus' Sermon on the Mount recorded in Matthew 5–7. In this one short sermon, Jesus used fifty-six metaphors![125] Now when you consider that the sermon can be read slowly in about ten minutes, that amounts to about 5.6 metaphors per minute or one metaphor every ten seconds!

Let me try to illustrate how Jesus used word pictures to explain and help us remember truth. Below I have listed the first part of twenty phrases from the Sermon on the Mount. Some are statements leading up to a word picture and others are word pictures leading up to a statement or another word picture. See if you can complete each sentence in your mind. As you do this, consider the kinds of the word pictures Jesus used.

Blessed are you when men ...
Let your light shine before men in such a way ...
For truly I say to you, until heaven and earth pass away ...

For I say to you, that unless your righteousness ...
You have heard that it was said, 'You shall not commit adultery'; but I say to you ...
And if your right hand makes you stumble ...
Therefore you are to be perfect, as ...
But you, when you pray, go into ...
Do not lay up for yourselves treasures upon earth ...
No one can serve two masters; for ...
For this reason I say to you, do not be anxious for ...
Look at the birds of the air, that they do ...
And which of you by being anxious can add ...
Or what man is there among you, when his son shall ask him for ...
If you then, being evil, know how to give good gifts to your children, ...
Enter by the narrow gate; for ...
Beware of the false prophets, who come to you in ...
Not everyone who says to Me, 'Lord, Lord,' will ...
Therefore everyone who hears these words of Mine, and acts upon them, ...
And everyone who hears these words of Mine, and does not act upon them, ...

So how did you do? Did you find it easy to finish the thought presented by each statement? Now it could be that you have purposely memorized that section of Scripture before. But most people, who have not tried to memorize it, but merely read it many times, would find it fairly easy to finish those statements. Why are those sentences easy to remember? Could it be that they are easy to remember because of the word pictures?

Think about this hypothetical scenario. What if Jesus had not used all those word pictures in the Sermon on the Mount? Would it still be one of the greatest sermons ever delivered? What if Jesus had preached the same truth but had reduced it all to abstract propositions? Would you be able to understand those propositions better without the word pictures? Would they be as easy to remember? Would they be easier to apply?

I think not. God does things on purpose. His word presents truth in word pictures to help us understand, remember and apply the truth.

Now let me ask you, 'Do you try to preach like that?' If not, why not? If it helps to put your mind at ease, I do not preach like Jesus either, but I wish I could. Maybe you're thinking, 'Tell me how and I will see what I can do.' I will do my best in the chapter entitled, 'Do-it-yourself word pictures'. Many homiletics books warn against using too much illustrative material. Martyn Lloyd-Jones says, 'Illustrations are just servants, and you should use them sparsely and carefully.'[126] Donald Demaray chimes:

> Bunched up illustrations, or pictures strung together as beads on a string, do not make good homiletics. At best, that procedure creates an expectation of entertainment. Moreover, a welter of pictures confuses meanings, and the real point, if known, gets lost in the shuffle.[127]

I smile when I read homiletics books that say, 'Do not use too much metaphor, simile, or illustration.' It makes me want to ask the question, 'You mean, don't be like Jesus?' It is true that large amounts of word pictures can obscure the truth, but not always. Jesus did tell many parables so that some might not see and understand the truth. Yet the same parables were designed to help believers understand more about the Kingdom (Matt. 13:11-17). Jesus, like the writers of Scripture, often used word pictures in a continuous string. I believe they did this in order to help people to understand the truth they were teaching. When they did use many word pictures they were not entertaining, or obscuring the truth, or failing in their homiletical delivery. Spurgeon, a voluminous user of word pictures, warned against using too many illustrations when he said: 'While we thus commend illustrations for necessary uses, it must be remembered that they are not the strength of a sermon any more than a window is the strength of a house; and for this reason, among others, they should not be too numerous. Too many openings for light may seriously detract from the stability of the building.'[128] It is true that any word picture which detracts from the truth should be excluded. We will discuss that in more detail later.

For now, we need to come to some conclusions about word pictures and their implementation in expository preaching. It grieves me when I hear an expositor rightly divide the Word of Truth, but shoot over people's heads with dry, abstract language. It also grieves me when I hear an excellent communicator preach a sermon that tortures a text of Scripture and neuters it of any doctrine. I think many expositors are so repulsed by the quarter of an inch deep preaching of many preachers that they have worked hard not to be like them in every way. This often means being very technical and abstract.

But back to our questions. Why was it appropriate for Jesus to preach the word using a plethora of word pictures but inappropriate for Bible expositors today to do so? Who would dare accuse Jesus of mishandling the word of God? He preached perfect sermons! He was the Word of God! Why is it that expository preachers will read someone like Thomas Watson or C. H. Spurgeon and say, 'Wow, that man really knew how to preach!' but when it comes to their own preaching ministry they are quick to say, 'You shouldn't use too many illustrations, stories, metaphor, or simile.' I think we need to re-examine *how* we are to present the information we receive from our exegesis of the word of God. I am not saying that we should give up precision. I am not saying that we should ignore grammar and syntax. I am not saying that we should forfeit the application of sound hermeneutical principles. I am merely trying to point out that Jesus did not give people art supplies; he painted pictures for them. He did not give them the raw ingredients; he cooked them up into an attractive dish.

Warren Wiersbe, in his book *Preaching and Teaching with*

Imagination, has a chapter entitled, 'Skeletons in the Pulpit, Cadavers in the Pews.'[129] I love that! Not only is it a great word picture, it illustrates what I am talking about. Without trying to do a detailed exegesis of an uninspired chapter title, that chapter title teaches me an important lesson. If Bible expositors are abstract and lifeless in the pulpit, they will make spiritual corpses out of their people in the pews. Jesus was never lifeless. He was always picturesque, tangible and descriptive. We should be like that when we preach the Word.

Another thing that concerns me is that Bible expositors (like myself) will sometimes preach a sermon on one of Jesus' word pictures and be so diligent to dissect it into its individual parts that the congregation cannot see the picture! It is like taking a famous painting of Rembrandt, cutting it up into very small pieces, sorting out the pieces into colour groups, and then standing in the pulpit with the fragments and saying, 'Isn't that an incredible painting?' Sometimes stories are best left as stories and not turned into lessons on grammar and syntax. Remember, when Jesus first spoke the stories he gave, they worked in their non-dissected form.

In order to keep from desecrating one of Jesus' priceless works of art, I try to illuminate his pictures with more pictures. I try to show people the focal point of the picture. I try to consider the response of the original audience, what gave rise to Jesus' painting in the first place and what Jesus intended for us to learn from his painting. I then try to point out practical applications for people today in parallel circumstances. I may zoom in on a fine detail now and then, but I try not to mutilate a work of art with too many abstract dissections. Compared to many, I am a poor art exhibitor, but I keep pressing on toward the mark.

One more illustration from Jesus' ministry, then we will look at word pictures in the New Testament epistles.

Jesus' greatest enemies were the religious leaders of Israel. From the miraculous muting and subsequent opening of Zacharias' mouth onward, the leaders of Israel had been exposed to mountains of incontrovertible evidence confirming that Jesus was indeed the long-awaited Messiah. They so resented Jesus' ministry that at first they wanted to discredit him, but soon after, they fixed their hopes on murder. Everywhere Jesus went it seemed that the Pharisees were lurking in the shadows like cockroaches. They searched for even a crumb of accusation against him but could not find one. After they had made many failed attempts, Jesus decided to 'expose them' in the sight of the multitude. In the first twelve verses of Matthew 23, Jesus, speaking to the multitude, tears off the hypocritical mask of Pharisaical religion. Then in verses 13-36, Jesus turns his verbal guns on the Pharisees themselves. The verbal bombs came in like inescapable mortars, blowing their self-righteousness to pieces. Jesus verbally beat them into dust with word pictures. He tarred and feathered them in the sight of the multitude. I have listed a sampling of word pictures below from Matthew 23. Learn from the Master:

> But woe to you, ... hypocrites, ... you shut off the kingdom of heaven from men; ... hypocrites, ... you devour widows' houses, ... hypocrites, ... you travel about on sea and land to make one proselyte; and when he becomes one, you make him twice as much a son of hell as yourselves. Woe to you, blind guides, ... You fools and blind men; ... hypocrites! For you tithe mint and dill and cummin, and have neglected the weightier provisions of the law: ... You blind guides, who strain out a gnat and swallow a camel! ... hypocrites! ... you clean the outside of the cup and of the dish, but inside they are full of robbery and self-indulgence. You blind Pharisee, first clean the inside of the cup and of the dish, so that the outside of it may become clean also... hypocrites! For you are like whitewashed tombs which on the outside appear beautiful, but inside they are full of dead men's bones and all uncleanness ... hypocrites! ...You serpents, you brood of vipers, how shall you escape the sentence of hell?

You can see why the religious leaders heightened their efforts to kill Jesus. You can imagine the humiliation and disgrace that Jesus heaped upon them in the sight of the multitude. You can see the crowd gathered around Jesus. You can imagine small pockets of religious leaders mixed in among them, whispering to one another about how they might accuse Jesus. You can picture their horror as Jesus defrocked them while the multitude looked on. They could not run, that would have made them look like cowards. They had already tried to out-argue Jesus, but he had silenced them. There they were, like trapped rats, being devoured by the Lion of Judah.

Jesus spoke the greatest discourses ever uttered, and he did it by using graphic and concrete word pictures. Wisdom cries out at the street corner.

Use of word pictures in the New Testament epistles

We conclude our brief summary of word pictures in the Scriptures with a whirlwind tour of the New Testament epistles.

First, let us start with Paul since he was the major contributor to the New Testament canon. Paul makes it clear in his writings that he was interested only in preaching the word. As we saw in the previous chapter 'Hey! You can't do that!', Paul was not against using word pictures generously. We learned that in the last epistle he ever wrote, 2 Timothy, Paul used forty-five word pictures in the first two chapters alone. Of course, that only proves that he used word pictures towards the end of his life, but what about his other twelve epistles? Let us look at the book of Romans.

If there ever was a book that was theological and doctrinal, it is the book of Romans. The first verse alone gives us three word pictures, 'Paul, *a bond-servant* of Christ Jesus, *called* as an apostle, *set apart* for the gospel of God' (Rom. 1:1). In verse two, Paul confirms the legitimacy of the gospel of Jesus Christ, by pointing out that it was 'promised beforehand through His prophets in the holy Scriptures' (Rom. 1:2). This phrase is a word picture because it connects what is new, unfamiliar, and abstract (the gospel of Jesus Christ) to what is concrete, what has been seen, experienced and accepted (Hebrew Scriptures). Paul continues to sprinkle different kinds of word pictures throughout the book of Romans. Consider how he uses vivid terms in 1:20-27. Note how explicit and concrete he is in his description of the reprobate. He gives specific examples to bring clarity and understanding to the doctrine of depravity.

> For since the creation of the world His invisible attributes, His eternal power and divine nature, *have been clearly seen, being understood through what has been made,* so that they are without excuse. *For even though they knew God, they did not honor Him as God, or give thanks; but they became futile in their speculations, and their foolish heart was darkened.* Professing to be wise, they became fools, *and exchanged the glory of the incorruptible God for an image in the form of corruptible man and of birds and four-footed animals and crawling creatures.* Therefore God gave them over in the lusts of their hearts to impurity, that their bodies might be dishonored among them. *For they exchanged the truth of God for a lie, and worshipped and served the creature rather than the Creator,* who is blessed forever. Amen. For this reason God gave them over to degrading passions; *for their women exchanged the natural function for that which is unnatural, and in the same way also the men abandoned the natural function of the woman and burned in their desire toward one another, men with men committing indecent acts and receiving in their own persons the due penalty of their error* (Rom. 1:20-27, emphasis mine).

The rest of the book of Romans is no different. In 1:29-32, Paul gives twenty concrete examples of depraved behaviour. In Chapter 2, he continues giving examples, illustrations and samples of carnal thinking and behaviour. In 3:4, 10-18, Paul uses cross-references to illustrate, prove and bring clarity to the total depravity of man. In Chapter 4, he uses an extended word picture where Abraham is the subject. In Chapter 5, he compares Adam with Christ. In Chapter 6, among many other word pictures, he effectively uses the slave metaphor.

This continues until the end of the book. If you stop and think about a specific section in Romans, you will begin to recall some of the many word pictures Paul used. When Paul speaks of the more abstract and hard to understand doctrine of election and sovereign choice in Romans 9, he has many word pictures. He uses Abraham, Sarah, Isaac, Rebekah, Esau, Jacob, Moses, Pharaoh, the potter and the clay, and quotes from both Hosea and Isaiah. Paul's epistles do not read like the more abstract systematic theologies on my bookshelves. His letters are much more lucid and understandable. Granted, Paul does write letters 'in which are some things hard to understand' (2 Pet. 3:16), but think how much harder they would be to understand if Paul used abstract language! Romans is one of, if not the, greatest theological work ever written on the doctrine of salvation. Yet it is very lucid because it is saturated with various kinds of word pictures. Now if Paul used word pictures to communicate theology and doctrine, shouldn't we do the same from the pulpit? We move on to the book of Hebrews.

I am sure you realize that the book of Hebrews is very Jewish in its orientation. Like the rest of the New Testament epistles, Hebrews is very rich in word pictures. As the author of Hebrews argues the superiority of Christ, word pictures abound. Many Scripture quotations and comparisons can be found throughout the book. Christ is presented as better than angels, better than Moses, than Moses' house, as a better Sabbath rest, a better high priest from a better priestly order, a better sacrifice and offering a better covenant. These, of course, are just some of the larger word pictures used in the book of Hebrews. The book is also full of metaphor and simile. One of my favourite similes is used at the end of Hebrews 6. I can especially relate to it, having been a commercial fisherman: 'This hope we have as an anchor of the soul, a hope both sure and steadfast and one which enters within the veil, where Jesus has entered as a forerunner for us, having become a high priest forever according to the order of

Melchizedek' (Heb. 6:19-20). Here the author of Hebrews uses 'anchor', 'enters within the veil', 'forerunner' and 'Melchizedek' to illustrate the sufficiency of hoping in Christ.

Another section of Hebrews that is rich in illustrative word pictures is the great faith chapter, Hebrews 11. Faith is one of the great themes of the Bible which is why the author of Hebrews spends so much time in that chapter using word pictures to describe faith. In that chapter alone the author of Hebrews mentions eighteen specific individuals! He mentions specific places, specific events and even describes specific ways men and women of faith were put to death. All of these word pictures illustrate what faith is and how faith acts.

Consider how you have defined faith in the past in your preaching ministry. Did you do it as the author of Hebrews did or did you give them an abstract definition with no illustration? I have used the following definition of faith on various occasions without illustrating it: 'Faith is a volitional commitment to place one's trust in the person and work of Christ.' Sometimes I have quoted Hebrews 11:1, 'Now faith is the assurance of things hoped for, the conviction of things not seen.' Both of those definitions are abstract. Note that the author of Hebrews does not hesitate to give a concise, abstract definition of faith, but he does not stop there. He takes great pains in illustrating what faith is and what faith does. That is what people need. They need the concise technical definition and then they need word pictures to explain it.

What about James? Did he use word pictures? Just asking the question makes me see the answer in my mind as I recall some of the graphic ways James presents the truth. James used a wide variety of great word pictures. Notice how some of the word pictures from chapter one are still effective 2,000 years after they were written! First, he begins with several illustrations taken from nature:

But let him ask in faith without any doubting, for the one who doubts is like the surf of the sea driven and tossed by the wind (Jas. 1:6).

And let the rich man glory in his humiliation, because like flowering grass he will pass away. For the sun rises with a scorching wind, and withers the grass; and its flower falls off, and the beauty of its appearance is destroyed; so too the rich man in the midst of his pursuits will fade away (Jas. 1:10-11).

Then James uses hunting and reproduction terminology:

But each one is tempted when he is carried away and enticed by his own lust. Then when lust has conceived, it gives birth to sin; and when sin is accomplished, it brings forth death (Jas. 1:14-15).

After that he uses natural observations about light:

Every good thing bestowed and every perfect gift is from above, coming down from the Father of lights, with whom there is no variation, or shifting shadow (Jas. 1:17).

Women can really relate to this one:

For if anyone is a hearer of the word and not a doer, he is like a man who looks at his natural face in a mirror; for once he has looked at himself and gone away, he has immediately forgotten what kind of person he was (Jas. 1:23-24).

If you know about horses this one is for you:

If anyone thinks himself to be religious, and yet does not bridle his tongue but deceives his own heart, this man's religion is worthless (Jas. 1:26).

James continues to do this for the rest of his epistle. He presents doctrine and theology through common experiences that almost everyone is familiar with. I find this helpful because it tells me what *kind* of word pictures have lasting value. One more example from James. In Chapter 3, when speaking of the increased judgment upon teachers and the power of the tongue, James gives these illustrations: a horse illustration (vv. 2-3), a nautical illustration (v. 4), a forest fire illustration (v. 5), a hell illustration (v. 6), a circus illustration (vv. 7-8), a spring illustration (v. 11), and a fig tree, olive tree and vine illustration (v. 12). All those illustrations to describe the tongue!

Moving right through the New Testament epistles, let us focus our attention for a brief moment on Peter. Peter gives us two epistles to examine. In 1 Peter we are given two word pictures in the first verse when Peter says, 'Peter, an apostle of Jesus Christ, to those who reside as *aliens, scattered*' (1 Pet. 1:1). Peter continues using word pictures all the way through the epistle. Here are some samples from Chapter 1: 'sprinkled with His blood' (v. 2); 'caused us to be born again' (v. 3); 'to obtain an inheritance which is imperishable and undefiled and will not fade away, reserved in heaven for you' (v. 4); 'more precious than gold', and 'tested by fire' (v. 7); 'as obedient children' (v. 14); 'precious blood, as of a lamb unblemished and spotless' (v. 19). Peter, like all the other writers of all the other books of the Bible, uses a significant number of word pictures in his first epistle. His second epistle is no different. He uses many smaller word pictures and refers to his approaching death as 'the laying aside of my earthly dwelling' (2 Pet. 1:14). He contrasts his experience on the Mount of Transfiguration with the reliability of the word of God (2 Pet. 1:17-19, cf. Matt. 17:1ff). Teaching about false teachers in Chapter 2, he illustrates God's certain judgment of them and his ability to rescue the persecuted, by reminding us that even angels who did not keep their proper abode were judged, the people of Noah's time were judged, as were the cities of Sodom and Gomorrah (2 Pet. 2:4-5). All three illustrations teach us about the universality of God's justice and the last two illustrations show us how he is able to rescue the righteous from the wicked. Note these other word pictures in chapter 2:

But these, like unreasoning animals, born as creatures of instinct
to be captured and killed, reviling where they have no
knowledge, will in the destruction of those creatures also be
destroyed, suffering wrong as the wages of doing wrong. They
count it a pleasure to revel in the daytime. They are stains and
blemishes, reveling in their deceptions, as they carouse with
you, having eyes full of adultery and that never cease from sin,
enticing unstable souls, having a heart trained in greed, accursed
children; forsaking the right way they have gone astray, having
followed the way of Balaam, the son of Beor, who loved the
wages of unrighteousness, but he received a rebuke for his own
transgression; for a dumb donkey, speaking with a voice of a
man, restrained the madness of the prophet. These are springs
without water, and mists driven by a storm, for whom the black
darkness has been reserved (2 Pet. 2:12-17).

Peter does an effective job of describing God's judgment
of the ungodly false teachers. He sees them as vermin, rodents
and wild beasts that are better off captured and killed. That
reminds me of my childhood growing up in the mountains. I
used to trap different kinds of animals around my house and
kill them. Mice and rats were pests that found their way into
our food pantry and ground squirrels got into our vegetable
garden. They were to be 'captured and killed'. That is how
Peter describes the false teachers. God will one day capture
and kill them with the second death. He also sees these
deceivers as 'spots and blemishes' which ruin sound doctrine.
It reminds me of the time my wife bought me a nice dress shirt
and the first time I wore it my pen leaked ink on it. It instantly
became a cleaning rag. Peter also describes false teachers as
given over to immorality 'having eyes full of adultery'. What
a picture! Peter knew how to use word pictures.

We have already discussed word pictures in narrative and
prophecy which would include John's Gospel and the book of
Revelation. Anyone who has read those books knows that
they are heaped full of word pictures. John builds his Gospel
around seven illustrative miracles. Revelation even paints

some Picasso-type word pictures, describing bizarre creatures like beasts with seven heads and ten horns, a dragon, and a woman clothed with the sun. But what about John's epistles? If you have studied John's first epistle before, you know that he is fighting against the inroads made by Gnosticism. John wants his readers to know that Jesus was not just a spirit, or a concept, or a non-physical personification of a divine idea. He wants them to know that Jesus was flesh and blood. He was human. That is why he starts 1 John with these words, 'What was from the beginning, what we have heard, what we have seen with our eyes, what we beheld and our hands handled, concerning the Word of Life' (1 John 1:1). With that one verse he lays his theological cards down on the table. Jesus was a real physical individual. John continues with the light and darkness motif that he likes to use in all his writings (e.g. John 1:4, 5, 7-9; 3:19-21; 1 John 1:5-7; 2:8-11; Rev. 21:24; 22:5). The entire book of 1 John presents a number of word picture test cases that one can look to for assurance of salvation. I counted seventeen 'probably not saved' indicators and nineteen 'probably are saved' indicators. Each indicator is a concrete example (a word picture) that helps the reader know if true saving faith is present.[130] After John gives all of these concrete illustrations he says in 1 John 5:13: 'These things I have written to you who believe in the name of the Son of God, in order that you may know that you have eternal life.' The 'these things' are the many tests John mentions up until 5:13. John in essence is saying, 'If you see the evidence of true saving faith in your life you can know that you have eternal life.' Like James 2, John stresses that assurance of one's salvation is not predicated on the evidence of a past religious experience but on the present evidence of regeneration. According to John, the person with no righteousness in his life has no assurance. John favours smaller word pictures in his last two epistles but his writings as a whole show that he relied on them heavily to communicate the doctrine of God.

Finally, we come to the last author of the last epistle of the

Bible, Jude. Jude uses word pictures in nearly every verse of his twenty-five verse epistle. Both James and Jude grew up with Jesus and maybe this is where they learned Jesus' style of presenting truth. I will quote one section from Jude – four verses. See how many word pictures you can count:

> But these men revile the things which they do not understand; and the things which they know by instinct, like unreasoning animals, by these things they are destroyed. Woe to them! For they have gone the way of Cain, and for pay they have rushed headlong into the error of Balaam, and perished in the rebellion of Korah. These men are those who are hidden reefs in your love feasts when they feast with you without fear, caring for themselves; clouds without water, carried along by winds; autumn trees without fruit, doubly dead, uprooted; wild waves of the sea, casting up their own shame like foam; wandering stars, for whom the black darkness has been reserved forever (Jude 10-13).

I hope I have convinced you that the Bible is indeed an encyclopedia of word pictures. It is a great resource for expository preachers. Consider all the various kinds of word pictures we have been exposed to in this quick survey! Word pictures are everywhere in the Bible! The reason for this is that God created us to learn by comparison and analogy. I find it reassuring that the authors of Scripture rarely say: 'Now that metaphor really means...' or 'That string of similes means...'. No, they just use them, knowing that their readers will see the connection. It is somewhat of a mystery how they work, but they do. It seems that the starker the contrast, the more clearly they communicate. I have read much on the subject but I think the best way to explain why they work is that God made us to learn by comparison.

The best lesson to take away from this chapter is: make an effort to notice word pictures when you read your Bible. Be impacted by their vividness and the truths they teach. Then remember Jesus' conclusion to the parable of the good Samaritan, 'Go and do the same.'

'Preach the word; be instant in season, out of season' (2 Tim.4:2). The minster must not be idle. Sloth is as inexcusable in a minister as sleeping in a sentry. John the Baptist was a *voice crying* (Matt. 3:3). A dumb minister is of no more use than a dead physician. A man of God must work in the Lord's vineyard.

A godly man loves the Word preached, which is a commentary upon the Word written. The Scriptures are the sovereign oils and balsams; the preaching of the Word is the pouring of them out. The Scriptures are the precious spices; the preaching of the Word is the beating of these spices, which causes a wonderful fragrance and delight (Thomas Watson).

7

DO IT YOURSELF WORD PICTURES

Practical ideas for using word pictures in your preaching and teaching

I have always been a 'do it yourself' man. It runs in my family. I have three brothers and all of us have the 'I can do that' gene passed down from our father. From rebuilding engines to building houses, from pouring concrete to repairing our own appliances, we like to do it ourselves. It is loathsome for us even to think of hiring someone else to do something we can do (even if we don't know how to do it). That has got us into trouble many times – just ask our wives. Now what is interesting about the Hughes brothers is that we all know how to do everything (at least we think we do), but we all know how to do it in a different way. That becomes apparent when we get together to work on a family project, as when we gathered a couple of summers ago to build our parents a garage. There we all were, four 'experts' who knew how to get the job done four different ways. It is difficult when they do not realize that my way is best; but being the youngest, I do not always get my way.

That scenario is similar to preachers and preaching. It does not matter how long you have been a preacher. You may have preached for a short time or have spent forty years in the pulpit, but you believe you are an expert and your way is best. 'They are my gifts,' you think to yourself, 'I can use them the way I think they should be used for the glory of God.' There is some truth in this. Other people's ways of doing things might not be the best for you personally. Usually you have to discover by trial and error what works best for the way God has gifted you.

I bring that up to let you know before we begin looking at
'ways to do it' that some of the ideas I have listed below may
not work for you. That is to be expected. You will have to
learn by trial and error. One writer describes how Thomas
Guthrie learned by trial and success in his ministry:

> Dr. Guthrie tells that at the commencement of his ministry he
> determined that he would so preach as to compel the attention of
> his hearers. In order to do this, he carefully watched his
> congregation, to see what caught and fixed their attention most
> readily. V hen he discovered that it was the illustrations used, he
> set himself to cultivate that faculty to the fullest extent; and by
> so doing gained the ear of the crowd.[131]

No matter how you get the job done, it has to get done.
Experimentation will reveal what works best for you.
Spurgeon said, 'There is no better way of teaching the art of
pottery than by making a pot.'[132] You have to prepare sermons
and preach them to find out how to use word pictures
effectively. You cannot be told what will work best for you.
The Scriptures give no biblical mandates for how to employ
word pictures in preaching. What I will show you I have
discovered by trial and error, or stolen from other thieves.
David Burrell, speaking of how to do it, says that 'the wise
preacher must not only use his imagination with effect but
must cultivate it, and form the habit of using it; and must curb
it withal; and must regard it as one of his homiletic assets to be
wholly consecrated to the service of God'.[133] Instruction,
integrated with application, confined by biblical doctrine, will
yield proficiency in using word pictures.

If you are still not convinced that word pictures are an
important communication technique for the Bible expositor, I
want you to know that I am finished trying to convince you. If
you are not persuaded by now, I am afraid that I have laboured
over you in vain. Yet, even if you are only slightly convinced,
I would encourage you to do some test sermons. Try a word

picture here and there and see what kind of feedback you get from your congregation. Then try to use more and see what happens. I am not saying you should seek to entertain people. I am encouraging you to engage them so that they can grow to be like Jesus. If you think that word pictures are only entertaining devices, then go back and read the prophets. Preach like Jesus, like Paul, like the authors of Scripture, and Thomas Watson. I believe the Lord will bless you if you do and your people will love you for the truth you help them understand.

One more bit of counsel before we look at the specifics. Becoming an excellent preacher is hard work. One has said, 'Read the pastoral epistles some time and note all the words that describe the preaching ministry;' words such as 'diligence', 'work', 'workman', 'labour', 'study', 'persevere', 'take pains', 'be absorbed'. Sermon preparation is a 'work' of the ministry. Quick fixes are a myth. John Henry Jowett warns, 'Preaching that costs nothing will accomplish nothing, and that if the study is a lounge, the pulpit will be an impertinence. What an offense to both God and man a careless, slipshod, ill-wrought sermon is!'[134] You will never be an excellent preacher if you do not work hard at it. The things below must be applied with diligence. If some of them do not bear fruit, then try using a different tool. If you persist, God will help you find the way.

Notice how others use word pictures in their writing and speaking

This may seem obvious to you and now that you have made it this far you are probably aware that you need to do that. I have enjoyed teaching this material to other people because I hear, 'I never noticed how many word pictures my favourite authors used until you taught me about word pictures.' That, my friends, is half the battle. Training your mind to 'see' word pictures, instead of just reading and accepting them, will greatly increase your expertise in using them. I notice them when I read newspapers, when I read comics, when I read theological journals, when I am reading just about anything. When I notice an especially effective word picture, I think to myself, 'I need to remember that one or I could modify that and use it to illustrate....' Hopefully this book will turn on the observation light so that you will begin to see word pictures (or the lack thereof) in whatever you are listening to or reading. Every word picture you see will become a lighthouse (did you see that one?) showing you the way. Each word picture will be a small lesson.

Let me give you a few examples of what I mean by noticing how others use word pictures in their writings. I have just grabbed a magazine out of our magazine rack to show you what I mean. The magazine is called *Birds and Blooms*. Reading through it I come to a section entitled 'Setting the Table'. It describes how different people have attempted to keep squirrels from getting in their bird feeders. Then I read, 'While squirrels are known to penetrate most feeder defenses, we've heard from lots of subscribers who believe their ingenious barriers have helped them win the battle.'[135] Now do you think you could use that in a sermon? Let me be more specific. Do you think that that sentence might help you create a word picture to illustrate sin and temptation? Here is an example of what might be done. You are preaching on sin and temptation that week and need some illustrations. We will start with a fairly long word picture:

> We have a bird feeder outside our kitchen window. It is hanging in mid air from a chain attached to the eave of our roof. At first we did not have problems with squirrels eating the birdseed but soon they found out how to climb onto our roof, down the chain, and into the bird feeder. So we added a slippery metal cone directly above the feeder to keep the squirrels from climbing down the chain and getting to the bird seed. That worked for a while, but soon the squirrels found that they could climb up the side of the house, sit on the edge of the window box and jump to the bird feeder. That made us move the feeder farther away from

the house on a pole. (Now at this point people are thinking to themselves, What does this have to do with temptation? That is good. Word pictures that produce that sort of reaction are often the best kind. I will explain more about that in a minute.)

Satan and his demons are like squirrels. They are watching you right now, looking for weakness in your life. Maybe they have already found that weakness and have successfully enticed you to sin. If that is the case, then you must confess your sin and increase your defences. You must install some Scripture barriers lest you find your walk with the Lord eaten away by the squirrels. But be warned, as soon as you think that you have conquered that sin, Satan will often find another way around your defences. Then you must go back to the word of God and prayer and erect more defences still.

That word picture might work really well in places where people are familiar with bird feeders and problems with squirrels. They will have a greater experiential reservoir to draw from. But even if a person has never had a bird feeder and lives in the inner city, they will still be able to 'see' what you are saying.

Let me give you another possible word picture that is a bit smaller:

Squirrels learn to penetrate most bird feeder defences over a period of time. It seems that whatever barriers you put up they find another way to get at the seed. In the same way Satan often learns to penetrate your defences over a period of time. Like a squirrel, he usually does not try to destroy the barriers you have erected; he tries to go round them. Satan will always seek to tempt you at a point of weakness.

Let me give you another one. This time I will remove the squirrel but keep all of the word picture language from our original sentence:

Satan can penetrate man-made defences. It does not matter how many ingenious barriers you put up, they will not help you overcome temptation. You cannot fight a battle against Satan with man-made devices.

I will conclude this experiment with some shorter word pictures:

Satan is a squirrel who will try to snatch away the seed of the Word as soon as it is set out for your people to eat.

or

Satan is like a squirrel that is ever searching to find a way into your bird feeder. He will not stop trying to tempt you until you are dead.

or

Ingenious man-made barriers are worthless against temptation. Satan always finds a way around them.

or

Satan's arrows are able to penetrate even ingenious man-made barriers. The Christian who relies on his own resources has lost the battle before the trumpet sounds.

That is what I mean by noticing how others use word pictures when you are reading. Yes, I could have been reading some great Christian classic or the biography of a famous missionary – it matters not. Word pictures are everywhere in almost all kinds of writing and speech. Once you begin to notice them you can put them to theological use and make them work for you. They are like labourers you do not have to feed or pay. They will serve you in your sermons if you will give them a chance. Once you have the pictures, you can cut, paste and copy them for ongoing use in your preaching. Soon your mind will begin to swim with pictures. Below are four quotations where Watson uses the word 'prison'. Notice how he can take one graphic word and use it in many ways.

A godly man is heavenly in his disposition. He sets his affections on things above (Col. 3:2). He sends his heart to heaven before he gets there; he looks upon the world as but a beautiful prison and he cannot be much in love with his fetters, though they are made of gold. A holy person contemplates glory and eternity; his desires have got wings and have fled to heaven.[136]

Will not anyone be willing to exchange a dark prison for a king's palace? Will he not exchange his brass for gold? You who become godly change for the better: you change your pride for humility, your uncleanness for holiness. You change a lust that will damn you for a Christ who will save you. If men were not besotted, if their fall had not knocked their brains out, they would see that is it the most rational thing in the world to become godly.[137]

The coolest part of hell is hot enough, but there are some who shall have a hotter place in hell than others. All shall go into that fiery prison, but some sinners God will thrust into the dungeon.[138]

When the archangel's trumpet sounds, the bodies of believers shall come out of the grave to be made happy, as the chief butler came out of the prison, and was restored to all his dignity at the court; but the bodies of the wicked shall come out of the grave, as the chief baker out of prison, to be executed (Gen. 40:21-22).[139]

A good lesson to learn is that often the word pictures which have the greatest impact are those which contain the greatest contrasts. Jesus said in Matthew 23:24 to the Scribes and the Pharisees, 'You strain out a gnat, and swallow a camel.' Gnats and camels have nothing to do with hypocrisy, until they are turned into metaphor or simile. Spurgeon advises, 'Do not say what everybody expected you would say. Keep your sentences out of ruts.'[140] Later he explains: 'Brethren, take them at unawares. Let your thunderbolt drop out of a clear sky. When all is calm and bright let the tempest rush up, and by contrast make its terrors all the greater.'[141] Do not try to hold your word pictures by the hand. Put them out there and let them do their work. Arthur Hoyt says, 'Illustration should be used with directness. It is a mistake ever to apologize for them or to prepare an audience for them. Like humor, the virtue of illustration is often in its surprise.'[142] Keep these things in mind as you use word pictures in your preaching.

Note the extensive use of word pictures in the Scriptures as you read, study and meditate on your Bible

I have already encouraged you to do this in the chapter entitled 'An encyclopedia of word pictures'. Yet I would like to pass on to you a few gems I have found before we move on.

First, as you read the Bible, observe how word pictures are constructed. Notice their simplicity and how many of them are timeless in familiarity. Then go and do likewise. You can try stealing word pictures or portions of biblical narrative and using them to illustrate other things. Let me show you:

> A godly wife is a lamp unto her husband's feet and a light unto his path.

or,

> You must lay the axe of repentance to the root of every sin, then with confession throw it into the fire.

or,

> Have you ever thought that you have murdered your favourite sin only to have its blood cry out to you from the ground and beg you to resurrect it?

or

> Some are swallowed up in the belly of false teaching and when they finally find the truth, it is as if they are vomited up on dry land and start obeying God for the first time.

The Puritans were very good at these kinds of word pictures. They were so well acquainted with the Bible that they were constantly borrowing word pictures and biblical narrative to construct their own. Notice how Watson uses the imagery from Hebrews in the quotation below:

> A great faith is like an oak that spreads its roots deep and is not easily blown down (Col. 2:7). A great faith is like the anchor or cable of a ship that holds it steady in the midst of storms. A Christian who is steeled with this heroic faith is settled in the mysteries of religion.[143]

Notice in the quotation below the assortment of biblical imagery that Watson employs:

> Ignorance is the womb of lust. Vapors arise most in the night. The black vapors of sin arise most in a dark ignorant soul. Satan casts a mist before a sinner so that he does not see the flaming sword of God's wrath. The eagle first rolls himself in the sand and then flies at the stag, and by fluttering its wings, so bedust the stag's eyes that it cannot see, and then it strikes it with its talons. So Satan, that eagle or prince of the air, first blinds men with ignorance and then wounds them with his darts of temptation.[144]

Another important use of word pictures in the Bible is to focus on them and try to develop them. So often we read a word picture and just move on. Let me give you a couple of examples. Suppose you are teaching on Isaiah 40:31: 'Yet those who wait for the LORD will gain new strength; They will mount up with wings like eagles, they will run and not get tired, they will walk and not become weary.' Now a verse like this is very picturesque. We have the option of merely getting to the abstract point of it, 'God will give you spiritual strength if you wait on him,' or you can amplify the meaning of it. Here is an amplification of the phrase 'gain new strength' that might work well, especially with children:

I have two boys at home who have remote control cars. Their cars use rechargeable batteries. If you play with them for a long time the batteries begin to run out of energy. Whenever they are not hooked up to the battery charger they are losing energy. If you run the cars too long without recharging the batteries, the cars will stop running all together. The good news is that the batteries can be recharged, but you have to wait awhile. This is how it is being a Christian. God is like a spiritual battery charger. You are like a rechargeable battery. You need to wait on God. If you do, he will recharge you and give you new strength. If you fail to wait on him you will run out of spiritual energy and your spiritual growth will stop. If this happens, you need to start trusting God again. As long as you wait on God and trust in him, he will always keep you charged up to serve him.

Here is another amplification, of the phrase 'mount up with wings as eagles':

Have you ever been outside and noticed a hawk, an eagle, or some other bird soaring effortlessly way up high in the wind currents? It is amazing how they do not even need to flap their wings. They do not need to hold themselves up because the wind does it for them. They merely need to put themselves in the right place and they can float in the air as long as the wind currents are right. That is how it is for us as Christians. If we put our trust in God and wait on him, he will lift us up and cause us to soar on the wings of the Spirit.

You can use word pictures from the Bible, you can amplify them, and you can try copying the *style* of word pictures recorded in the word of God. You might want to create your own parable and then give a spiritual interpretation of it as Jesus did. But take the warning of one who said, 'Parable making, like proverb making, looks easy until one attempts it.'[145] For example, you could take the illustration just given about the two boys with remote control cars and turn it into a parable. You could say:

Let me tell you a parable about two boys who lived in the same house. Both of them received remote control cars for Christmas. These cars were powered by rechargeable batteries. Every morning and every evening the two boys would play with their cars. One boy would faithfully put his batteries in the battery charger every morning when he got up and every night before he went to bed. Because of this his car never ran out of energy. The other boy was always anxious to do other things and would often forget to recharge his batteries. Because of this his car would stop working when he needed it the most.

From there you could give your spiritual interpretation, 'Hear the interpretation of the parable of the rechargeable batteries.' Since Jesus did not interpret all of his parables I will leave you to figure out that parable on your own.

Now you may be thinking to yourself, 'Oh, a parable like that is childish. It is intellectually insulting.' If that is what you think, you need to read some of Jesus' parables again. Jesus used simple things like fishing, shepherding, gardening, farming, baking and making sure that you had enough oil for your lamp (which was the rechargeable flashlight of the first century), to teach theology and doctrine about the kingdom. Sometimes 'childish things' are just the ticket. Daniel Kidder observes:

> Anyone who will sit down with a little child, or a class of children, and apply himself to the task of entertaining and instructing them for half an hour will find himself instinctively resorting to comparisons, narratives, and the kindred means of illustration, which have only to be adapted to children of a larger growth to answer the very end now proposed.[146]

You do not have to compromise accuracy or content in order to be easy to understand. Our seminary educations should not be used as a ladder to store things high on the top shelf beyond the reach of the average man but should be used to bring the most complex theological truths down to where even a child can reach them. One spiritual principle clearly understood by your congregation is better than a thousand nebulous ones that they neither understand nor know how to apply. Borrow and mimic word pictures in the Bible.

Ask God to help you to think of simple, effective ways to express the truth of his word as Jesus did

This may seem obvious to some of you. After all, every expositor knows that we need to pray about all things at all times (e.g. Luke 18:1; Eph. 6:18; Phil. 4:6; 1 Thess. 5:17). Yet, how many of you have recently asked God to help you to illustrate or explain his word so that people could understand your sermons? So often, we jump into our sermon preparations without taking the time to ask God for help. I am ashamed every time I catch myself doing that very thing. Prayer is like oil to the preacher. It helps him work without breaking down. James Rosscup states that 'Preachers who follow the biblical model take prayer very seriously. In sermon preparation, they steep themselves in prayer.'[147] It was John Owen who said something to this effect, 'He who spends more time in the pulpit in front of his people, than he does in his prayer closet on their behalf, is but a sorry watchman indeed.' Watson said:

> A *godly man* cannot live without prayer. A man cannot live unless he takes his breath, nor can the soul, unless it breaths forth its desire to God. As soon as the babe of grace is born, it cries; no sooner was Paul converted than 'behold, he prayeth (Acts 9:11).
>
> A godly man is on the mount of prayer every day; he begins the day with prayer; before he opens his shop, he opens his heart to God. We burn sweet perfumes in our houses; a godly man's house is 'a house of perfume'; he airs it with the incense of prayer; he engages in no business without seeking God.[148]

We need to plead with God to help us to teach his word in an understandable way. How can we expect to go about the spiritual duty of sermon preparation and preaching in the power of the flesh? We must keep the words of Jeremiah in mind, 'Thus says the LORD, "Cursed is the man who trusts in mankind and makes flesh his strength, and whose heart turns away from the LORD" ' (Jer. 17:5). When we trust in our strength during sermon preparation, by default, we are turning our hearts away from God. We cannot expect God to bless our preaching when we are running from his will.

Use word pictures from nature
Everyone has some experience of God's creation. People know what grass is and what flowers are and that there are countless grains of sand at the beach. We need to remember that creation is a 'theology proper' manual. 'The heavens are telling of the glory of God; and their expanse is declaring the work of His hands;' 'For since the creation of the world His invisible attributes, His eternal power and divine nature, have been clearly seen, being understood through what has been made, so that they are without excuse' (Ps. 19:1; Rom. 1:20). Those verses tell me that we can learn about God through his creation. Granted, the natural man suppresses the natural revelation of God in unrighteousness (Rom. 1:18). But believers should learn to see God in his creation. It is the preacher's job to help them do so. David Burrell, speaking of word pictures in nature, points out:

> The best of preachers, namely Christ, was a consummate master of this art. His sermons were picturesque to the last degree. He found 'tongues in trees, sermons in stones, books in the running brooks' and homiletic figures in everything. Consequently he was never dull, however profound; but was always impressive and well within the intellectual range of average men.[149]

Jesus used creation as an illustration encyclopedia. He used natural phenomena to explain spiritual truths about God. Notice how he uses the familiar things of creation:

And why are you anxious about clothing? Observe how the lilies of the field grow; they do not toil nor do they spin, yet I say to you that even Solomon in all his glory did not clothe himself like one of these. But if God so arrays the grass of the field, which is alive today and tomorrow is thrown into the furnace, will He not much more do so for you, O men of little faith (Matt. 6:28-30)?

Jesus shows us how flowers and grass teach us about the sufficiency of God's provision. Is this what you see when you go outside? Notice how Watson uses flowers:

A pious soul meditates on the truth and holiness of the Word. He not only has a few transient thoughts, but leaves his mind steeping in the Scripture. By meditation, he sucks from this sweet flower and ruminates on holy truths in his mind.

Many love the Word preached only for its eloquence and notion. They come to a sermon as to a music lecture (Ezek. 33:31-32) or as to a garden to pick flowers, but not to have their lusts subdued or their hearts bettered. These are like a foolish woman who paints her face but neglects her health.

Believers are Christ's garden; their graces are flowers; their savory discourse is the fragrant scent of these flowers.[150]

When it rains or the sun shines, what do you learn about God? This is what Jesus saw:

But I say to you, love your enemies, and pray for those who persecute you in order that you may be sons of your Father who is in heaven; for He causes His sun to rise on the evil and the good, and sends rain on the righteous and the unrighteous (Matt. 5:44-45).

If we did not have the sun or the rain, we would not be able to live. The sunshine and the rain are gracious provisions of God. We need to see them as that, and we need to teach our people to see them as that too. We also need to realize that God sends these blessings on all men regardless of how wicked they are. They illustrate his universal grace. We need to be like that too and love others in the same way. Jesus saw in the sun and the rain God's unconditional love and gracious provision. This is one way you can find word pictures in nature. Ask yourself, 'What does that tell me of God?'

Another important reason to look at and ponder things in creation is that they provide word pictures that are universal and timeless. Many volumes of word pictures can be discovered right outside the door of your office or home. Have you ever picked up a rock, stubbed your toe on one or sat on one? You probably have. What did they teach you about God besides the fact that he made them. Let us ponder for a moment the great gallery of word pictures that can be unpacked from a single rock. The word 'rock' is used figuratively in the Bible more times than it is used literally. Moses saw myriads of rocks while watching his father-in-law's sheep in the desert. He looked at them, threw them, sat on them, walked on them, and probably used them for shade and for tools.

Look and see how many different ways Moses uses 'rock' figuratively in Deuteronomy 32 alone. First he uses 'rock' as a name of God:

> The Rock! His work is perfect,
> For all His ways are just;
> A God of faithfulness and without injustice,
> Righteous and upright is He (Deut. 32:4).

Then he uses rock to illustrate that God is able to do the impossible:

> He made him ride on the high places of the earth,
> And he ate the produce of the field;
> And He made him suck honey from the rock,
> And oil from the flinty rock (Deut. 32:13).

Then he uses 'rock' to describe God's ability to save:

> But Jeshurun grew fat and kicked –
> You are grown fat, thick, and sleek –
> Then he forsook God who made him,
> And scorned the Rock of his salvation (Deut. 32:15).

Then he uses 'rock' to describe God as creator:

> You neglected the Rock who begot you,
> And forgot the God who gave you birth (Deut. 32:18).

He uses 'rock' to describe God's ability to strengthen for victory and God's being greater than idols:

> How could one chase a thousand,
> And two put ten thousand to flight,
> Unless their Rock had sold them,
> And the Lord had given them up?
> Indeed their rock is not like our Rock,
> Even our enemies themselves judge this (Deut. 32:30, 31).

Finally he also uses 'rock' facetiously to describe the futility of trusting in idols. This is interesting because he started the chapter using 'rock' to describe God:

> And He will say, 'Where are their gods,
> The rock in which they sought refuge (Deut. 32:37)?

Now can you remember the last time you used a rock to illustrate a biblical truth? What have you been waiting for? Moses did not exhaust all the word pictures latent in the word rock. Everyone knows what a rock is, that is why rocks make good word picture material. I encourage you to do a concordance search and read all hundred and thirty-something occurrences of the word 'rock' or 'rocks' in the Bible. You will be amazed at the creativity of the biblical authors. The Psalms alone will give you a degree in 'rock word pictures'. Notice some of the ways that Watson used the word 'rock' in his preaching:

The reason why so many prayers suffer shipwreck is because they split against the rock of unbelief. Praying without faith is shooting without bullets. When faith takes prayer in hand, then we draw near to God.

The test of a pilot is seen in a storm; so the test of a Christian is seen in affliction. That man has the right art of navigation who, when the boisterous winds blow from heaven, steers the ship of his soul wisely, and does not dash upon the rock of impatience.

It is not our holding to God, but his holding to us that preserves us. A little boat tied fast to a rock is safe, and so are we, when we are tied to the 'rock of ages.'[151]

If you take time to look at things in nature you will see how even a simple object found in God's creation can be used to teach many spiritual truths.

Consider what is 'like' or 'as' the truth that you are teaching This is an exercise that I do when I need to come up with a word picture for some truth that I am trying to explain. I state the truth and say to myself, 'This truth is like....' Then something usually comes to mind. If something does not come to mind, then I get some rest and try again. But usually they come slowly and pick up momentum. I try to think of comparable things until I find a couple of word pictures that will set the truth on fire. As one person said, 'The stories or pictures you use must storm the inner citadel of the soul.'[152]

Some will argue that you should never use more than one illustration per truth. It is true that you can over illustrate, but how much illustration is 'over illustration'? It is a hard concept to quantify. Jesus sometimes gave his parables in 'threes'. He did this to help his listeners to understand the truth better. When teaching about the lost he uses the parables of the lost sheep, the lost coin and the lost son. When teaching about the gathering of the righteous and wicked at the end of the age, Jesus tells the parables of the treasure hidden in the field, a merchant seeking fine pearls and the dragnet. All three parables teach a slightly different aspect of the same thing. That is why several 'like' or 'as' comparisons are not only allowable but sometimes necessary to cover various aspects of the truth you are trying to communicate. Please do not get me wrong, I am not saying that you need to use three metaphors or similes to illustrate everything you say. I am merely pointing out that the Bible does not give us a 'set amount' that is the 'right amount'. As a general rule, I believe that the more complex the doctrine, the more illustrations should be used to clarify the meaning of it. If you are using small word pictures, you may want to use more than three, but if they are larger, you should probably use fewer. Excessive illustration will tend to bore and under illustration may tend to keep your hearers in the dark.

You will have to experiment and get feedback from your congregation to find an even balance. Getting feedback is a good practice, by the way. Find a mixed group of people in your church and periodically hand them an observation form and ask them to criticize your sermon. Give them specific things to look for such as: Did the preacher communicate the context of the passage clearly? Did the preacher explain the text clearly? Did the preacher give practical ways to apply the text? Do you have any suggestions for how the preacher might have improved his sermon? Ask them not to put their names on the forms. That will give them the opportunity to be more frank with you. Read what people say. Listen to their criticism and encouragement. I am not saying you should ignore what the Bible says about preaching and do what your congregation tells you to do. I say this because it will help you to become a better preacher. Don't ever compromise a biblical mandate or be a man-pleaser. But take time to learn from your people. Your people will let you know if you are effectively communicating the word.

Let me give you an example of some feedback I received from two individuals. Occasionally I will walk out from behind the pulpit and address people. I do not make a practice of wandering around all over the place like a game show host, I merely step out into view now and then so that people can see me. This is representative of the feedback I received from that practice: 'That makes me really uncomfortable when you do that. It makes me want to tell you to go back behind the pulpit;' 'I think that is really effective because it makes me pay attention better. It makes me feel like you are talking just to me.' Sometimes you will get contradictory feedback that shows that you cannot please everyone. But I did learn something from those comments. I learned that when I crawled out from behind my wooden fortress people felt 'confronted'. Later I spoke at a college retreat where I was told to 'let 'em have it!' So taking what I had learned, I stood eight feet from them and 'let 'em have it'. I noticed something interesting. Everyone paid attention. No one fell asleep. Several seminary students said that it was 'really intense'. Those are good things to know.

In the same way you need to get feedback from your people when you use different kinds of word pictures. Try something like this. Pick one type of word picture, let us say a simile. Then, in several parts of your sermon, try shooting off several rounds of similes and see if people notice. See if they mention those sections of your sermon. If the rest of your sermon is dry and abstract, a few volleys of similes will show up like a lighthouse on a dark night. Look how Jesus used similes:

> Therefore He was saying, 'What is the kingdom of God *like*, and *to what shall I compare it?* It is *like* a mustard seed, which a man took and threw into his own garden; and it grew and became a tree; and the birds of the air nested in its branches.' And again He said, '*To what shall I compare* the kingdom of God? It is *like* leaven, which a woman took and hid in three pecks of meal, until it was all leavened' (Luke 13:18-21, emphasis mine).

Notice how Watson uses similes:

To be learned and ungodly is like a devil transformed into an angel of light; to be beautiful and ungodly is like a lovely picture hung in an infected room; to be honorable in the world and ungodly is like an ape in purple, or like that image which had a head of gold on feet of clay (Dan. 2:32-33). It is godliness that ennobles and consecrates the heart, making God and angels fall in love with it.[153]

When you figure out what the text means by what it says, ask yourself, 'What is this like?' Ask yourself, 'To what shall I compare this truth?' That will get your word picture machine working and soon your mind will start manufacturing similes and metaphors.

Practise thinking of word pictures during moments of free time

I realize that pastors do not tend to have much free time, and when they do, they usually think about something other than word pictures. Here are some moments of free time that I use for word picture conjuring. First, I do it when I am driving. Usually when I am driving I will listen to tapes or the radio, but when I am driving around towards the end of the week, when I am trying to get my sermon finished, I like to think of word pictures. If I was preaching on God's wrath poured out against unrepentant sinners, I might think that unrepentant sinners are targets, punch bags, cars to be demolished, paper boxes to be crushed and burned, fuel for the furnace, wood for the fire, traitors to be shot, criminals waiting on death row, etc. I say them out loud sometimes as I drive around. This teaches me to think in word pictures. If you can train yourself to do that automatically it will greatly enhance your preaching. It is great when you are preaching away and suddenly word pictures come into your mind.

We have quite a bit of free time that we often do not redeem for heaven. We can think of word pictures in the shower, while working in the garden, when filling our car up with petrol, or when grocery shopping. A miracle could happen –

we might give up watching TV. One of the most fruitful times I have found to think of word pictures is when driving with someone else who is in the ministry. All you need is two or more preachers in a car who start thinking of word pictures out loud. I have found that to be very entertaining and always helpful. Preachers tend to feed off of each other. Soon you will have more word pictures than you can use.

Reduce the truth that you are trying to teach to a basic concept, then think of persons, places and things that illustrate that truth

This is something else I have tried. First, I ask myself, 'What am I trying to teach?' or 'What basic concept describes or is parallel to what I am trying to say?' I try to distill what I need to teach into its elemental form. Then I start asking questions about that basic proposition. 'What is like...?' or 'What is not like...?' or 'What is it to be compared to...?' Let us say you are teaching about the painful consequences of sin. First, you boil that truth down into its fundamental principle–painful consequences. Then you ask yourself what kind of things bring with them painful consequences? These are some of the things that come to my mind which bring about painful consequences: slamming your finger in the car door, picking up a bee, touching something hot, falling down, tripping, slipping, poking yourself in the eye, drinking and driving, playing with guns, speaking rashly, telling lies, taking drugs. Now once you have that part of the exercise done, the rest is easy. All you need to do is compare those things with sin and its consequences. You might say something like this:

> Have you ever slammed your finger in the car door? It hurts doesn't it? You probably did not do it on purpose, but why did it happen? Usually it happens because you let down your guard. You stopped thinking about what you were doing. But isn't it interesting how slamming your finger in the car door makes you pay attention after that? In the same way, God has a way of

building painful consequences into sinful behaviour. Those consequences are designed to get you to pay attention to what you are doing.

or,

Sin is pleasurable for a time but always has painful consequences. Playing with a loaded weapon can be fun too, until someone accidently pulls the trigger and kills himself.

Once you have some ideas, then it is just a matter of getting them arranged on the canvas so that they point to the truth. They do not need to be any particular size; they only need to illuminate the truth. Tailor them to your sermon. Robert McCraken says: 'One original illustration, suggested to your own mind by a walk in the country, or by a round of pastoral calls, is worth a whole cyclopedia of borrowed material.'[154] Once you get to the place where you can generate word pictures effortlessly, you will slay them in the pews. 'Your own meditations ought to yield your best illustrations.'[155] Reduce the truth you are trying to teach into its basic concept, think of parallels, then forge them into spiritual weapons.

Take a person, place, or thing and try to think of as many spiritual parallels as you can

Here is another word picture drill you can try. It is the opposite of the method above. Instead of starting with a truth and thinking of a word picture, you first think of a person, place, or thing. Then you see how many spiritual truths you can illustrate with it. Let us say you think of a tree. If you prefer, you can think of just tree word pictures, or you can think of all the parts of a tree: roots, branches, leaves, fruit and flowers. Now you are ready to start exercising. I recommend that you do several sets to get your word picture muscles in shape. If you do a search of the words listed above, i.e., 'root/s, branch/es, leaf or leaves, fruit and flower/s,' with Bible software, you will discover over seven hundred occurrences!

And you probably are able to guess by now that many usages are figurative. 'The axe is already laid at the root of the trees;' 'bring forth fruit in keeping with repentance;' 'every tree that does not bear good fruit is cut down and thrown into the fire;' 'I shall raise up for David a righteous branch;' 'Judah shall again take root downward and bear fruit upward.' If you need some help, the biblical writers will show you how to make word pictures out of persons, places and things. Jay Adams gives us good advice for finding illustrations also:

> As the first order of business every morning when you enter your study (after prayer) look around at, listen to, smell, touch what is there. Look at things you never noticed before – cracks in plaster, holes in rugs, scratches in the desk; they all contain messages if you will only read them carefully. Listen to that hum, the bird singing outside, the sound of water gurgling through a pipe in the wall. What are these sounds telling you? Nothing? Then listen, imagine, think, think, think! Run your hand over the smooth surface of the desk, the rough texture of a concrete block in the outside wall – is there a truth hidden there? Of course – at least 50 illustrations are hidden in that block alone, if you will attune yourself to them! That pen lying on your desk, like the human beings who may use it, has potential to bless or curse others; those pages of crumpled, discarded thought in the wastebasket have a word to speak about God's attitude toward humanistic ideas; that telephone, which is your link with the outside; all these items, and thousands of others like them, are available to you for use. Focus on one – say the telephone – see how many different aspects of it provide illustrations. Why, the telephone alone could keep you busy manufacturing illustrations for a month.[156]

Many illustrations are waiting to be found in persons, places and things. Familiar objects make truth easier to understand. When you use them in illustrations, it is like a mental shoehorn that allows the truth to slide in. Let me give you one more thing you might want to try.

Think how you would communicate what you are teaching to a new believer or to a child who has little or no Bible knowledge

Let us say someone in your church leads his next-door neighbour to the Lord and brings him to your Bible study. You are teaching about 'walking in the Spirit' from Galatians 5. It is a challenging concept to teach to mature believers, let alone someone who has no spiritual knowledge. Now if you say, 'You need to walk in the Spirit,' imagine what that person might be thinking. He is going to be thinking of the 'Twilight Zone'. He is going to be thinking of walking the dog and how maybe walking the Spirit is the same thing. Oh, did you say *in the Spirit?* So maybe it is like getting in a car and driving around. He does not have a clue what 'walking in the Spirit' is. You need to help him understand. You need to *show him* what Paul meant when he said, 'walk in the Spirit'. Here is one suggestion:

> Walking in the Spirit is a command that takes effort. It is like choosing to swim against the current. When you placed your faith in Christ, God gave you his Spirit. The Spirit will encourage you and enable you to obey God's word from within. The Spirit is not like a drill sergeant who makes you obey but a coach who encourages you. He comes alongside you to help you do what is right. When you read the Bible, God will be speaking to you and his Spirit will encourage you to obey. As when you obey your coach, you must engage your will. You must make an effort to do what he says. If you do not make any effort to obey God's word, you will not be walking in the Spirit. When you are not walking in the Spirit you will be carried downstream by the currents of your own lusts and end up in the dead sea.

Remember, it is important for people to see the truth, but it is really important that you show them the truth so that they can understand what you are saying. The person with no knowledge of the Bible needs some familiar things to help them grasp the unfamiliar things of God's word. The example above might be one of several attempts to help someone to 'see' what the Bible is saying. That is why it is often helpful to give more than one word picture. Each word picture will help bring definition to the doctrine you are trying to teach. Now you may be saying to yourself, 'I could do better than that.' Praise God! Go for it. Believe me, I want you to do better than that. The point is that it is better to use simplistic and sometimes silly word pictures than NO word pictures at all. A silly word picture will deliver the truth better than an abstract proposition. Let me give you another example. This is one I used when I taught about the mercy and grace of God:

> Mercy and grace both flow from the goodness of God to satisfy the thirst of the sinner. Both are unexpected friends dispatched from heaven to help in a time of need. Grace gives undeserved good to the sinner while mercy withholds the deserved wrath of God. Mercy is like a father who protects his sinful daughter when judgment comes courting; but before judgment is able to find her, grace captures her heart and sneaks her through the window of salvation. When judgment finally arrives, the daughter is no longer eligible, for she is happily married in the arms of grace.

Here is another to help you to 'get the picture'. This next paragraph was used in a Bible study in an attempt to illustrate the abstract doctrines of sovereignty, providence and concurrence, and how they relate to God's accomplishing his sovereign decree (not an easy task):

> God is like an archer who is sovereign over the bow. He has the power and wisdom to do what he wishes with the bow. The bow is God's will. The archer can point the bow in any direction he wants. In the archer's quiver is a multitude of arrows which are situations that God has chosen to use to accomplish his decree. God, by his sovereignty, directs the bow (his will) to launch the arrows (the individual situations) at the target (which is his decree). When the arrows are launched they encounter wind,

turbulence, gravity, etc. These things are like the movements of God's creation. They are man's will concurring with God's will. Often they seem to run contrary to God's will. But, because the Archer is sovereign over the bow and the arrow, he is able to hit the bull's-eye, his perfect will or decree, every time he shoots.

Notice that a word picture like that is 'technical'. It needed to be because of the difficulty in describing how several doctrines work together. But even though the word picture is technical it still offers some concrete comparisons for the believer to latch on to. Again, the example is not perfect and could be improved upon. But the point is that an immature believer needs to have something to relate Bible doctrine to, especially if it is the first time he has heard about that specific doctrine. Henry Ward Beecher said:

> I have seen an audience, time and again, follow an argument, doubtfully, laboriously, almost suspiciously, and look at one another, as much as to say, 'Is he going right?' – until the place is arrived at, where the speaker says, 'It is like ...' and then they listen eagerly for what it is like; and when some apt illustration is thrown out before them, there is a sense of relief, as though they said, 'Yes, he is right.'[157]

Even if people understand the doctrine you are preaching they can always use another good word picture to help them understand it better. Again this is where feedback might come in handy. If you are brave enough, as you are shaking hands and hugging babies after the service, hand out a few questionnaires and self-addressed stamped envelopes. Ask a few people to fill them in and post them to you. On the questionnaire ask them what things they learned about the doctrine of 'whatever you preached on'. Ask them specific questions about the main thrust of the text and see if the truth went to the heart or if it bounced off onto the floor. Then you will see if you are communicating. A wife is also a good resource for this. So are the elders of your church. Blackwood tells this story of John Henry Jowett: 'Almost every week Jowett used to select a small group of friends who would sit before him on the ensuing Sunday morning – a different group each week – and then use them as a sort of homiletical proving ground.'[158] Get feedback from young or new believers and see if they are learning what you are trying to teach them. One more thing: be sitting down when you read what they say and remember that even Christ 'learned obedience from the things which he suffered' (Heb. 5:8).

The practical steps I have mentioned have worked for me. I think that they will work for you too. Try them one at a time and see if they do the trick. If you have problems at first, do not sound the retreat. I have been working on this for four years and I am still not very good at it, but I am much better than I was. Be encouraged by this story:

> When Jowett began to preach, he did not seem to be unusually gifted. But by God's blessing upon his ceaseless labors he soon began to be an inspiring pulpit interpreter of the Bible for the common people. His experience shows that the way for the godly pastor to develop this power is to love his people, feed his soul daily on the Book, and work hard on every sermon.[159]

[The minister must be] a plain preacher, suiting his matter and style to the capacity of his audience *(I Cor. 14:19)*. Some ministers, like eagles, love to soar aloft in abstruse metaphysical notions, thinking they are most admired when they are least understood. They who preach in the clouds, instead of hitting their people's conscience, shoot over their heads.

The word is a hammer (Jer. 23:29). Every blow of the hammer is to fasten the nails to the building; so the preachers words are to fasten you the more to Christ; they weaken themselves to strengthen and settle you. This is the grand design of preaching, not only for the enlightening, but for the establishing of souls; not only to guide them in the right way, but to keep them in it (Thomas Watson).

8

BURMESE TIGER TRAPS

Pitfalls to avoid when using word pictures

When I was growing up, one of my favourite cartoon series was the Bugs Bunny Roadrunner show. My favourite character was 'Wile E. Coyote – Suuuuper Genius'. I loved all the contraptions he made even though none of them ever worked. I longed to see him finally catch the Roadrunner. One of the Coyote's 'fail proof' traps was the 'Burmese Tiger Trap'. It was a large pit dug into the ground with a cover stretched over the top that was painted to look just like the road surface. He reckoned that the Roadrunner would come sprinting down the road and fall right into the hole. Then he would jump in and have a roadrunner sandwich for lunch. But it never worked. The Roadrunner was too fast, or too light, or had too much help from the animators. He would go right over the top of the trap and even stand on it and nothing would happen. This would make the Coyote quite frustrated, and he would try the trap out on himself to see why it did not work. Immediately he would plunge into the pit. You can probably guess or remember what was waiting for him at the bottom. Yes, it was a large Burmese tiger with a bad temper, sharp teeth and long claws. The moral of the story is crystal clear. Never fall into a Burmese Tiger Trap. When using word pictures there are some Burmese Tiger Traps that you need to avoid. I hope that the warnings that we are about to look at will be like guard rails to keep you from falling into the tiger trap.

Do not use word pictures to play the entertainer
A temptation exists to cross over the line from expository preaching to entertaining. That should be avoided like a

Burmese Tiger Trap. Humour has a small place in the pulpit, but, for the most part, preaching is serious business. 'Teachers will incur a stricter judgment' (Jas. 3:1). Anything that attracts attention to the person of the preacher or away from the word of God is to be avoided at all costs. You are there to shed light on the Scriptures, not to draw attention to yourself.

We must remember that God has created us with a sense of humour (at least most of us) and has also allowed us to receive pleasure from a wide variety of things. In your reading of the Bible, you have probably come across some humorous passages. Let me point out a few that have given me a chuckle. First, the story of Elijah and the prophets of Baal on Mount Carmel contains some humour (1 Kings 18). After Elijah sets up the 'challenge of the gods contest', all the prophets of Baal assemble and call upon their god to consume the sacrifice. They are being watched by the nation, and in a desperate masochistic frenzy, they try everything they can to make their imaginary god respond. Then comes the humorous part when the text reads: 'And it came about at noon, that Elijah mocked them and said, "Call out with a loud voice, for he is a god; either he is occupied or gone aside, or is on a journey, or perhaps he is asleep and needs to be awakened" ' (1 Kings 18:27). A word study of the text will reveal that most English versions of the Bible have toned down what Elijah was really saying. But even in the toned down form, it oozes with sarcasm and is rather funny. Isaiah had a similar sense of humour when he ridiculed the idol worshippers of his day with these words:

> To whom then will you liken God? Or what likeness will you compare with Him? As for the idol, a craftsman casts it, a goldsmith plates it with gold, and a silversmith fashions chains of silver. He who is too impoverished for such an offering selects a tree that does not rot; He seeks out for himself a skillful craftsman to prepare an idol that will not totter (Isa. 40:18-20).

Jeremiah perfected Isaiah's idol mocking and said:

For the customs of the peoples are delusion; Because it is wood
cut from the forest, the work of the hands of a craftsman with a
cutting tool. They decorate it with silver and with gold; They
fasten it with nails and with hammers so that it will not totter.
Like a scarecrow in a cucumber field are they, and they cannot
speak; They must be carried, because they cannot walk! Do not
fear them, For they can do no harm, Nor can they do any good
(Jer. 10:3-5).

Those texts are humorous to a small degree. They teach us
that worshipping idols is laughable, ridiculous and futile. It is
like worshipping and serving a scarecrow in a cucumber field.
Now if you are thinking to yourself, 'I don't know about the
legitimacy of using humour,' consider Jesus' words to the
Scribes and Pharisees: 'have you never read?'[160] a phrase
which Jesus liked to use when addressing the 'experts' in the
law. When you consider that the Scribes and Pharisees were
fanatics about the Hebrew Scriptures, that is quite the
question. The Scribes were the 'copy machines' of the sacred
text. The Pharisees would often memorize huge portions of
the Bible. They would wrangle and discuss microscopic
textual minutiae. They could tell you how many letters were
in each book and what the middle letter was to the Hebrew
canon. With the crowds and their peers looking on Jesus says
to them, 'have you never read?' I would love to have seen one
of those encounters. It makes me wonder if Jesus said it with
a smile on his face or not. I am sure it spawned some laughter
from a few in the crowd.

Having said that, I would not make an effort to insert
humour for humour's sake. You may think of something
funny off the cuff or you may say something funny by
accident and those things are fine, if kept in moderation. I
know in my own preaching ministry that people will often
break out into laughter when I least expect it. It surprises me

and often causes me to lose my train of thought. I had this happen to me recently when preaching on the book of Job. I explained in detail how Job had lost his family, his servants, his livestock and even his health. I then said, 'The only thing he had left was his wife, and look at the text to see what a blessing she turned out to be.' This was very humorous to my congregation and I never planned it to be so. Other times when I have tried to be funny two people laugh and hundreds of others sit there stone-faced. Also, do not think that just because you have a funny story that it is your obligation before God and men to entertain your congregation with it from the pulpit. Do not insert humour into your sermons merely to make them humorous. Charles Brown warns against the misuse of humour when he says:

> There are preachers who, once possessed of an interesting story or clever illustration, become impatient to use it. They can hardly wait for Sunday to come. They will employ that illustration in the next sermon preached even though it has to be dragged in by the hair of its head.[161]

Remember that the pulpit is not a place to tickle the funny bone but to strike the heart. The words 'reprove', 'rebuke' and 'exhort' do not allow for much entertaining (2 Tim. 4:2). You should not try to make your people feel happy, or even sad for that matter. If you are aiming at any 'feeling', it should be to make them feel 'accurate' about themselves. If they are sinning, they should feel guilt; and if they are walking in obedience, they should feel joy and thankfulness to the Lord. I believe that part of what Paul was condemning in 1 Corinthians 1 and 2 was man-centred, entertainment-oriented elocution and rhetoric. Entertaining from the pulpit will exalt the preacher and focus attention on him rather than the word of God.

Having put up the barbed wire fence around humour, I believe there may be an exception to what I have just said.

Preachers may find it helpful to use some humour at the beginning of a sermon or actually before the preaching of the word begins. Humour can be an effective 'ice breaker' or 'opener' to a sermon. I have seen this done many times by godly expositors, and it has a way of calming the beast in the crowd. It helps focus their attention on what is going to be said next. It can cause them to drop their armour so that the arrows of truth may enter in. But never use humour that will not pass inspection with God. Remember, you have not been sent to bring entertainment to your people, but the sword of the Spirit.

Avoid over-illustrating the truth
The idiom, 'flogging a dead horse' comes to mind when I say, 'Do not over-illustrate.' Word pictures should be used to clarify, explain and focus attention on the truth but not to beat it into dust. By over-illustrating we run the risk of discrediting ourselves and boring people with God's word. I would like to give you a mathematical formula for how many word pictures one should use to illustrate a truth and what length they should be, but I am afraid I cannot. I can say this: give them as many as it takes to help them to understand. If one will do, then that is enough. Being verbose is not a virtue. Also remember: 'That which is perfectly clear cannot be helped by illustration.'[162] A window that is spotless is best left alone; by further cleaning you waste cleaning supplies and run the risk of smudging the glass. Ezra Rhoades says:

> Consider that always your illustration is for the sake of your truth, not vice versa. Over illustration is quickly tiresome, it gives the sense of superficiality, it leads to the suspicion that you are laboring to be poetic or eloquent or that you are substituting ornament for further material. Too many raisins spoil the pudding. Too many pictures spoil your wall.[163]

Spurgeon, who used an abundance of illustrations, also warned against abuses:

Flowers upon the table at a banquet are well enough; but as
nobody can live upon bouquets, they will become objects of
contempt if they are set before us in lieu of substantial viands.
The difference between a little salt with your meat and being
compelled to empty the salt-cellar is clear to all; and we could
wish that those who pour out so many symbols, emblems,
figures and devices would remember that nausea in oratory is
not more agreeable than in food.[164]

So how many word pictures are enough? Jesus, I believe,
used a maximum number of them. The authors of Scripture
often presented truth with many small word pictures. As
mentioned earlier, Jesus sometimes gave parables in sets of
three. All that is to say that I do not have an answer. You need
to use as many as it takes to drive the truth home. Sometimes
you have to hit a nail more than once to get it driven in flush.
If you have a big hammer, and you swing really hard, you can
sometimes sink the nail in with one blow – if the wood is not
too hard. If you have a smaller hammer, or the wood is hard,
then several blows are usually necessary. If you hit the nail too
many times, the hammer will damage the wood. You do not
want that to happen.

Do not use word pictures to gain the approval of men
This not only includes 'entertaining' as mentioned above, but
every kind of man-pleasing. We must remember that when we
stand before God's people to preach the word there is only one
person we need to please and that person is the Lord Jesus
Christ. He is the one who has saved us, who has given us gifts
and empowered us with his Spirit. Shall we use God's good
gifts to steal his glory? How ridiculous it is even to ask such
a question. Yet, is that not what we do when we feed our own
lusts in the pulpit? We must remember that we are not our
own: we have been bought with a price. We are soldiers
enlisted in the King's army to serve him, and everyone knows
that traitors are shot. There is a subtle difference between

desiring that people pay attention to the *Word* and desiring that they pay attention to *you*. Your task is not to make sure that they like what you are saying.

When reading men like Thomas Watson we can think to ourselves, 'I wish I could preach like he did so that I could be well-liked and famous.' That kind of attitude is a millstone that will quickly bring us low in God's sight. Those who are truly saved will love you if you are faithful to the text and preach the whole counsel of God's word. But again, the one you should seek to please is God. What if Jeremiah had tried to get people to like him? His ministry would have been a disgrace. Yet Jeremiah, like many of the prophets, faithfully preached the Word, seeking to obey God in the midst of a crooked and perverse generation. Paul said, 'Therefore also we have as our ambition, whether at home or absent, to be pleasing to him' (2 Cor. 5:9). When you are tempted to be a man-pleaser, remember this admonition from the author of Hebrews, 'Therefore, since we receive a kingdom which cannot be shaken, let us show gratitude, by which we may offer to God an acceptable service with reverence and awe; for our God is a consuming fire' (Heb. 12:28-29).

Do not make word pictures too long
Do not make your word pictures so long that people get lost and cannot find their way back to the text. Jesus told some pretty long stories in his preaching and teaching ministry, but remember that he was a perfect preacher. We must be careful with long stories because they can take people away from the text of God's word rather than focus attention on it. If you have to say, 'Now where was I?' after giving a word picture, you have wandered too far away from the text. Long word pictures, if used incorrectly, can be like leading someone out into a forest and then ditching them. You cause them to get 'lost' so that they cannot find their way back to the text without the help of a 'rescue review'. If you need to 'review' after an illustration, it merely betrays the fact that your

illustration failed to serve its purpose. The whole purpose of word pictures is to focus people on the text, not to lead them away from it. I remember creating a parable one time that was about three minutes long. Several people said that they liked 'the story', but no one mentioned that it was a good illustration of the truth that I was preaching. A few days later I received an unsigned letter in the post with a mild rebuke encouraging me to 'stick with the text'. Usually unsigned mail contains a grenade with the pin pulled. You open the letter and 'Ka-boom!' I have learned that vengeance is theirs, they will repay. That was not one of the most pleasurable moments in my preaching career, but it was an educational one. Make sure that all longer word pictures are crafted so that people can clearly see how they relate to the text of Scripture.

Do not use complicated word pictures that need excessive explanation. Sometimes you must give some context to a word picture. That is legitimate. Jesus did this when giving parables at times. He would say something like, 'There was a certain ...' and then would give some context to the parable. But be sensitive to what the 'average' person understands. You may have a degree in physics and understand how a spectrometer works, but that does not mean that your people do.

Avoid extra-complicated or detailed word pictures
The better illustrations, as mentioned before, are usually simple ones that everyone can easily understand. John Broadus pointed out:

> Many a preacher wonders why his vision of truth, which stirs him so profoundly, falls flat, not realizing that his words gave no familiar pictures. His hearers were farmers, perhaps, while his pictures were of city life, problems, scenery.[165]

Make sure that your word pictures do not, like Saul, stand head and shoulders above your people.

Again, an exception exists for every general rule. If you happened to be preaching at a Sunday morning service held by the Astrophysicists of America Association, a spectrometer illustration would be right at home. In fact I have discovered that word pictures that relate to what people deal with every day are extra effective. If you are preaching to a crowd that has expertise in a particular field, then by all means meet them where they live. But if you do decide to do this, be careful that you know what you are talking about. One bit of misinformation can discredit you in their eyes. I remember preaching a sermon once on *'the manifold wisdom of God'* from Ephesians 3:10. I had just been working on my car and so I said something like this:

> Under the bonnet of the car that you drive is an engine. Attached to your engine is a device called an exhaust manifold. The exhaust manifold receives exhaust fumes from each cylinder and brings them all together and focuses them into a single pipe which is called an exhaust pipe. In a similar way God has chosen to bring together and focus his manifold wisdom on the church. The church receives the many aspects of God's grace which is put on display for angelic majesties. The church is designed to display the 'manifold' wisdom of God.

That particular word picture was pushing the limits. Most people know that they have an engine in their car, and most people know that they have an exhaust pipe. Yet, many do not understand mechanical things and how an internal combustion engine works. For them, that particular illustration probably created as much confusion as clarity. Even if they got the point they might have been sidetracked into thinking about how their engines worked. On the positive side, I am sure that many of those who did have some knowledge of mechanics probably understood the text better because of the illustration. After giving that message the only person who commented on that particular illustration was a man who was a car mechanic by profession. He loved it. That taught me that if I have a specialized audience, I might want to use specialized word pictures; but if I have a general audience I should use universal ones.

Do not make your congregation wish they had a dictionary
Of all the kinds of preachers in existence, I believe expository preachers are more guilty of making their people long for dictionaries than any other. We tend to be more academic, more precise, more theological. We tend to use more theological language like, 'the anthropocentric hamartiological nature of man is evident in this text' or 'the use of the ineffable tetragrammaton with the Hiphil shows us a causal relationship.' Words like that throw people's minds into a mental traffic jam. It causes them to lose focus on the text and the echo of 'What did he just say?' rings in their ears. If your people are stuck, they can't follow you. Big words can be mental bogs which are usually best reserved for theological four-wheelers in the seminary classroom.

Have you ever considered how many theological terms we use ending in 'ence' and 'tion' that never appear in the Bible? You might want to take notice of how many of those terms pop out of your mouth when preaching. If you do decide to use theological jargon in the pulpit, make sure you paint a graphic definition. Help your people 'see' what the terms mean. I remember recently going to the Evangelical Theological Society's annual meeting. During several of the sessions that I attended, the theological slang terms were so thick that I thought they were speaking in a different language. I felt like asking for an interpreter so that we could receive edification. All that to say, do not make your people wish they had a theological dictionary.

Conclusion
Word pictures are one of the most productive and effective means of communicating the word of God. It is my desire that expositors will shy away from abstract preaching. What good

is a sermon that people cannot follow, understand or
remember? We must keep in mind that expository preaching
does not have as its goal exegesis, but communicating the
word of God. We are to 'feed the sheep' by preparing
nutritious meals not merely by throwing raw ingredients at
them. In the following pages I have included two appendices
to help you learn how to use word pictures. Appendix A is a
list of Thomas Watson's works. Appendix B is some of the
cream from Thomas Watson's sermons. I commend you to
God and the word of his grace:

> Devote yourselves to prayer, keeping alert in it with an attitude
> of thanksgiving; praying at the same time for us as well, that
> God may open up to us a door for the word, so that we may speak
> forth the mystery of Christ, for which I have also been
> imprisoned; in order that *I may make it clear* in the way I ought
> to speak (Col. 4:2-4, emphasis mine).

NOTES

1 Stephen D. Olford, *Anointed Expository Preaching,* (Nashville: Broadman & Holman Publishers, 1998) p. 4.

2 Sidney Greidanus, *Preaching Christ from the Old Testament,* (Grand Rapids: William B. Eerdmans Publishing, 1999) p. 231.

3 Haddon W. Robinson, *Biblical Preaching,* (Grand Rapids: Baker Book House, 1980) p. 20.

4 John F. MacArthur and the Master's Seminary Faculty, *Rediscovering Expository Preaching,* (Dallas: Word Publishing, 1992) pp. 23-24.

5 John R. W. Stott, *Between Two Worlds: The Art of Preaching in the Twentieth Century,* (Grand Rapids: William Eerdmans Publishing Company, 1982) pp. 125-26.

6 The Master's Seminary is located in Sun Valley, California on the campus of Grace Community Church. Its president is pastor/ teacher John MacArthur.

7 Andrew W. Blackwood, *Preaching from the Bible,* (New York: Abingdon – Cokesbury Press, 1941) p. 208.

8 Editor's note on the dustjacket of *The Duty of Self Denial and Ten Other Sermons by Thomas Watson,* by Thomas Watson, reprinted (Morgan: Soli Deo Gloria, no date).

9 John MacArthur, in the foreword to *The Mischief of Sin,* First published 1671; reprinted (Carlisle: The Banner of Truth Trust, 1992), p. vi.

10 Hamilton Smith, in the biographical introduction to *Gleanings from Thomas Watson,* First published 1915; reprinted (Morgan: Soli Deo Gloria, 1995), p. xi.

11 Malcolm H. Watts, in the preface to *Religion Our True Interest,* First published in 1682, reprinted (Edinburgh: Blue Banner Productions, 1992), p. vii.

12 Charles Spurgeon, in the 'Brief Memoir of Thomas Watson' in *A Body of Divinity,* by Thomas Watson, First printed as part of a larger work *A Body of Practical Divinity,* 1692; reprinted 1890; reprinted (Carlisle: The Banner of Truth Trust, 1958, revised edition 1965), p. x.

13 Spurgeon, *A Body of Divinity,* p. x.

[14] Smith, *Gleanings*, p. xii.

[15] J. I. Packer, *A Quest for Godliness,* (Wheaton: Crossway Books, 1990), p. 29.

[16] Spurgeon, *A Body of Divinity*, p. viii.

[17] Smith, *Gleanings*, p. xiii.

[18] Watts, *Religion,* p. viii.

[19] Spurgeon, *A Body of Divinity*, p. x.

[20] W. M. Symington, in the 'Life and Character of Charnock' found in Charnock's work *The Existence and Attributes of God,* (reprinted from 1853 edition, Grand Rapids: Baker Book House, 1979), pp. 7-8.

[21] Packer, *A Quest,* p. 75.

[22] From the back dustjacket of *A Body of Divinity.*

[23] Smith, *Gleanings*, p. xii.

[24] Thomas Watson, *The Godly Man's Picture,* First published in 1666; reprinted (Carlisle: The Banner of Truth Trust, 1992), pp. 87-88.

[25] Smith, *Gleanings,* p. xv.

[26] *Webster's New Collegiate Dictionary,* 1981.

[27] Haddon Robinson, *Biblical Preaching,* (Grand Rapids: Baker Book House, 1980), p. 182.

[28] Puritanism began to gain strength in 1558 when Queen Elizabeth enacted the settlement which gave certain religious freedoms to the Puritans. Later, as times grew tougher, Puritanism gained more strength. It seems that persecution was used by God like a purifying furnace which made their lives purer and their works sweeter.

[29] Robert J. McCraken, *The Making of a Sermon,* (New York: Harper & Brothers, 1956) p. 258.

[30] Thomas Watson, *The Godly Man's Picture,* First published in 1666; reprinted (Carlisle: The Banner of Truth Trust, 1992), pp. 14, 98, 123.

[31] Charles Spurgeon, 'Brief Memoir of Thomas Watson', in *A Body of Divinity,* p. vii.

[32] *Random House Webster's College Dictionary,* (1999), s.v. 'sensuous'.

[33] ibid, s.v. 'sensual'.

[34] Henry Grady Davis, *Design for Preaching,* (Philadelphia: Fortress Press, 1958), p. 271.

[35] Jay Adams in *The Preacher and Preaching,* ed. Samuel T. Logan, Jr., (Phillipsburg: Presbyterian and Reformed, 1986), p. 354.

[36] Jay Adams, *Preaching With Purpose,* (Grand Rapids: Zondervan Publishing House, 1982), p. 86.

[37] Watson, *The Godly Man's Picture,* pp. 147, 181, 186.

[38] Warren Wiersbe, *Preaching and Teaching With Imagination: The Quest for Biblical Ministry,* (Grand Rapids: Baker Book House, 1994), p. 44.

[39] Roy B. Zuck, *Basic Bible Interpretation,* (Wheaton: Victor Books, 1991), p. 221.

[40] McCraken, *The Making of a Sermon,* p. 258.

[41] Donald E. Demaray, *Pulpit Giants,* (Chicago: Moody Press, 1973), p. 40.

[42] Watson, *The Godly Man's Picture,* pp. 109, 127, 169.

[43] Watson, *The Godly Man's Picture,* pp. 66, 150, 180.

[44] Farris D. Whitesell, *Power in Expository Preaching,* (no city stated: Fleming H. Revell, 1963), p. 75.

[45] Halford E. Luccock, *The Minister's Workshop,* (New York: Abingdon–Cokesbury Press, 1944), p. 107.

[46] Ray G. Jordan, *You Can Preach,* (New York: Fleming H. Revell, 1951), p. 154.

[47] An example of one who strongly discourages using illustration books is Charles Brown who describes them as a 'delusion and a snare'. He says any preacher who has 'been foolish enough to purchase one, he had best burn it forthwith'. Charles Reynolds Brown, *The Art of Preaching,* (New York: MacMillan, 1922), p. 131.

[48] Two examples of Scripture illustration books that I like to use are *A Treasury of Scripture Knowledge* (Mclean: MacDonald Publishing, 1982) and *10,000 Illustrations from the Bible* (Grand Rapids: Baker Book House, 1990).

[49] David James Burrell, *The Sermon: Its Construction and Delivery,* (Chicago: Fleming H. Revell, 1913), p. 225.

[50] Watson, *The Godly Man's Picture,* pp. 63, 178, 195.

[51] Wiersbe, *Preaching and Teaching,* p. 26.

[52] Henry Ward Beecher, *Yale Lectures on Preaching,* (Boston: The Pilgrims Press, 1902), p. 110.

[53] John A. Broadus, *On the Preparation and Delivery of Sermons,* (New York: Harper & Brothers, 1944), pp. 282-3.

[54] Andrew W. Blackwood, *Preaching From the Bible,* (New York: Abingdon – Cokesbury Press, 1941), p. 197.

[55] Beecher, *Yale Lectures on Preaching,* p. 117.

[56] Jay E. Adams, *Truth Apparent: Essays on Biblical Preaching,* (Phillipsburg: Presbyterian and Reformed, 1982), p. 64.

[57] John Broadus, *On The Preparation and Delivery of Sermons,* (New York: Harper & Brothers, 1944), p. 279.

[58] *Webster's,* s.v. 'imagination'.

[59] John Broadus quoted by Whitesell, *Power in Expository Preaching,* p. 104.

[60] W. Macneile Dixon quoted by Donald E. Demaray in *An Introduction to Homiletics,* (Grand Rapids: Baker Book House, 1990), p. 139.

[61] Brown, *Art of Preaching,* p. 142.

[62] Henry Ward Beecher quoted by John Broadus, *On the Preparation and Delivery of Sermons,* p. 279.

[63] Thomas Watson, *A Body of Divinity,* pp. 70, 120-1.

[64] Thomas Watson, *All Things for Good,* First published 1663; reprint (Carlisle: The Banner of Truth Trust, 1986), pp. 107-9.

[65] Faris D. Whitesell, and Lloyd M. Perry, *Variety in Your Preaching,* (New York: Fleming H. Revell, 1954), p. 111.

[66] Charles Spurgeon, *Lectures to My Students,* (Grand Rapids: Zondervan Publishing House, 1954), p. 129.

[67] Watson, *The Godly Man's Picture,* p. 154.

[68] Daniel P. Kidder, *A Treatise on Homiletics,* (New York: Carlton & Porter, 1866), p. 239.

[69] Luccock, *The Ministers Work Shop,* p. 117.

[70] Burrell, *The Sermon: Its Construction and Delivery,* pp. 217-8.

[71] Geoffrey Thomas in *The Preacher and Preaching,* ed. Logan, p. 369.

[72] Sydney Smith quoted by Arthur S. Hoyt in *The Work of Preaching,* (New York: MacMillan, 1925), p. 262.

[73] Robinson, *Biblical Preaching,* p. 179.

[74] Paul B. Bull, *Lectures on Preaching and Sermon Construction,* (New York: The MacMillan Company, 1932), p. 268.

[75] Spurgeon, *Lectures,* p. 133.

[76] Wiersbe, *Preaching and Teaching,* p. 221.

[77] Spurgeon, *Lectures,* p. 127.

[78] W. B. Riley, *The Preacher and His Preaching,* (Wheaton: Sword

of the Lord Publishers, 1948), p. 114.

[79] Burrell, *The Sermon*, p. 217.

[80] ibid., pp. 223-24.

[81] Alex Montoya, quotation remembered from class lecture at The Master's Seminary.

[82] Spurgeon, *Lectures*, p. 127.

[83] A great personal struggle of mine, after graduating from seminary, was trying not to use terms such as predestination, sanctification, propitiation, redemption, reconciliation, providence, concurrence and a host of other 'common' abstract theological terms without defining them in a more understandable way. I still use those terms but work at showing people what they mean.

[84] William Evans, *How to Prepare Sermons and Gospel Address*, (Chicago: The Bible Institute Colportage Association, 1913), p. 136.

[85] Andrew W. Blackwood, *Expository Preaching For Today*, (Grand Rapids: Baker Book House, 1975), p. 49.

[86] Alford Ernest Garvie, *A Guide to Preachers* (New York: George H. Doran, 1906), p. 237.

[87] Thomas Watson, *Heaven Taken by Storm*, (First edition, New York: E. Low, 1810; reprinted, Ligonier: Soli Deo Gloria, 1992), p. 118.

[88] Simpson quoted by Batsell Barrett Baxter, *The Heart of Yale Lectures*, (New York: The MacMillan Company, 1947), p. 148.

[89] See οἰκοδομή (*oikodomē)*, Walter Bauer, Wilbur F. Gingrich, and Frederick W. Danker, *A Greek-English Lexicon of the New Testament and Other Early Christian Literature*, (Chicago: University of Chicago Press, 1979) pp. 558-9; or W. E. Vine, *Vine's Expository Dictionary of Biblical Words*, (Nashville: Thomas Nelson Inc., 1984) p. 194.

[90] *Webster's*, s.v. 'communicate'.

[91] ibid. s.v. 'communication'.

[92] See Leon Morris, *The First Epistle of Paul to the Corinthians*, vol. 7, *Tyndale New Testament Commentaries*, ed. R. V. G. Tasker, (Grand Rapids: William B. Eerdmans, 1978), p. 42.

[93] Johannes P. Louw and Eugene A. Nida, *Greek-English Lexicon of the New Testament based on Semantic Domains*, (New York: United Bible Societies, 1988-9), Logos Bible Software.

[94] John MacArthur in *Communicating with Power*, ed. Michael Duduit, (Grand Rapids: Baker Book House, 1996), p. 121.

[95] These terms and phrases were taken from 2 Timothy chapters 1 and 2.

[96] See Paul's sermons and defences in Acts 13:16-41; 13:46-47; 14:15-17; 17:22-31; 23:1-3; 26:1-29; 28:25-28.

[97] Spurgeon, *Lectures*, p. 127.

[98] Watson, *The Godly Man's Picture*, pp. 68, 76.

[99] Gerhard Kittel and Gerhard Friedrich, editors, *The Theological Dictionary of the New Testament, Abridged in One Volume*, (Grand Rapids: William B. Eerdmans Publishing Company, 1985); W. E. Vine, *Vine's Expository Dictionary of Old and New Testament Words*, (Grand Rapids: Fleming H. Revell, 1981), Logos Library System.

[100] See for examples Mt. 4:24; 8:16; 12:15; 15:30; Lk. 5:17; 9:11; Jn. 12:1, 9, 17; Acts 4:30; 5:16; 20:9-10.

[101] Charles Bridges, *The Christian Ministry*, First published in 1830; reprinted, (Carlisle: The Banner of Truth Trust, 1991), p. 310.

[102] Spurgeon, *Lectures*, p. 349.

[103] John MacArthur, 'Marks of the Faithful Preacher', Part 3, 2 Timothy 4:3-5, tape #55-22, (Word of Grace Communications, 1988).

[104] D. Martyn Lloyd-Jones, *Preachers and Preaching*, (Grand Rapids: Zondervan Publishing House, 1971), p. 227.

[105] R.C. Sproul, 'The Whole Man', *The Preacher and Preaching*, ed. Samuel T. Logan, (Phillipsburg: Presbyterian and Reformed, 1986), p. 114.

[106] Iain H. Murray, *Jonathan Edwards: A new Biography*, (Carlisle: The Banner of Truth Trust, 1987), pp. 186-91. According to Iain Murray, Edwards slowly changed from reading his sermon from a manuscript to preaching from an outline. This seems to have occurred about 1741 according to the manuscript evidence. But even when preaching from an outline, Edwards seems to have shunned many homiletic devices.

[107] John Piper, *The Supremacy of God in Preaching*, (Grand Rapids: Baker Book House, 1990), pp. 88-9.

[108] Sproul, 'The Whole Man', *The Preacher and Preaching*, p. 115.

[109] Answer to question 4, 'What is God?' in the 'Westminster

Shorter Catechism', quoted by Thomas Watson, *A Body of Divinity,* p. 39.

[110] Thomas Watson, *The Doctrine of Repentance,* (reprinted, Carlisle: The Banner of Truth Trust, 1987), p. 32.

[111] Watson, *A Body of Divinity,* p. 200.

[112] ibid., p. 17.

[113] Edward F. Markquart, *Quest for Better Preaching,* Minneapolis: Augsburg Publishing House, 1985), p. 150.

[114] Evans, *How to Prepare Sermons and Gospel Addresses,* p. 135.

[115] Demaray, *An Introduction to Homiletics,* p. 141.

[116] Piper, *The Supremacy of God in Preaching,* p. 88.

[117] See Ex. 29:18, 25, 41; Lev. 1:9, 13, 17; 2:2, 9, 12; 3:5, 16; 4:31; 6:15, 21; 8:21, 28; 17:6; 23:13, 18; Num. 15:3, 7, 10, 13, 14, 24; 18:17; 28:2, 6, 8, 13, 24, 27; 29:2, 6, 8, 13, 36.

[118] Thomas Watson, *Harmless as Doves* (reprinted, Geanies House, Fearn, Ross-shire: Christian Focus Publications, 1993) pp. 117-8.

[119] Thomas Watson, *A Body of Divinity,* p. 87.

[120] Watson, *The Godly Man's Picture,* p. 156.

[121] Watson, *A Body of Divinity,* pp. 62-3.

[122] Broadus, *On Preparation and Delivery of Sermons,* p. 284.

[123] Hoyt, *The Work of Preaching,* p. 263.

[124] Vernon, C. Stanfield, quoting Ian Macpherson, *Homiletics,* (Grand Rapids: Baker Book House, 1970), p. 45.

[125] Brown, *The Art of Preaching,* p. 125.

[126] Jones, *Preachers and Preaching,* p. 233-4.

[127] Demaray, *An Introduction to Homiletics,* p. 146.

[128] Spurgeon, *Lectures,* p. 252.

[129] I highly recommend Warren Wiersbe's book *Preaching and Teaching with Imagination: The Quest for Biblical Ministry,* (Grand Rapids: Baker Book House, 1994). Wiersbe approaches the subject of word pictures from the 'what makes them work' perspective. Do not be scared away by the title. It has some very helpful information for expository preachers.

[130] These verses contain 'not saved' indicators: 1 Jn. 1:6, 8,10; 2:4, 9,11, 15, 19, 22-23; 3:8, 10, 15,17; 4:5, 8, 20; 5:10, 12. These verses contain 'saved' indicators: 1 Jn. 1:7, 9; 2:3, 5,10,17,19,23; 3:7, 9, 16, 18-19, 21, 24; 4:6, 7, 13-19; 5:12. All these 'tests' are the 'these things' referred to in 1 Jn. 5:13.

[131] John Edwards, *A Primer of Homiletics*, (London: The Epworth Press, 1932), p. 75-6.

[132] Spurgeon, *Lectures*, p. 349.

[133] Burrell, *The Sermon*, p. 231.

[134] John Henry Jowett paraphrased by McCraken in, *The Making of the Sermon*, p. 71.

[135] Editors, 'Setting the Table,' *Birds and Blooms*, Collectors edition (21), 1999, p. 19.

[136] Watson, *The Godly Man's Picture*, p. 104.

[137] ibid., p. 201.

[138] Watson, *The Mischief of Sin*, p. 92.

[139] Watson, *A Body of Divinity*, p. 307.

[140] Spurgeon, *Lectures*, p. 137.

[141] ibid., p. 138.

[142] Hoyt, *The Work of Preaching*, p. 269.

[143] Watson, *The Mischief of Sin*, p. 151.

[144] Watson, *The Doctrine of Repentance*, p. 107.

[145] Burrell, *The Sermon*, p. 223.

[146] Kidder, *A Treatise on Homiletics*, p. 245.

[147] James E. Rosscup in *Rediscovering Expository Preaching*, (Dallas: Word Publishing, 1992), p. 63.

[148] Watson, *The Godly Man's Picture*, p. 88.

[149] Burrell, *The Sermon*, p. 219.

[150] Watson, *The Godly Man's Picture*, pp. 62, 66, 141.

[151] Watson, *The Godly Man's Picture*, pp. 90, 124, 215.

[152] Demaray, *An Introduction to Homiletics*, p. 144.

[153] Watson, *The Godly Man's Picture*, p. 191.

[154] McCraken, *The Making of a Sermon*, p. 265.

[155] Ezra Rhoades, *Case Work in Preaching*, (New York: Fleming H. Revell, 1952), p. 84.

[156] Jay E. Adams, *Truth Apparent: Essays on Biblical Preaching*, (Phillipsburg: Presbyterian and Reformed, 1982), p. 58.

[157] Henry Ward Beecher quoted by Baxter, *The Heart of Yale Lectures*, p. 152.

[158] Blackwood, *Preaching from the Bible*, p. 213.

[159] ibid., p. 215.

[160] See Mt. 12:3, 5; 19:4; 21:16; 22:31. Jesus was speaking to men obsessed with reading, studying, memorizing and copying the Scriptures.

[161] Brown, *The Art of Preaching,* pp. 130-1.
[162] Hoyt, *The Work of Preaching,* p. 265.
[163] Rhoades, *Case Work in Preaching,* p. 82.
[164] Spurgeon, *Lectures,* p. 354.
[165] Broadus, *On the Preparation and Delivery of Sermons,* p. 287.

APPENDIX: A LIST OF WATSON'S WORKS

(These are the known works of Thomas Watson. They are available today, in one form or another. See Bibliography for full reference of works available today.)

1. *All Things for Good*, Banner of Truth Trust, (formerly *A Divine Cordial*). An exposition of Rom. 8:28, first published in 1663.

2. *Art of Divine Contentment*, Soli Deo Gloria. An exposition of Phil. 4:2, first published in 1652.

3. *The Beatitudes*, Banner of Truth Trust. An exposition of Matt. 5:1-12, first published in 1660.

4. *A Body of Divinity*, Banner of Truth Trust. At first a single larger work, it has now been divided up into three works: 1) *A Body of Divinity*, 2) *The Lord's Prayer*, and 3) *The Ten Commandments*, first published in 1692.

5. *The Christian Soldier*,the title of the edition published by Robert More; printed by E. Low in 1810. It is now being printed as *Heaven Taken By Storm* from Soli Deo Gloria, the first edition was published in 1669.

6. *A Divine Cordial*, Banner of Truth Trust, now called *All Things for Good*. An exposition of Romans 8:28, first published in 1663.

7. *The Doctrine of Repentance* Banner of Truth Trust, first published in 1668.

8. *Discourses on Important and Interesting Subjects*. At first two volumes published in Glasgow in 1829, it has recently been reprinted in one volume by Soli Deo Gloria, *The Sermons of Thomas Watson*.

9. *The Duty of Self Denial*, Soli Deo Gloria. This work was formerly, *Sermons on Several Subjects Preached by Mr. Thomas Watson,* first published in 1675. The present edition by Soli Deo Gloria has several other sermons added.

10. *The Fight of Faith Crowned: The Remaining Sermons of Thomas Watson*, Soli Deo Gloria, 1996.

11. *Gleanings from Thomas Watson*, Soli Deo Gloria. This work has many quotations of Watson which are not referenced, first published in 1915.

12. *Godly Man's Picture, Drawn With a Scripture Pencil, or Some Characteristic Marks of a Man Going to Heaven*, Banner of Truth Trust, first printed in 1666.

13. *Harmless as Doves*, Christian Focus Publications, 1993. A collection of Watson's sermons.

14. *Heaven Taken by Storm*, Soli Deo Gloria, first published in 1669.

15. *The Lord's Prayer*, Banner of Truth. An exposition of Matthew 6:9-13. Formerly part of the larger work *A Body of Practical Divinity*, first published in 1692.

16. *Mischief of Sin*, Soli Deo Gloria, 1994, first published in London by Thomas Parkhurst in 1671.

17. *Plea for the Godly and Other Sermons by Thomas Watson*, Soli Deo Gloria. This book is a collection of Watson's sermons and contains one of Watson's farewell sermons which he gave at the time of his ejection from St Stephen's. Many of these sermons are contained in another work published by Christian Focus Publications called *Harmless as Doves*.

18. *Practical Notes of the Third Chapter of Malachi verses 16, 17 and 18.* Later published under the title *Religion Our True Interest* by Blue Banner Productions, first printed in 1682.

19. *Puritans on Conversion*, Soli Deo Gloria. Watson is the third author of this work contributing his sermon 'One Thing Necessary', a sermon which is also found in *The Sermons of Thomas Watson*.

20. *Religion Our True Interest*, Blue Banner Publications. An exposition of Malachi 3:16-18, with a final section on Psalm 119:65, first published in 1692 as *Practical Notes of the Third Chapter of Malachi verses 16, 17, and 18.*

21. *The Sermons of Thomas Watson*, Soli Deo Gloria. A collection of Watson's sermons, first published in 1829.

22. *The Select Works of Rev. Thomas Watson*, United Presbyterian Board of Publication, 1871. (Most of these sermons are contained in *The Body of Divinity, The Ten Commandments, The Lord's Prayer, and Harmless as Doves,* except for his farewell sermon which is found in *The Selected Works* ... and also in *A Plea for the Godly,* by Soli Deo Gloria.

23. *Sermons on Several Subjects Preached by Mr. Thomas Watson.* These Sermons are found in *The Duty of Self Denial,* Soli Deo Gloria.

24. *The Ten Commandments*, Banner of Truth Trust. Formerly part of *A Body of Practical Divinity,* first published in 1692.

THE ART GALLERY

*A select topical index of some of
Thomas Watson's best word paintings*

It is my hope that these choice quotations from Watson's works will be used as tutor to teach you, not merely as a safe from which to steal. There is nothing wrong with occasionally quoting a quotable person, but it is my desire that this index be used to *prime the word picture pump of your mind* so that you will learn to generate your own word pictures and use them effectively to illustrate biblical truth. Store bought cakes are rarely better than home-made ones.

The writings from which the quotations are selected are identified by the following abbreviations:

MS	Mischief of Sin
ATFG	All Things for Good
GMP	Godly Man's Picture
BP	Body of Divinity
HD	Harmless as Doves
DR	Doctrine of Repentance

Adultery – Adultery is the shipwreck of chastity, the murder of conscience. MS p. 33

Affections – A godly man is heavenly in his disposition. He sets his affections on things above (Col. 3:2). He sends his heart to heaven before he gets there; he looks upon the world as but a beautiful prison and he cannot be much in love with his fetters, though they are made of gold. A holy person contemplates glory and eternity; his desires have got wings and have fled to heaven. GMP p. 104

Affliction – A sick-bed often teaches more than a sermon. ATFG p. 27

Affliction – God intermixes mercy with affliction. He steeps his sword of justice in the oil of mercy. There was no night so dark but Israel had a pillar of fire in it. There is no condition so dismal but we may see a pillar of fire to give us light. GMP p. 126

Affliction – The test of a pilot is seen in a storm; so the test of a Christian is seen in affliction. That man has the right art of navigation who, when the boisterous winds blow from heaven, steers the ship of his soul wisely, and does not dash upon the rock of impatience. GMP p. 124

Affliction – As the hard frosts in winter bring on the flowers in the spring, and as the night ushers in the morning-star, so the evils of affliction produce much good to those that love God. ATFG p. 27

Affliction – Sin is like the tree that breeds the worm, and affliction is like the worm that eats the tree. There is much corruption in the best heart; affliction does by degrees work it out, as the fire works out the dross from the gold. ATFG p. 29

Affliction – Afflictions quicken our pace on the way to heaven. It is with us as with children sent on an errand. If they meet with apples or flowers by the way, they linger and are in no great hurry to get home, but if anything frightens them, then they run with all the speed they can to their father's house. So in prosperity, we gather the apples and flowers and do not give much thought to heaven, but if troubles begin to arise and the times grow frightful, then we make more haste to heaven and with David 'run the way of God's commandments' (Ps. 119:32). GMP pp. 125-6

Affliction – There is more malignity in a drop of sin than in a sea of affliction, for sin is the cause of affliction, and the cause is more than the effect. The sword of God's justice lies quiet in the scabbard till sin draws it out. Affliction is good for us: 'It is good for me that I have been afflicted' (Ps. 119:71). Affliction causes repentance (2 Chron. 33:12). The viper, being stricken, casts up its poison; so, God's rod striking us, we spit away the poison of sin. Affliction betters our grace. Gold is purest, and juniper sweetest, in the fire. Affliction prevents damnation (1 Cor. 11:32). DR p. 49

Affliction – When God lays men upon their backs, then they look up to heaven. God's smiting His people is like the musician's striking upon the violin, which makes it put forth melodious sound. How much good comes to the saints by affliction! When they are pounded they send forth their sweetest smell. Affliction is a bitter root, but it bears sweet fruit. ATFG p. 56

Affliction – The magnet of mercy does not draw us so near to God as the cords of affliction. When Absalom set Joab's corn on fire, then he came running to Absalom (2 Sam. 14:30). When God sets our worldly comforts on fire, then we run to Him, and make our peace with Him. When the prodigal was pinched with want, then he returned home to his father (Luke 15:18). When the dove could not find any rest for the sole of her foot, then she flew to the ark. When God brings a deluge of affliction upon us, then we fly to the ark of Christ. Thus affliction makes us happy, in bringing us nearer to God. Faith can make use of the waters of affliction, to cause us to swim faster to Christ. ATFG p. 31

Affliction – Augustine, 'Affliction is God's flail to thresh off our husks; not to consume, but to refine.' There is no good in sin; it is the spirit and quintessence of evil. Sin is worse than hell; for the pains of hell are a burden to the creature only; but sin is a burden to God. BD p. 136

Affliction – Oh, how good it is, when sin has bent the soul awry from God, that affliction should straighten it again! ATFG p. 28

Affliction – Christ never wounds but to heal; the rod of affliction is to recover the sick patient. David's bones were broken that his soul might be healed. God uses affliction as the surgeon does his lance, to let out the venom and corruption of the soul, and make way for a cure. HD p. 139

Affliction – Our hearts are foul and sinful. Our gold is mixed with dross, our stars with clouds. Now, when affliction consumes pride, formality, hypocrisy, when God's lance lets out our spiritual abscess, then we are bettered by affliction. MS p. 46

Affliction – Affliction is God's furnace where He melts His gold. MS p. 45

Affliction – Afflictions work for good, as they are the means of loosening our hearts from the world. When you dig away the earth from the root of a tree, it is to loosen the tree from the earth; so God digs away our earthly comforts to loosen our hearts from the earth. A thorn grows up with every flower. God would have the world hang as a loose tooth which, being twitched away, does not much trouble us. ATFG p. 29

Anger – When lust or rash anger burns in the soul, Satan warms himself at this fire. Men's sins feast the devil. BD p. 134

Anxiety – When the strings of the lute are snarled up, the lute is not fit to make music. So when a Christian's spirit is perplexed and disturbed, he cannot make melody in his heart to the Lord. GMP p. 120

Anxiety – An impatient man is like a troubled sea that cannot rest (Isa. 57:20). He tortures himself upon the rack of his own griefs and passions, whereas patience calms the heart, as Christ did the sea, when it was rough. GMP p. 123

Apostasy – The apostate drops as a windfall into the devil's mouth. BD p. 2

Apostasy – 'The apostate (says Tertullian) seems to put God and Satan in the balance, and having weighed both their services, prefers the devil's service, and proclaims him to be the best master: and, in this sense may be said to put Christ to open shame' (Heb. 6:6). He will never suffer for the truth, but be as a soldier that leaves his colors, and runs over to the enemy's side; he will fight on the devil's side for pay. BD p. 2

Apostasy – No one is so fit to make an apostate as a lukewarm professing Christian. GMP p. 214

Assurance – A believer can sail to heaven, though the tide of reason and the wind of temptation are against him. MS p. 152

Assurance – If you have assurance of your justification, do not abuse it. It is abusing assurance when we grow more remiss in duty; as the musician, having money thrown him, leaves off playing. BD p. 258

Assurance – Assurance will be a golden shield to beat back temptation, and will triumph over it. BD p. 254

Assurance – The plow goes before the seed be sown; the heart must be plowed up by humiliation and repentance, before God sows the seed of assurance. BD p. 252

Assurance – Faith will make us walk, but assurance will make us run: we shall never think we can do enough for God. Assurance will be as wings to the bird, as weights to the clock, to set all the wheels of obedience running. BD p. 253

Assurance – The jewel of assurance is best kept in the cabinet of a humble heart. BD p. 260

Atheism – He that says there is no God is the wickedest creature that is; he is worse than a thief, for he takes away our goods, but the atheist would take away our God from us. BD p. 43

Attitude – Oh, sinner, do not wonder that it is so bad with you, but rather wonder that it is no worse! Are you in the deep of affliction?

It is a wonder you are not in the deep of hell! If Jesus Christ was brought low, is it a wonder that you are brought low? MS p. 22

Bad company – It is a kind of hell to be in the company of the wicked, where we cannot choose but hear God's name dishonored. It was a capital crime to carry the image of Tiberius, engraved on a ring or coin, into any sordid place. Those who have the image of God engraved on them should not go into any sinful, sordid company. I have only ever read of two living people who desired to keep company with the dead, and they were both possessed of the devil (Matt. 8:28). GMP p. 141

Bad company – Take heed of coming into infected company, lest you take the infection; the wicked are devils to tempt to sin. Lot was the world's wonder that lived in Sodom when it was a pest-house, yet did not catch the disease. HD p. 154

Bad company – The breath of sinners is infectious. They are like the dragon which 'cast a flood out of his mouth' (Rev. 12:15). They cast a flood of oaths out of their mouths. Wicked tongues are set on fire by hell (Jas. 3:6). The sinner finds match and gunpowder, and the devil finds fire. GMP p. 186

Believers – Believers are Christ's garden; their graces are flowers; their savory discourse is the fragrant scent of these flowers. GMP p. 141

Blood of Christ – Christ's blood is a softening blood. There is nothing so hard but may be softened by this blood. It will soften a stone. Water will soften the earth, but it will not soften a stone; but Christ's blood mollifies a stone. It softens a heart of stone. It turns a flint into a spring. The heart, which before was like a piece hewn out of rock, being steeped in Christ's blood, becomes soft and the waters of repentance flow from it. How was the jailer's heart dissolved and made tender when the blood of sprinkling was upon it! 'Sirs, what must I do to be saved?' (Acts 16:30). His heart was hot like melting wax. God might set what seal and impression He would upon it. MS p. 126

Blood of Christ – As the merit of Christ's blood pacifies God, so the virtue of it purifies us. It is the King of heaven's bath. It is a laver to wash in. It washes a crimson sinner milk white. 'The blood of Jesus cleanseth us from all our sin,' (1 Jn. 1:7). The Word of God is a looking glass to show us our spots, and the blood of Christ is a fountain to wash them away (Zech. 13:1). MS p. 125

Boasting – Christian, though you do not break forth into a flame of scandal, yet you have no cause to boast, for there is much sin raked up in the embers of your nature. You have the root of bitterness in you, and would bear as hellish fruit as any, if God did not either curb you by His power, or change you by His grace. ATFG p. 47

Call of God – When God calls a man by His grace, he cannot but come. You may resist the minister's call, but you cannot the Spirit's call. The finger of the blessed Spirit can write upon a heart of stone, as once He wrote His law upon tables of stone. God's words are creating words; when He says, 'Let there be light', there was light, and when He says, 'Let there be faith,' it shall be so. When God called Paul, he answered to the call. 'I was not disobedient to the heavenly vision' (Acts 26:19). God rides forth conquering in the chariot of His gospel; He makes the blind eyes see, and the stony heart bleed. If God will call a man, nothing shall lie in the way to hinder; difficulties shall be united, the powers of hell shall disband. 'Who hath resisted his will?' (Rom. 9:19). God bends the iron sinew, and cuts asunder the gates of brass (Ps. 107:16). When the Lord touches a man's heart by His Spirit, all proud imaginations are brought down, and the fort-royal of the will yields to God. ATFG pp. 108-9

Call of God – God so calls as He allures; He does not force, but draw. The freedom of the will is not taken away, but the stubbornness of it is conquered. 'Thy people shall be willing in the day of thy power' (Ps. 110:3). ATFG p. 107

Call of God – As chastity distinguishes a virtuous woman from a harlot, so holiness distinguishes the godly from the wicked. It is a holy calling; 'For God hath not called us unto uncleanness, but unto holiness' (1 Thess. 4:7). Let not any man say he is called of God, that lives in sin. Has God called you to be a swearer, to be a drunkard? Nay, let not the merely moral person say he is effectually called. What is civility without sanctity? It is but a dead carcass strewed with flowers. The king's picture stamped upon brass will not go current for gold. The merely moral man looks as if he had the King of heaven's image stamped upon him; but he is not better than counterfeit metal, which will not pass for current with God. ATFG p. 108

Call of God – Others are more stubborn and knotty sinners, and God comes to them in a rough wind. He uses more wedges of the law to break their hearts; He deeply humbles them, and shows them they are damned without Christ. Then having ploughed up the fallow ground of their hearts by humiliation, He sows the seed of consolation. He presents Christ and mercy to them, and draws their wills, not only to accept Christ, but passionately to desire, and faithfully to rest upon Him. ATFG p. 107

Christ – There is no other Savior. 'Neither is there salvation in any other' (Acts 4:12). As there was but one ark to save the world from drowning, so there is but one Jesus to save sinners from damning. BD p. 161

Concurrence – While the wicked resist the will of God's precept, they fulfill the will of His permissive decree (Acts 4:28). God commands one thing, they do the contrary; to keep the Sabbath, and they profane it. While they disobey His command, they fulfill His permissive decree. If a man sets up two nets, one of silk, the other of iron, the silken net may be broken, not the iron; so while men break the silken net of God's command, they are taken in the iron net of His decree; while they sit backward to God's precepts, they row forward to His decrees; His decrees to permit their sin, and to punish them for their sin permitted. BD p. 71

Concurrence – When a man rides on a lame horse, his riding is the cause why the horse goes, but the lameness is from the horse itself. Herein is God's wisdom, that the sins of men carry on His work, yet He has no hand in them. BD p. 75

Confession – Confession purges out sin. Augustine called it 'the expeller of vice'. Sin is a bad blood; confession is like the opening of a vein to let it out. Confession is like the dung-gate, through which all the filth of the city was carried forth (Neh. 3:13). Confession is like pumping at the leak; it lets out that sin which would otherwise drown. Confession is the sponge that wipes the spots from off the soul. DR p. 35

Confession – Pharaoh confessed he had sinned (Exod. 9:27), but when the thunder ceased he fell to his sin again: 'he sinned yet more, and hardened his heart' (Exod. 9:34). Origen calls confession the vomit of the soul whereby the conscience is eased of that burden which did lie upon it. Now, when we have vomited up sin by confession we must not return to this vomit. What king will pardon that man who, after he has confessed his treason, practices new treason? DR p. 32

Confession – Our hearts must go along with our confessions. The hypocrite confesses sin but loves it, like a thief who confesses to stolen goods, yet loves stealing. How many confess pride and covetousness with their lips but roll them as honey under their tongue. DR p. 29

Confession – Those iniquities which men hide in their hearts shall be written one day on their foreheads as with the point of a diamond. They who will not confess their sin as David did, that they may be pardoned, shall confess their sins as Achan did, that they may be stoned. It is dangerous to keep the devil's counsel; 'He that covers his sins shall not prosper' (Prov. 28:13). DR p. 32

Confession – Confession must be voluntary. It must come as water out of a spring, freely. The confession of the wicked is extorted, like the confession of a man upon a rack. When a spark of God's wrath flies into their conscience, or they are in fear of death, then they will fall to their confessions. Balaam, when he saw the angel's naked sword, could say, 'I have sinned' (Num. 22:34). But true confession drops from the lips as myrrh from the tree or honey from the comb, freely. 'I have sinned against heaven, and before thee' (Luke 15:18): the prodigal charged himself with sin before his father charged him with it. DR p. 29

Conscience, seared – Men are brought low indeed when the sound of Aaron's bell will not awaken them. No sermon will stir them.

They are like the blacksmith's dog that can lie and sleep near the anvil when all the sparks fly about. Conscience is in a lethargy. Once a man's speech is gone and his feeling lost, he draws on apace to death. So when the checks of conscience cease and a man is sensible neither of sin nor wrath, you may ring out the bell. He is past hope of recovery. Thus some are brought low, even to a reprobate sense. This is the threshold of damnation. MS p. 8

Conscience – Worldly things can no more relieve a troubled mind than a silk stocking can ease a broken leg. MS p. 9

Conscience – Though we must be humble, yet not base. It is unworthy to prostitute ourselves to the lusts of men. What is sinfully imposed ought to be zealously opposed. Conscience is God's diocese, where none has the right to visit, but He who is the Bishop of our souls (1 Pet. 2:25). He must not be like hot iron, which may be beaten into any form. A brave spirited Christian will rather suffer, than let his conscience be violated. ATFG pp. 122-3

Conscience – Let us not purchase the world with the loss of a good conscience. What wise man would damn himself to grow rich? or pull down his soul, to build up an estate? Be like Christ in a holy contempt of the world. BD p. 202

Conscience – The dog has a mind to the bone, but is afraid of the club; so men have a mind to lust, but conscience stands as the angel, with flaming sword, and affrights: they have a mind to revenge, but the fear of hell is a curb-bit to check them. There is no change of heart; sin is curbed, but not cured. A lion may be in chains, but is a lion still. BD p. 244

Contention – Beware of the devil's couriers – I mean such as run on his errand, and make it their work to blow the coals of contention among Christians, and render one party odious to another. GMP p. 145

Contentment – When Christians complain at their condition, they forget that they are servants, and must live on the allowance of their heavenly Master. You who have the least bit from God will die in His debt. GMP p. 39

Conversion – Such as have had godly parents, and have sat under the warm sunshine of religious education, often do not know how or when they were called. The Lord did secretly and gradually instil grace into their hearts, as the dew falls unnoticed in drops. ATFG pp. 106-7

Conviction – A man is convinced of sin, he sees he is a sinner and nothing but a sinner; the fallow ground of his heart is broken up (Jer. 4:3). As the husbandman breaks the clods, then casts in the seed, so God, by the convincing work of the law, breaks a sinner's heart, and makes it fit to receive the seeds of grace. Such as were never convinced are never called. 'He shall convince the world of sin' (Jn. 16:8). Conviction is the first step in conversion. BD p. 224

Covetousness – Beware of covetousness: 'men shall be covetous ... having a form of godliness, but denying the power' (2 Tim. 3:5). One of Christ's own apostles was caught with a silver bait. Covetousness will make a man betray a good cause and make shipwreck of a good conscience. GMP p. 210

Creation – If a man should go into a far country, and see stately edifices there, he would never imagine that these built themselves, but that some greater power had built them. To imagine that the work of creation was not framed by God, is as if we should conceive a curious landscape to be drawn by a pencil without the hand of an artist. BD p. 40

Creation – Every star in the sky, every bird that flies in the air, is a witness against the heathen. A creature could not make itself. BD p. 116

Creation – The creation is the heathen man's Bible, the ploughman's primer, and the traveler's perspective glass, through which he receives a representation of the infinite excellencies which are in God. The creation is a large volume, in which God's works are bound up; and this volume has three great leaves in it, heaven, earth, and sea. BD p. 113

Creation – To create requires infinite power. All the world cannot make a fly. God's power in creating is evident; because He needs no instruments to work with; He can work without tools; because He needs no matter to work upon; He creates matter, and then works upon it; and because He works without labor; 'He spake, and it was done' (Ps. 33:9). BD p. 78

Creation – The world is like a curious piece of tapestry, in which we may see the skill and wisdom of Him that made it. BD p. 116

Crucifixion – The cross of Christ is the ladder by which we ascend to heaven. His crucifixion is our coronation. BD p. 174

Crucifixion – The balm-tree weeps out its precious balm, to heal those that cut and mangle it; so Christ shed His blood, to heal those that crucified Him. BD p. 175

Death – Men unprepared, being summoned by the king of terror before the tribunal, go as the prisoner to the bar to receive their fatal doom. I think the thoughts of it are enough to put them either into frenzy or despair. Would it not be sad for a man to have his house on fire, and the fire so fierce that he has not time to get out his goods? Such is the case of many at death. A fever has set their house of clay on fire, and they are snatched away so suddenly that they have no time to make provision for their souls. MS p. 87

Death – Death, like a whirlwind, may blow down the tree of the body, but it cannot blast the fruit of our graces. The trees of righteousness carry their fruit with them: 'their works follow them' (Rev. 14:13). The Christian who abounds in holiness may say with Simeon in Luke 2:29, 'Lord, now let Your servant depart in peace.' He who bears but a little fruit departs in safety; but he who bears much fruit departs in peace. HD p. 185

Death – Death can no more be stopped in its race than the sun. Death's scythe cuts asunder the royal scepter. God's messenger of death finds out every man. MS p. 84

Death – Death shall stop the bottle of tears, and open the gate of Paradise. A believer's dying day is his ascension day to glory. ATFG p. 57

Death – As the husbandman waits till his seed sown springs up, as the merchant waits for the coming home of his ship, so we should wait till death comes to ship us over to another world. MS p. 90

Death – Death so changes the body and puts it into such a frightful dress that none fall in love with it but the worms. MS p. 83

Death – Death smites a believer as the angel smote Peter on his side and made his chains fall off, Acts 12:7. So death smites a believer and makes the chains of his sins fall off. MS p. 51

Death – Death approaching changes a man's opinion about sin. Before, he looked upon sin as merely a matter of merriment. He thought swearing an oath, drinking to excess, and wasting his precious time in vanity was but a light thing. He said of sin, as Lot did of Zoar, 'Is it not a little one?' (Gen. 19:20). But when he sees death's grim face appear, he now has other apprehensions of sin than he had before. The wine that showed its color in the glass and smiled at him now bites like a serpent (Prov. 23:32). Those sins which before were thought to be light as feathers are now like talents of lead ready to sink him. MS pp. 81-2

Death – The servant that has been all day working in the vineyard longs till evening comes, when he shall receive his pay. How can they who have lived, and brought no glory to God, think of dying with comfort? They cannot expect a harvest where they sowed no seed. How can they expect glory from God who never brought any glory to Him? O in what horror will they be at death! The worm of conscience will gnaw their souls, before the worms can gnaw their bodies. BD p. 20

Deception – Is it not strange that two should live together, and eat and drink together, yet not know each other? Such is the case of a sinner. His body and soul live together, work together, yet he is unacquainted with himself. He knows not his own heart, nor what a hell he carries about him. Under a veil a deformed face is hid. Persons are veiled over with ignorance and self-love; therefore they see not what deformed souls they have. The devil does with them as the falconer with the hawk. He blinds them and carries them hooded to hell. DR p. 19

Depravity – Original sin is like that tree, in Daniel 4:23, though the branches of it were hewn down, and the main body of it, yet the stumps and root of the tree were left. Though the Spirit be still weakening and hewing down sin in the godly, yet the stump of original sin is left. It is a sea that will not, in this life, be dried up. BD p. 147

Depravity – The sin of our nature is like a sleeping lion, the least thing that awakens it makes it rage. Though the sin of our nature seems quiet, and lies as fire hid under the embers, yet if it be a little stirred and blown up by temptation, how quickly may it flame forth into scandalous evils! Therefore we need always to walk watchfully. 'I say to you all, Watch' (Mk. 13:37). A wandering heart needs a watchful eye. BD p. 148

Depravity – As the bishop of Alexandria, after the people had embraced Christianity, destroyed all their idols but one, that the sight of that idol might make them loathe themselves for their former idolatry; so God leaves original sin to pull down the plumes of pride. Under our silver wings of grace are black feet. BD p. 148

Depravity – If we look within us, here we see our sins represented to us in the glass of conscience; lust, envy, passion. Our sins are like vermin crawling in our souls. 'How many are my iniquities' (Job 13:23)? Our sins are as the sands of the sea for number, as the rocks of the sea for weight. BD p. 201

Depravity – Let God's afflicting hand lie upon men, though their strength to sin is abated, yet not their appetite. When they grow old, their lusts grow young. Unless the daystar of grace arises in their hearts and alters their course, they will never leave sinning till they have sinned themselves to the devil. A bowl running down hill seldom stops in the middle. MS p. 60

Depravity – Original sin is the cause of all actual sin. It is the kindling wood of sin, it is the womb in which all actual sins are conceived. BD p. 146

Depravity – Original sin may be compared to that fish Pliny speaks of, a sea-lamprey, which cleaves to the keel of the ship and hinders it when it is under sail. Sin hangs weights upon us so that we move but slowly to heaven. O this adherence of sin! Paul shook the viper which was on his hand into the fire (Acts 28:5), but we cannot shake off original corruption in this life. Sin does not come as a lodger for a night, but as an indweller: 'sin that dwelleth in me' (Rom. 7:17). It is with us as with one who has a hectic fever upon him; though he changes the air, yet still he carries his disease with him. Original sin is inexhaustible. This ocean cannot be emptied. Though the stock of sin spends, yet it is not at all diminished. The more we sin, the fuller we are of sin. Original corruption is like the widow's oil which increased by pouring out. DR p. 73

Depravity – Reason and conscience are bound like prisoners with the chains of lust. By sinning still, men have contracted a custom of evil. Jeremiah 13:23, 'Can the Ethiopian change his skin or the leopard his spots?' Custom in sin stupefies conscience. 'Tis like a gravestone laid upon a man. Oh, how hard their conversion who go on still in their trespasses! That tree will hardly be plucked up which has been long rooting in the earth. How hard will they find it to be plucked up out of their natural estate who have been many years rooting in sin! He who had been possessed with the devil from his youth up found it harder to have the devil cast out of him, Mk. 9:21. MS p. 58

Depravity – I note hence the blindness of every sinner. He does not see that evil in sin which should make him leave it. He sins still. To this day, the veil is upon his heart. Sin is the spirit and quintessence of evil, but the unregenerate person is enveloped with ignorance. If he dies in sin, he is damned irrecoverably. But he sports with his own damnation – he sins still. Sin has made him not only sick but senseless. Though sin has death and hell following it, yet he is so blind that he sins still. MS p. 55

Depravity – If a wicked man could be fetched out of hell and brought back into a capacity of mercy, yet he would in a second life follow his lusts and sin himself into hell again. MS p. 57

Depravity – Men roll sin as honey under their tongue. 'They drink iniquity as water' (Job 15:16). Like a hydropsical person, that thirsts for drink, and is not satisfied; they have a kind of drought in them, they thirst for sin. Though they are tired out in committing sin, yet they sin. 'They weary themselves to commit iniquity' (Eph.

4:19); as a man that follows his game while he is weary, yet delights in it, and cannot leave it off (Jer. 9:5). Though God has set so many flaming swords in the way to stop men in their sin, yet they go on in it; which all shows what a strong appetite they have to the forbidden fruit. BD p. 144

Despair – Despair is a God-affronting sin. It is sacrilege; it robs God of His crown-jewels, His power, goodness, and truth. How Satan triumphs to see the honor of God's attributes laid in the dust by despair! Despair casts away the anchor of hope, then the soul must sink. What will a ship do in a storm without an anchor? MS p. 10

Discontent – Discontent is a sin which puts us upon sin. 'Fret not thyself to do evil' (Ps. 37:8). He that frets will be ready to do evil: fretting Jonah was a sinning Jonah (Jon. 4:9). The devil blows the coals of passion and discontent, and then warms himself by the fire. Oh, let us not nourish this angry viper in our breast. Let this text produce patience, 'All things work together for good to them that love God' (Rom. 8:28). ATFG p. 61

Divinity of Christ – Look upon Christ's divine nature. Christ may be fitly compared to Jacob's ladder, which reached from earth to heaven (Gen. 28:12). Christ's human nature was the foot of the ladder, which reaches to heaven. BD p. 163

Doctrine – Knowledge of the grounds of religion much enriches the mind. It is a lamp to our feet; it directs us in the whole course of Christianity, as the eye directs the body. Knowledge of fundamentals is the golden key that opens the chief mysteries of religion; it gives us a whole system and body of divinity, exactly drawn in all its lineaments and lively colors; it helps us to understand many of those difficult things which occur in the reading of the word; it helps to untie many Scripture knots. BD p. 4

Doctrine – That the ship may be kept from overturning, it must have its anchor fastened. Knowledge of principles is to the soul as an anchor to the ship, that holds it steady in the midst of the rolling waves of error, or the violent winds of persecution. BD p. 4

210 Expository Preaching With Word Pictures

Election – Election is the cause of our calling, and calling is the sign of our election. Election is the first link of the golden chain of salvation, calling is the second. He who has the second link of the chain is sure of the first. As by the stream we are led to the fountain, so by calling we ascend to election. Calling is an earnest and pledge of glory. 'God has chosen you to salvation, through sanctification' (2 Thess. 2:13). BD p. 224

Evangelism – Every star adds a luster to the sky; every convert is a member added to Christ's body and a jewel adorning His crown. GMP p. 185

Evangelism – [The godly man] is not content to go to heaven alone but wants to take others there. Spiders work only for themselves, but bees work for others. A godly man is both a diamond and a magnet – a diamond for the sparkling luster of grace and a magnet for his attractiveness. He is always drawing others to embrace piety. GMP pp. 183-4

Faith – Faith is the oil which feeds the lamp of hope. Faith and hope are two turtle-dove graces; take away one, and the other languishes. If the sinews are cut, the body is lame; if this sinew of faith is cut, hope is lame. GMP p. 28

Faith – Faith and fear go hand in hand. Faith keeps the heart cheerful, fear keeps the heart serious. Faith keeps the heart from sinking in despair, fear keeps it from floating in presumption. ATFG p. 20

Faith – Faith will be of more use to us than any grace; as an eye, though dim, was of more use to an Israelite than all the other members of his body, a strong arm, or a nimble foot. It was his eye looking on the brazen serpent that cured him. It is not knowledge, though angelic, not repentance, though we could shed rivers of tears, could justify us; only faith, whereby we look on Christ. 'Without faith it is impossible to please God' (Heb. 11:6). BD p. 218

Faith – Faith is in the soul as fire among metals; it refines and purifies. Morality may wash the outside, faith washes the inside. 'Having purified their hearts by faith' (Acts 15:9). BD p. 219

Faith – A great faith is like an oak that spreads its roots deep and is not easily blown down, Col. 2:7. A great faith is like the anchor or cable of a ship that holds it steady in the midst of storms. A Christian who is steeled with this heroic faith is settled in the mysteries of religion. MS p. 151

Faith – Faith excites repentance; it is like the fire to the still which makes it drop. GMP p. 28

Faith – Let me tell you, all you who are yet in your natural estate, your souls are mortgaged. If your land were mortgaged, you would endeavor to redeem it. Your souls are mortgaged: sin has mortgaged them, and has laid your souls to pawn, and where do you think your souls are? The pawn is in the devil's hand, therefore a man in the state of nature is said to be 'under the power of Satan' (Acts 26:18). Now there are but two ways to fetch home the pawn, and both are set down in Acts 20:21; 'Repentance towards God, and faith towards our Lord Jesus Christ.' Unravel all your works of sin by repentance, honor Christ's merits by believing: divines call it saving faith, because upon this wing the soul flies to the ark Christ, and is secured from danger. HD pp. 117-8

Faith – Faith is the applying of Christ's merits. A plaster, though it be ever so rare and excellent, yet if it be not applied to the wound, will do no good; though the plaster be made of Christ's blood, yet it will not heal, unless applied by faith. The brazen serpent was a sovereign remedy for the cure of those that were stung; but if they had not looked upon it, they received no benefit. So though there be healing virtue in Christ, yet unless we look upon Him by the eye of faith, we cannot be cured. HD p. 152

Faith – Faith is a world-conquering grace (1 Jn. 5:4). It overcomes the world's music and crucible; it steels a Christian with divine courage, and makes him stand immovable, like a rock in the midst of the sea. GMP p. 44

Faith – When men begin to distrust the promise, then they quarrel at Providence. When faith grows low, passions grow high. MS p. 3

Faith – As fire is to the chemist, so is faith to the Christian; the chemist can do nothing without fire, so there is nothing done without faith. Faith makes Christ's sacrifice ours. 'Christ Jesus my Lord' (Phil. 3:8). It is not gold in the mine that enriches, but gold in the hand. Faith is the hand that receives Christ's golden merits. BD p. 176

Faith – The promises are full of riches, justification, adoption, glory: faith is the key that unlocks this cabinet of the promises, and empties out their treasure into the soul. HD p. 161

Faith – Never did any look upon Christ with a believing eye, but He was made like Christ. A deformed person may look on a beautiful object, and not be made beautiful; but faith looking on Christ transforms a man, and turns him into his similitude. BD p. 219

Faith – As the chameleon is changed into the color of that which it looks upon, so faith, looking on Christ, changes the Christian into the similitude of Christ. BD p. 219

Faith – Faith is a cure-all – a remedy against all troubles. It is a godly man's sheet anchor that he casts out into the sea of God's mercy, and is kept from sinking in despair. GMP p. 29

Faith – Faith is a quickening grace, the vital artery of the soul. 'The just shall live by faith' (Hab. 2:4). Life makes us capable of adoption, dead children are never adopted. It makes us Christ's brethren, and so God comes to be our Father. BD p. 234

Fall of man – So when Adam grew careless of God's command, and left off the garment of his innocency, he caught a sickness; he could stay no longer in the garden, but lay bedrid; his sin has turned the world which was a paradise into a hospital. HD p. 121

Fall of man – Sin dug Adam's grave. BD p. 152

Fall of man – Free-will was a sufficient shield to repel temptation. The devil could not have forced him unless he had given his consent. Satan was only a suitor to woo, not a king to compel; but

Adam gave away his own power, and suffered himself to be decoyed into sin; like a young gallant, who at one throw loses a fair lordship. BD p. 137

False profession – How many are painted only with the vermilion of a profession, whose seeming luster dazzles the eyes of the beholders, but within there is nothing but petrification! Hypocrites are like the swan, which has white feathers, but black skin; or like the lily, which has a fair color, but a bad scent. 'Thou hast a name that thou livest, and art dead' (Rev. 3:1). GMP p. 15

False profession – Sinners desire Christ only for shelter. The Hebrews never chose their judges except when they were in some imminent danger. Godless persons never look for Christ except at death, when they are in danger of hell. GMP p. 53

False teachers – Now, such as are not settled in religion, will, at one time or other, prove wandering stars; they will lose their former steadfastness, and wander from one opinion to another. Such as are unsettled are of the tribe of Reuben, 'unstable as water', (Gen. 49:4); like a ship without ballast, overturned with every wind of doctrine. Beza writes of one Belfectius, that his religion changed as the moon. The Arians had every year a new faith. These are not pillars in the temple of God, but reeds shaken every way. BD p. 1

False teaching – A man may as well damn his soul by error as vice, and may as soon go to hell for a drunken opinion as for a drunken life. HD p. 115

Fear of men – When we are advocates in a bad cause, pleading for any impious, unjustifiable act; when we baptize sin with the name of religion, and with our oratory wash the devil's face, this is to be the servants of men. In these cases, a godly person will not so unman himself as to serve men. He says, like Paul, 'If I yet pleased men, I should not be the servant of Christ' (Gal. 1:10); and like Peter, 'We ought to obey God rather than men' (Acts 5:29). GMP p. 43

Fellowship – As the stones in an arch help to strengthen one another, one Christian by imparting his experience, heats and quickens another. 'Let us provoke one another to love, and to good works' (Heb. 10:24). How does grace flourish by holy conference! A Christian by good discourse drops that oil upon another, which makes the lamp of his faith burn the brighter. ATFG p. 22

Fellowship – Walk with them that are holy. 'He that walketh with the wise shall be wise' (Prov. 13:20). Be among the spices and you will smell of them. Association begets assimilation. Nothing has a greater power and energy to effect holiness than the communion of saints. BD p. 87

Fellowship – Be often among the godly. They are the salt of the earth, and will help to season you. Their counsel may direct, their prayers may enliven you. Such holy sparks may be thrown into your breasts as may kindle devotion in you. It is good to be among the saints to learn the trade of godliness: 'He that walketh with the wise men shall be wise' (Prov. 13:20). GMP p. 208

Foolishness – How is a fool tested but by showing him an apple and a piece of gold? If he chooses the apple before the gold, he is judged to be a fool and his estate is beggared. How many such idiots there are who prefer husks before manna, the gaudy, empty things of this life before the Prince of Glory! Will not Satan beggar them at last for fools? GMP pp. 54-5

Forgiveness – 'He will cast all our sins into the depths of the sea' (Mic. 7:19). Sin shall not be cast in like a cork which rises up again, but like lead which sinks to the bottom. GMP p. 10

Forgiveness – When a creditor forgives a debtor, he does it freely. Pardon of sin is a fine thread, spun out of the heart of free grace. GMP p. 9

Forgiveness – The pardoned soul is out of the gunshot of hell (Rom. 8:33). GMP p. 11

Fruitfulness – It is the very definition of a branch in Christ that 'it bears fruit' (Jn. 15:2). As a man differs from a beast by reason, a beast differs from a plant by sense, a plant differs from a hypocrite by fruit. Fruitfulness puts a difference between the sound tree and the hollow tree. HD p. 182

Glorification – Sanctification and glory differ only in degree: sanctification is glory in the seed, and glory is sanctification in the flower. BD p. 242

Glorifying God – We glorify God, when we are God-admirers; admire His attributes, which are the glistening beams by which the divine nature shines forth; His promises which are the charter of free grace, and the spiritual cabinet where the pearl of price is hid; the noble effects of His power and wisdom in making the world which is called 'the work of His fingers' (Ps. 8:3). To glorify God is to have God-admiring thoughts; to esteem Him most excellent, and search for diamonds in this rock only. BD p. 7

Glorifying God – Glorifying God consists in four things: 1. Appreciation, 2. Adoration, 3. Affection, 4. Subjection. This is the yearly rent we pay to the crown of heaven. BD p. 7

Glory – The streams of glory are not like the water of a conduit, often stopped, so that we cannot have one drop of water; but those heavenly streams of joy are continually running. Oh how should we despise this valley of tears where we now are, for the mount of transfiguration! how should we long for the full enjoyment of God in Paradise! Had we a sight of that land of promise, we should need patience to be content to live here any longer. BD p. 25

Glory – Virtue leads to glory. First you cleanse the vessel, and then pour in wine. God does first cleanse us by grace, and then pour in the wine of glory; the silver link of grace draws the golden link of glory after it: indeed grace differs little from glory; grace is glory in the bud, and glory is grace in the flower. In short, glory is nothing else but grace commencing and taking its degrees. HD pp. 166-7

Godliness – Will not anyone be willing to exchange a dark prison for a king's palace? Will he not exchange his brass for gold? You who become godly change for the better: you change your pride for humility, your uncleanness for holiness. You change a lust that will damn you for a Christ who will save you. If men were not besotted, if their fall had not knocked their brains out, they would see that it is the most rational thing in the world to become godly. GMP p. 201

Godliness – Godliness has truth for its foundation; it is called 'the way of truth' (Ps. 119:30). Godliness is a ray and beam that shines from God. If God is true, then godliness is true. GMP p. 12

Godliness – To be learned and ungodly is like a devil transformed into an angel of light; to be beautiful and ungodly is like a lovely picture hung in an infected room; to be honorable in the world and ungodly is like an ape in purple, or like that image which had a head of gold on feet of clay (Dan. 2:32-33). It is godliness that ennobles and consecrates the heart, making God and angels fall in love with it. GMP p. 191

Godliness – The dew lies on the leaf, the sap is hidden in the root. The moralist's religion is all in the leaf; it consists only in externals, but godliness is a holy sap which is rooted in the soul: 'in the hidden part thou shalt make me to know wisdom' (Ps. 51:6). GMP pp. 12-13

Godliness – There is a great deal of difference between a stake in the hedge and a tree in the garden. A stake rots and moulders, but a tree, having life in it, abides and flourishes. When godliness has taken root in the soul, it abides to eternity; 'His seed remaineth in him' (1 Jn. 3:9). Godliness being engraved in the heart by the Holy Ghost, as with the point of a diamond, can never be erased. GMP p. 14

Godliness – Godliness is a spiritual queen, and whoever marries her is sure of a large dowry with her. GMP p. 7

Godliness – We sucked in sin as naturally as our mother's milk, but godliness is 'the wisdom from above' (Jas. 3:17). It is breathed in from heaven. God must light up the lamp of grace in the heart. Weeds grow of themselves; flowers are planted. Godliness is a celestial plant that comes from the New Jerusalem. Therefore it is called a 'fruit of the Spirit' (Gal. 5:22). A man has no more power to change himself than to create himself. GMP p. 13

Godliness – Godliness is the intricate embroidery and workmanship of the Holy Ghost. A soul furnished with godliness is damasked with beauty, it is enameled with purity. This is the clothing of wrought gold which makes the King of heaven fall in love with us. GMP p. 202

Goodness of God – The goodness of God works for good, as it ushers in all blessings. The favors we receive are the silver streams which flow from the fountain of God's goodness. ATFG p. 15

Goodness of God – He is a sea of goodness without bottom and banks. ATFG p. 66

Gospel – God rides forth conquering in the chariot of His gospel; He conquers the pride of the heart, and makes the will, which stood out as a fort-royal, to yield and stoop to His grace; He makes the stony heart bleed. BD p. 223

Grace – The life of sin is the death of the soul. A sinner has all the signs of one that is dead; he has no pulse; for the affections are the pulse of the soul; his pulse does not beat after God. He has no sense: 'Who being past feeling' (Eph. 4:19). Dead things have no beauty, there is no beauty in a dead flower; dead things are not capable of privilege; the dead heir is not crowned. But grace is the vital artery of the soul; it does not only irradiate, but animate; therefore it is called 'the light of life' (Jn. 8:12). And believers are said to have their grave clothes pulled off, and to be alive from the dead (Rom. 6:13). By grace the soul is grafted into Christ the true vine (Jn. 15:5), and is made not only living but lively (1 Pet. 1:3). Grace puts forth a divine energy into the soul. HD p. 160

Grace – Grace to the soul, as light to the eye, as health to the body. Grace does to the soul, as a virtuous wife to her husband, 'She will do him good all the days of her life' (Prov. 31:12). ATFG p. 20

Grace – Grace is a Christian's armor of proof, which does more than any other armor can; it not only defends him, but puts courage into him. HD p. 163

Grace – See the great difference between sin and grace. Sin brings a man low, but grace lifts him high. Sin tumbles him in the ditch, but graces sets him upon the throne. MS p. 36

Grace – A good conscience can sleep in the mouth of a cannon. Grace is a Christians coat of mail, which fears not the arrow or bullet. True grace may be shot at, but can never be shot through. Grace puts the soul into Christ, and there it is safe, as the bee in the hive, as the dove in the ark: 'There is no condemnation to them which are in Christ Jesus' (Rom. 8:1). HD pp. 165-6

Grace – Every man is by sin bound in fetters. A man that is in fetters, if you use arguments, and persuade him to go, is that sufficient? There must be a breaking of his fetters, and setting him free, before he can walk. So it is with every natural man; he is fettered with corruption; now the Lord by converting grace must file off his fetters, nay, give him legs to run too, or he can never obtain salvation. ATFG p. 113

Guilt – Guilt clips the wings of prayer so that it cannot fly to the throne of grace, but forgiveness breeds confidence. GMP p. 11

Guilt – If you love worldly things, they cannot remove trouble of mind. If there be a thorn in the conscience, all the world cannot pluck it out. ATFG p. 92

Guilt – Sin puts teeth into the cross. Guilt makes affliction heavy. A little water is heavy in a lead vessel, and a little affliction is heavy in a guilty conscience. MS p. 7

Heart – The heart and sin are like two lovers who cannot endure to be parted. MS p. 55

Heart – A hard heart is the anvil on which the hammer of God's justice will be striking to all eternity. DR p. 84

Heart – The heart of a man by nature is like a garrison which holds out in war. Though articles of peace are offered, though it is straightly besieged and one bullet after another is shot, yet the garrison holds out. So the heart is a garrison that holds out against God. Though He uses entreaties, gives warnings, shoots bullets into the conscience, yet the garrison of the heart holds out. The man will not be reclaimed; he sins still. He is said to have a brow of brass, in regard to his impudence, and a sinew of iron, in regard to his obstinance (Isa. 48:4). MS p. 56

Heart – The heart is deadly wicked (Jer. 17:9). It is a lesser hell. In the heart are legions of lusts, stubbornness, infidelity, hypocrisy, sinful desires; it boils as the sea with passion and revenge. 'Madness is in their heart while they live' (Eccl. 9:3). The heart is the devil's workhouse, where all mischief is framed. BD p. 144

Heart of man – As black vapors which arise out of fenny, moorish grounds, cloud and darken the sun, so out of the natural man's heart arise black vapors of sin, which cast a cloud upon God's glory. ATFG p. 112

Heart – As the viper has his teeth hid in the gums, so that if one should look into his mouth he would think it a harmless creature; so though there be much corruption in the heart, yet the heart hides it, and draws a veil over, that it be not seen. HD p. 132

Heart – The hearts of the best are like Peter's sheet, on which there were a number of unclean creeping things (Acts 10:12). This primitive corruption is bitterly to be wailed because we are never free from it. It is like a spring underground, which though it is not seen, yet it still runs. We may as well stop the beating of the pulse as stop the motions of sin. DR p. 73

Heart – A piece of lead, while it is in the lump, can be put to no use, but melt it, and you may then cast it into any mold, and it is made useful. So a heart that is hardened into a lump of sin is good for nothing, but when it is dissolved by repentance, it is useful. A melting heart is fit to pray. DR p. 76

Heart – Original sin, though latent in the soul, and as a spring which runs underground, often breaks forth unexpectedly. Christian, you cannot believe that evil which is in your heart, and which will break forth suddenly, if God should leave you. 'Is thy servant a dog that he should do this great thing' (2 Kings 8:13)? Hazael could not believe he had such a root of bitterness in his heart, that he should rip up the women with child. Is thy servant a dog? Yes, and worse than a dog, when that original corruption within is stirred up. If one had come to Peter and said, Peter, within a few hours you will deny Christ, he would have said, 'Is your servant a dog?' But alas! Peter

did not know his own heart, nor how far that corruption within
would prevail upon him. The sea may be calm, and look clear; but
when the wind blows how it rages and foams! So though now your
heart seems good, yet when temptation blows, how may original
sin discover itself, making you foam with lust and passion. BD pp.
145-6

Heaven – Heaven is not like Noah's ark, where the clean beasts and
the unclean entered. No unclean beasts come into the heavenly ark;
for though God suffer the wicked to live awhile on earth, He will
never suffer heaven to be pestered by such vermin. Are they fit to
see God who wallow in wickedness? Will God ever lay such vipers
in His bosom? 'Without holiness no man shall see the Lord' (Heb.
12:14). It must be a clear eye that sees a bright object: only a holy
heart can see God in His glory. Sinners may see God as an enemy,
but not as a friend; Many have an affrighting vision of Him, but not
a beatific vision; they may see the flaming sword, but not the mercy
seat. BD p. 245

Heaven – An ignorant man looks at a star and it appears to him like
a little silver spot, but the astronomer, who has his instrument to
judge the dimension of a star, knows it to be many degrees bigger
than the earth. So a natural man hears of the heavenly country that
it is very glorious, but it is at a great distance. And because he has
not a spirit of discernment, the world looks bigger in his eye. But
such as are spiritual artists, who have the instrument of faith to
judge heaven, will say it is by far the better country and they will
hasten there with the sails of desire. GMP p. 112

Hell – If there is anyone who makes religion a political engine to
carry on their sin more smoothly, these shall lie in the hottest place
of hell. MS p. 96

Hell – How many souls have been blown into hell with the wind of
popular applause? HD p. 115

Hell – If God in this life ordains His arrows against persecutors (Ps.
7:13), then surely He will make them His standing mark in hell, at
which He will be shooting to all eternity. MS p. 96

Hell – The pleasures of sin are but for a season, but the torments of the wicked are for ever. Sinners have a short feast, but a long reckoning. BD p. 62

Hell – The loss of the soul is an eternal loss; for the soul once lost, is lost for ever; the sinner and the furnace shall never be parted (Isa. 33:14). As the sinner's heart will never be emptied of sin, so God's vial shall never be emptied of wrath: it is an eternal loss. HD p. 117

Hell – The coolest part of hell is hot enough, but there are some who shall have a hotter place in hell than others. All shall go into that fiery prison, but some sinners God will thrust into the dungeon. MS p. 92

Hell – Every sin is a drop of oil upon hell's flame. MS p. 68

Hell – Surely, there is not a greater sign of a man ripe for hell, than this, not only to lack grace, but to hate it. ATFG p. 83

Hell – Eternity is a sea without bottom and banks. After millions of years, there is not one minute in eternity wasted; and the damned must be ever burning, but never consuming, always dying, but never dead. 'They shall seek death, but shall not find it' (Rev. 9:6). The fire of hell is such, as multitudes of tears will not quench it, length of time will not finish it; the vial of God's wrath will be always dropping upon a sinner. As long as God is eternal, He lives to be avenged upon the wicked. Oh eternity! eternity! who can fathom it? Mariners have their plummets to measure the depths of the sea; but what line or plummet shall we use to fathom the depth of eternity? The breath of the Lord kindles the infernal lake, (Isa. 30:33), and where shall we have engines or buckets to quench that fire? Oh eternity! If all the body of earth and sea were turned to sand, and all the air up to the starry heaven were nothing but sand, and a little bird should come every thousand years, and fetch away in her bill but the tenth part of a grain of all that heap of sand, what numberless years would be spent before that vast heap of sand would be fetched away! Yet, if at the end of all that time, the sinner might come out of hell, there would be some hope; but that word 'Ever' breaks the heart. 'The smoke of their torment ascendeth up for ever and ever.' What a terror is this to the wicked, enough to put them into a cold sweat, to think, as long as God is eternal, He lives for ever to be avenged upon them! BD pp. 62-3

Hell – Some think it hard that for the sins committed in a few years they should undergo perpetual torment, but here lies the justice and equity of it. It is because sinners have an everlasting principle of sin in them. Their stock of corruption would never be quite spent. They have a never-dying appetite to sin, which is justly punished with a never-dying worm. MS pp. 69-70

Holiness of God – By looking into the transparent glass of God's holiness, we see our own blemishes and so learn to bewail them. DR pp. 121-2

Holy Spirit in conversion – The Word is the instrumental cause of our conversion, the Spirit is the efficient. The ministers of God are only the pipes and organs; it is the Spirit blowing in them that effectually changes the heart. 'While Peter spake, the Holy Ghost fell on all them that heard the word' (Acts 10:44). It is not the farmer's industry in ploughing and sowing, that will make the ground fruitful, without the early and latter rain. So it is not the seed of the Word that will effectually convert, unless the Spirit puts forth His Sweet influence, and drops as rain upon the heart. Therefore the aid of God's Spirit is to be implored, that He would put forth His powerful voice, and awaken us out of the grave of unbelief. If a man knock at a gate of brass, it will not open; but if he come with a key in his hand, it will open: so when God, who has the key of David in His hand (Rev. 3:7) comes, He opens the heart, though it be ever so fast locked against Him. ATFG p. 106

Holy Spirit – While the heart is hard, it lies like a log, and is not wrought upon either by judgments or mercies, but when God's Spirit comes in, He makes a man's heart as tender as his eye and now it is made yielding to divine impressions. GMP p. 70

Humiliation of Christ – He came not in the majesty of a king, attended with His life-guard, but He came poor; not like the heir of heaven, but like one of an inferior descent. The place He was born in was poor; not the royal city Jerusalem, but Bethlehem, a poor obscure place. He was born in an inn, and a manger was His cradle, the cobwebs His curtains, the beasts His companions; He descended of poor parents. One would have thought, if Christ would have come into the world, He would have made choice of some queen or personage of honor to have descended from; but He comes of mean obscure parents, for that they were poor appears by their offering. 'A pair of turtledoves' (Luke 2:24), which was the usual offering of the poor (Lev. 12:8). Christ was so poor, that when He wanted money He was fain to work a miracle for it (Matt. 17:27). When He died He made no will. He came into the world poor. BD p. 196

Humiliation of Christ – Christ was not ambitious of titles or of honor. He declined worldly dignity and greatness as much as others seek it. When they would have made Him a King, He refused it; he chose rather to ride upon the foal of an ass, than be drawn in a chariot; and to hang upon a wooden cross, than to wear a golden crown. BD p. 202

Humiliation of Christ – That Christ should clothe Himself with our flesh, a piece of earth which we tread upon; oh infinite humility! Christ's taking our flesh was one of the lowest steps of His humiliation. He humbled Himself more in lying in the virgin's womb than in hanging on the cross. It was not so much for man to die, but for God to become man was the wonder of humility. 'He was made in the likeness of men' (Phil. 2:7). BD p. 196

Humility – It is hard to prescribe a just measure of humiliation. It is the same in the new birth as in the natural. Some give birth with more pangs, and some with fewer. But would you like to know when you are bruised enough? When your spirit is so troubled that you are willing to let go those lusts which brought in the greatest income of pleasure and delight. When not only is sin discarded but you are disgusted with it, then you have been bruised enough. The medicine is strong enough when it has purged out the disease. The soul is bruised enough when the love of sin is purged out. GMP p. 227

Humility – Though the saints have their golden graces, yet they have their leprous spots; seeing sin has made us vile, let it make us humble; seeing it has taken away our beauty, let it take away our pride; if God (saith Austin [Augustine]) did not spare the proud angels, will He spare you, who are but dust and rottenness? O look upon your boils and ulcers, and be humble! Christians are never more lovely in God's eyes, than when they are loathsome in their own; those sins which humble, shall never damn. HD p. 129

Humility – Humility was never a loser. The emptier the vessel is, and the lower it is let down into the well, the more water it draws up. So the more the soul is emptied of itself, and the lower it is let down by humility, the more it fetches out of the well of salvation. MS p. 134

Humility – When Moses' face shined, he covered it with a veil. When God's people shine most in grace, they are covered with the veil of humility. BD p. 156-7

Hypocrisy – The hypocrite thinks of nothing but self-interest; the sails of his mill move only when the wind of promotion blows. He never dives into the waters of the sanctuary except to fetch up a piece of gold from the bottom. GMP p. 98

Hypocrisy – As a comet may shine like a star, a luster may shine from their profession that dazzles the eyes of the beholders. 'Having a form of godliness, but denying the power' (2 Tim. 3:5). These are lamps without oil; whited sepulchers, like the Egyptian temples, which had fair outsides, but within spiders and apes. BD p. 243

Hypocrisy – The hypocrite deceives others while he lives, but deceives himself when he dies. GMP p. 16

Hypocrisy – Hypocrites are the chief guests the devil expects and he will make them as welcome as fire and brimstone can make them. GMP p. 102

Hypocrisy – The sorrow of hypocrites lies in their faces: 'they disfigure their faces' (Matt. 6:16). They make a sour face, but their sorrow goes no further, like the dew that wets the leaf but does not soak to the root. Ahab's repentance was in outward show. His garments were rent but not his spirit (1 Kings 21:27). Godly sorrow goes deep, like a vein which bleeds inwardly. The heart bleeds for sin: 'they were pricked in their heart' (Acts 2:37). As the heart bears a chief part in sinning, so it must in sorrowing. DR p. 21

Hypocrisy – Christian, if you mourn for hypocrisy, yet find this sin so potent that you cannot get the mastery of it, go to Christ. Beg of him that He would exercise His kingly office in your soul, that He would subdue this sin, and put it under the yoke. Beg of Christ to exercise His spiritual surgery upon you. Desire Him to lance your heart and cut out the rotten flesh, and that He would apply the medicine of His blood to heal you of your hypocrisy. GMP p. 19

Hypocrisy – The hypocrite feigns humility, but it is that he may rise in the world. He is a pretender to faith, but he makes use of it rather for a cloak than a shield. He carries his Bible under his arm, but not in his heart. His whole religion is a demure lie (Hos. 11:12). DR p. 68

Hypocrisy – The hypocrite seems to have his eyes nailed to heaven, but his heart is full of impure lustings. He lives in secret sin against his conscience. He can be as his company is and act both the dove and the vulture. DR p. 68

Hypocrisy – It is as great a shame to have the name of Christian, yet want sanctity, as to have the name of a steward and want fidelity; or the name of a virgin, and want chastity. It exposes religion to reproach, to be baptized into the name of Christ while unholy, and to have eyes full of tears on the sabbath, and on the week-day eyes full of adultery (2 Pet. 2:14); to be so devout at the Lord's table, as if men were stepping into heaven, and so profane the week after, as if they came out of hell; to have the name of Christian while unholy is a scandal to religion, and makes the ways of God evil spoken of. BD p. 248

Hypocrisy – How were the foolish virgins better for their 'blazing lamps', when they had no oil of grace? He who has only a painted holiness shall have a painted happiness. GMP p. 17

Hypocrisy – The hypocrite is not what he seems. A picture is like a man, but it lacks breath. The hypocrite is an effigy, a picture; he does not breathe forth sanctity. He is only like an angel on a signpost. A godly man answers to his profession as the transcript to the original. GMP p. 97

Hypocrisy – The hypocrite veils and smothers his sin. He does not cut off his sin but conceals it. Like a patient that has some loathsome disease in his body, he will rather die than confess his disease. GMP p. 97

Hypocrisy – The hypocrite or stage-player has gone a step beyond the moralist and dressed himself in the garb of religion. He pretends to a form of godliness but denies the power (2 Tim. 3:5). The hypocrite is a saint in jest. He makes a magnificent show, like an ape clothed in ermine or purple. The hypocrite is like a house with a beautiful facade, but every room within is dark. He is a rotten post fairly gilded. Under his mask of profession he hides his plague-sores. The hypocrite is against painting of faces, but he paints holiness. He is seemingly good so that he can be really bad. In Samuel's mantle he plays the devil. DR p. 68

Hypocrisy – The hypocrite is all for faith, nothing for works, like the laurel that makes a flourish but bears no fruit. GMP p. 173

Hypocrisy – Men are ambitious of credit, and wish to gain repute in the world, therefore they will dress themselves in the garb and mode of religion, so that others may write them down for saints. But alas, what is one better for having others commend him and his conscience condemn him? What good will it do a man when he is in hell that others think he has gone to heaven? Oh, beware of this! Counterfeit piety is double iniquity. GMP pp. 15-16

Hypocrisy – The hypocrite would rather have his faith commended than examined. He can no more endure a Scripture trial than counterfeit metal can endure a touchstone. He is like a man who has stolen goods in his house and is very unwilling to have his house searched. So the hypocrite has gotten some stolen goods that the devil has helped him to, and he is loathe to have his heart searched. Whereas true faith is willing to come to a trial. MS p. 138

Idleness – An idle person is the devil's tennis ball, which he bandies up and down with temptation till at last the ball goes out of play. GMP p. 169

Idolatry – God made man of the dust of the earth, and man makes a god of the dust of the earth. BD p. 106

Idolatry – Thus men make many gods. The apostle names the wicked man's trinity, 'The lust of the flesh, the lust of the eye, and the pride of life' (1 Jn. 2:16). The lust of the flesh is pleasure; the lust of the eye, money; the pride of life, honor. O take heed of this! Whatever you deify beside God will prove a bramble, and fire will come out of it and devour you (Judg. 9:15). BD p. 107

Idolatry – God does not like to have any creature set upon the throne of our affections; He will take away that comfort, and then He shall lie nearest our heart. If a husband bestows a jewel on his wife, and she so falls in love with that jewel as to forget her husband, he will take away the jewel so that her love may return to him again. A dear relation is this jewel. If we begin to idolize it, God will take away the jewel so that our love may return to Him again. GMP p. 122

Idolatry – Were it not a foolish thing to bow down to the king's picture, when the king is present? So it is to worship God's image, when God himself is present. BD pp. 47-8

Ignorance – Ignorance is the womb of lust. Vapors arise most in the night. The black vapors of sin arise most in a dark, ignorant soul. Satan casts a mist before a sinner so that he does not see the flaming sword of God's wrath. The eagle first rolls himself in the sand and then flies at the stag, and by fluttering its wings, so bedust the stag's eyes that it cannot see, and then it strikes it with its talons. So Satan, that eagle or prince of the air, first blinds men with ignorance and then wounds them with his darts of temptation. DR p. 107

Ignorance – A man in the dark is full of fear, he trembles every step he takes. Darkness is dangerous. He who is in the dark may quickly go out of the right way, and fall into rivers or whirlpools; so in the darkness of ignorance, we may quickly fall into the whirlpool of hell. ATFG p. 105

Image of God – On the king's coin his own image or effigy is stamped; so God stamped His image on man, and made him partaker of many divine qualities. BD p. 15

Immutableness of God – Expect to meet with changes in everything but God. BD p. 68

Immutableness of God – Oh trust in the immortal God! Like Noah's dove, we have no footing for our souls, till we get into the ark of God's unchangeableness. BD p. 69

Incarnation – He was born of a virgin, that we might be born of God. He took our flesh, that He might give us His Spirit. He lay in the manger that we might lie in paradise. He came down from heaven, that He might bring us to heaven. And what was all this but love? If our hearts be not rocks, this love of Christ should affect us. Behold love that surpasses knowledge (Eph. 3:19)! BD p. 196

Incarnation – It was real flesh that Christ took; not the image of a body, but a true body; therefore He is said to be 'made of a woman' (Gal. 4:4). As bread is made of wheat, and wine is made of the grape; so Christ is made of a woman: His body was part of the flesh and substance of the virgin. This is a glorious mystery, 'God manifest in the flesh'. In the creation, man was made in God's image; in the incarnation God was made in man's image. BD p. 192

Incarnation – Christ's taking flesh was a plot of free grace, and a pure design of love. God Himself, though Almighty, was overcome with love. Christ incarnate is nothing but love covered with flesh. As Christ's assuming our human nature was a master-piece of wisdom, so it was a monument of free grace. BD p. 194

Incarnation – Through the lantern of Christ's humanity we may behold the light of the Deity. Christ being incarnate makes the sight of the Deity not formidable, but delightful to us. BD p. 195

Infinitude of God – Though a thousand men behold the sun, there is light enough for them all: put never so many buckets into the sea, there is water enough to fill them. Though an innumerable company of saints and angels are to be filled out of God's fulness, yet God, being infinite, has enough to satisfy them. God has land enough to give to all His heirs. There can be no want in that which is infinite. BD p. 53

Joy – The oil of joy is poured chiefly into a broken heart: 'the oil of joy for mourning' (Isa. 61:3). In the fields near Palermo grow a great many reeds in which there is a sweet juice from which sugar is made. Likewise in a penitent heart, which is the bruised reed, grow the sugared joys of God's Spirit. God turns the water of tears into the juice of the grape which exhilarates and makes glad the heart. DR p. 102

Joy – Let me tell you, it is a sin not to rejoice. You disparage your Husband, Christ. When a wife is always sighing and weeping, what will others say? 'This woman has a bad husband.' Is this the fruit of Christ's love to you, to reflect dishonor upon Him? A melancholy spouse saddens Christ's heart. I do not deny that Christians should grieve for sins of daily occurrence, but to be always weeping (as if they mourned without hope) is dishonorable to the marriage relationship. 'Rejoice in the Lord always' (Phil. 4:4). Rejoicing brings credit to your husband. Christ loves a cheerful bride, and indeed the very purpose of God's making us sad is to make us rejoice. We sow in tears, so that we may reap in joy. The excessive sadness and contrition of the godly will make others afraid to embrace Christ. They will begin to question whether there is that satisfactory joy in religion which is claimed. Oh, you saints of God, do not forget consolation; let others see that you do not repent of your choice. It is joy that puts liveliness and activity into a Christian: 'the joy of the Lord is your strength' (Neh. 8:10). The soul is swiftest in duty when it is carried on the wings of joy. GMP p. 251

Joy – As in the spring-time, when the sun comes to our horizon, it makes a sudden alteration in the face of the universe: the birds sing, the flowers appear, the fig-tree puts forth her green figs; every thing seems to rejoice and put off its mourning, as being revived with the sweet influence of the sun; so when the Sun of Righteousness arises on the soul, it makes a sudden alteration, and the soul is infinitely rejoiced with the golden beams of God's love. BD p. 267

Joy – Joy stupefies and swallows up troubles; it carries the heart above them, as the oil swims above the water. BD p. 267

Joy – It reflects upon a master when the servant is always drooping and sad; sure he is kept to hard commons, his master does not give him what is fitting; so, when God's people hang their heads, it looks as if they did not serve a good master, or repented of their choice, which reflects dishonor on God. As the gross sins of the wicked bring a scandal on the gospel, so do the uncheerful lives of the godly. 'Serve the Lord with gladness' (Ps. 100:2). Your serving Him does not glorify Him, unless it be with gladness. A Christian's cheerful looks glorify God; religion does not take away our joy, but refines it; it does not break our violin, but tunes it, and makes the music sweeter. BD pp. 14-15

Joy – Joy is setting the soul upon the top of a pinnacle – it is the cream of the sincere milk of the word. Spiritual joy is a sweet and delightful passion, arising from the apprehension and feeling of some good whereby the soul is supported under present troubles, and fenced against future fear. BD p. 267

Judgment – If God threshes the wheat, He will burn the chaff. If the Lord afflicts those He loves, how severe will He be against those He hates? They will feel the second death, (Rev. 21:8). MS p. 40

Judgment – Such as will neither read the Bible themselves nor endure that their children should; such as will neither hear a good sermon themselves nor endure that their neighbors should; such as will stop the pipes which are to convey the water of life and who eclipse the lamps of the sanctuary – these shall receive greater damnation. 1 Thessalonians 2:16, 'Forbidding us to speak to the Gentiles that they might be saved, to fill up their sins alway, for the wrath is come upon them to the uttermost.' MS p. 93

Judgment – The enemies of Christ shall be but as so many clusters of ripe grapes, to be cast into the great wine-press of the wrath of God, and to be trodden by Christ till their blood come out. Christ will at last come off victor, and all His enemies shall be put under His feet. BD p. 190

Judgment – Offenders must come to punishment. The sinner's death-day, and dooms-day is coming. 'The Lord seeth that his day is coming' (Ps. 37:13). While there is a hell, the wicked shall be scourged enough; and while there is eternity, they shall lie there long enough; and God will abundantly compensate the faithful service of His people. BD p. 43

Judgment – Meditate much upon the day of judgment. Feathers swim upon the water, but gold sinks into it; so, light, feathery Christians float in vanity; they mind not the day of judgment; but serious spirits sink deep into the thoughts of it. BD p. 315

Judgment – Sure then that day is near at hand, for iniquity never more abounded than in this age, in which lust grows hot, and love grows cold. When the elect are all converted, then Christ will come to judgment. As he that rows a ferry-boat, stays till all the passengers are taken in, and then he will hasten away to judgment. BD p. 312

Justice of God – The justice of God, like the angel, stands with a drawn sword in its hand ready to strike, but sinners have not eyes as good as those of Balaam's ass to see the sword. God smites on men's backs, but they do not, as Ephraim did, smite upon their thigh (Jer. 31:19). It was a sad complaint the prophet took up: 'thou hast stricken them, but they have not grieved' (Jer. 5:3). That is surely reprobate silver which contracts hardness in the furnace. 'In the time of his distress did he trespass yet more against the Lord: this is that king Ahaz' (2 Chron. 28:22). A hard heart is a receptacle for Satan. As God has two places He dwells in, heaven and a humble heart, so the devil has two places he dwells in, hell and a hard heart. It is not falling into water that drowns, but lying in it. It is not falling into sin that damns, but lying in it without repentance: 'having their conscience seared with a hot iron' (1 Tim. 4:2). DR p. 62

Justice of God – The wicked man shall drink a sea of wrath, but not sip one drop of injustice. BD p. 92

Justification – Justification is a mercy spun out of the bowels of free grace. God does not justify us because we are worthy, but by justifying us makes us worthy. BD p. 227

Justification – Justification is the very hinge and pillar of Christianity. An error about justification is dangerous, like a defect in a foundation. Justification by Christ is a spring of the water of life. To have the poison of corrupt doctrine cast into this spring is damnable. It was a saying of Luther, 'that after his death the doctrine of justification would be corrupted'. In these latter times, the Arminians and Socinians have cast a dead fly into this box of precious ointment. BD p. 226

Knowledge – Many in the old world knew there was an ark, but were drowned, because they did not get into it. Knowledge which is not applied will only light a man to hell. It would be better to live a savage than to die an infidel under the gospel. Christ not believed in is terrible. Moses' rod, when it was in his hand, did a great deal of good. It wrought miracles; but when it was out of his hand, it became a serpent. So Christ, when laid hold on by the hand of faith, is full of comfort, but not laid hold on, will prove a serpent to bite. GMP p. 26

Knowledge – The knowledge of most people makes them more cunning in sin; these have little cause to glory in their knowledge. Absalom might boast of the hair of his head, but that hanged him; so these may boast of the knowledge of their head, but it will destroy them. GMP p. 25

Lordship of Christ – Submit to Christ willingly. All the devils in hell submit to Christ; but it is against their will; they are His slaves, not His subjects. Submit cheerfully to Christ's person and His laws. Many would have Christ their savior, but not their prince; such as will not have Christ to be their king to rule over them, shall never have His blood to save them. Obey all Christ's princely commands; if He commands love, humility, good works, be as the needle that points which way soever the magnet draws. BD p. 191

Love to others – The more we believe, the more we love: faith is the root, and love is the flower that grows upon it. 'Faith which worketh by love' (Gal. 5:6). ATFG p. 98

Love to God – Where there is love to God, there is a grieving for our sins of unkindness against Him. A child which loves his father cannot but weep for offending him. The heart that burns in love melts in tears. Oh! that I should abuse the love of so dear a Savior! Did not my Lord suffer enough upon the cross, but must I make Him suffer more? Shall I give Him more gall and vinegar to drink? How disloyal and disingenuous have I been! How have I grieved His Spirit, trampled upon His royal commands, slighted His blood! This opens a vein of godly sorrow, and makes the heart bleed afresh. 'Peter went out, and wept bitterly' (Matt. 26:75). ATFG pp. 75-6

Love to God – Peter's love at first was more infirm and languid, he denied Christ; but afterwards how boldly did he preach Him! When Christ put him to trial of his love, 'Simon, lovest thou Me?' (Jn. 21:16), Peter could make his humble yet confident appeal to Christ, 'Lord, thou knowest that I love Thee.' Thus that tender plant which before was blown down with the wind of temptation, now is grown into a cedar, which all the powers of hell cannot shake. ATFG pp. 102-3

Love of Christ – Among the several wonders of the magnet it is not the least, that it will not draw gold or pearl, but despising these, it draws the iron to it, one of the most inferior metals: thus Christ leaves angels, those noble spirits, the gold and pearl, and comes to poor sinful man, and draws Him into His embraces. BD p. 196

Love of money – Gain is the golden bait with which Satan fishes for souls: 'the sweet smell of money'. This was the last temptation he used with Christ: 'All these things will I give thee' (Matt. 4:9). But Christ saw the hook under the bait. Many who have escaped gross sins are still caught in a golden net. GMP p. 147

Love to others – A saint in this life is like gold in the ore, much dross of infirmity cleaves to him, yet we love him for the grace that is in him. A saint is like a fair face with a scar: we love the beautiful face of holiness, though there be a scar in it. The best emerald has its blemishes, the brightest stars their twinklings, and the best of the saints have their failings. You that cannot love another because of his infirmities, how would you have God love you? ATFG p. 82

Love – Let us be like Christ in mildness and sweetness. Let us pray for our enemies, and conquer them by love. David's kindness melted Saul's heart (1 Sam. 24:16). A frozen heart will be thawed with the fire of love. BD p. 200

Love of God – Christ has suffered more for His spouse than ever any husband did for a wife. He suffered poverty and ignominy. He who crowned the heavens with stars was Himself crowned with thorns. He was called a companion of sinners, so that we might be made companions of angels. He was regardless of His life; He leaped into the sea of His Father's wrath to save His spouse from drowning. GMP p. 245

Love to God – This may serve for a sharp reproof to such as have not a dram of love to God in their hearts – and are there such miscreants alive? He who does not love God is a beast with a man's head. Oh wretch! Do you live upon God every day, yet not love Him? If one had a friend that supplied him continually with money, and gave him all his allowance, were not he worse than a barbarian, who did not respect and honor that friend? Such a friend is God; He gives you your breath, He bestows a livelihood upon you, and will you not love Him? You will love your prince if he saves your life, and will you not love God who gives you your life? What magnet so powerful to draw love, as the blessed Deity? He is blind whom beauty does not tempt; he is sottish who is not drawn with the cords of love. When the body is cold and has no heat in it, it is a sign of death: that man is dead who has no heat of love in his soul to God. How can he expect love from God, who shows no love to Him? Will God ever lay such a viper in His bosom, as casts forth the poison of malice and enmity against Him?

This reproof falls heavy upon the infidels of this age, who are so far from loving God, that they do all they can to show their hatred of him. 'They declare their sin as Sodom' (Isa. 3:9). 'They set their mouth against the heavens' (Ps. 73:9), in pride and blasphemy, and bid open defiance of God. These are monsters in nature, devils in the shape of men. Let them read their doom: 'If any man love not the Lord Jesus Christ, let him be anathema-maranatha' (1 Cor. 16:22), that is, let him be accursed from God, till Christ's coming to judgment. Let him be heir to a curse while he lives, and at the dreadful day of the Lord, let him hear that heart-rending sentence pronounced against him, 'Depart, ye cursed.' ATFG pp. 72-3

Love to God – Many love God because He gives them corn and wine, and not for His intrinsic excellences. We must love God more for what He is, than what He bestows. True love is not mercenary. You need not hire a mother to love her child: a soul deeply in love with God needs not be hired by rewards. ATFG p. 68

Love to God – We can never love God as He deserves. As God's punishing us is less than we deserve (Ezra 9:13), so our loving Him is less than he deserves. ATFG p. 69

Love to God – How far are they from loving God, who are not at all affected with His dishonor? If they have but peace and trading, they lay nothing to heart. A man who is dead drunk, never minds nor is affected by it, though another be bleeding to death by him; so, many, being drunk with the wind of prosperity, when the honor of God is wounded and His truths lie a bleeding, are not affected by it. Did men love God, they would grieve to see His glory suffer, and religion itself become a martyr. ATFG p. 77

Love to God – Love is the incense which makes all our services fragrant and acceptable to God. ATFG p. 89

Love to God – Some drops of love may run beside to the creature, but the full stream must run towards God. The creature may have the milk of our love, but we must keep the cream for God. He who is above all, must be loved above all. 'There is none on earth whom I desire in comparison of Thee' (Ps. 73:25). BD p. 106

Love of God – He that loves God will have nothing to do with sin, unless to give battle to it. Sin strikes not only at God's honor, but

His being. Does he love his prince that harbors him who is a traitor to the crown? Is he a friend to God who loves that which God hates? The love of God and the love of sin cannot dwell together. ATFG p. 78

Loving others – A Christian in this life is like a good face full of freckles. You who cannot love another because of his imperfections have never yet seen your own face in the mirror. Your brother's infirmities may make you pity him; his graces must make you love him. GMP p. 140

Lust – Lust first bewitches with pleasure, and then comes the fatal dart. 'Till a dart strike through his liver' (Prov. 7:23). This should be as a flaming sword to stop men in the way of their carnal delights. Who for a drop of pleasure would drink a sea of wrath? BD p. 21.

Lust – Where ignorance reigns in the understanding, lust rages in the affections. BD p. 57

Lying – Though the bread of falsehood is sweet (Prov. 20:17), yet many vomit up their sweet morsels in hell. DR p. 67

Lying – Some are so wicked, that they will not only speak an untruth, but will swear to it; nay, they will wish a curse upon themselves, if that untruth be not true. I have read of a woman, one Anne Avarie, who in 1575, being in a shop, wished that she might sink if she had not paid for the wares she took, and fell down speechless immediately and died. BD p. 102

Lying – He that will lie in his trade shall lie in hell. BD 102

Lying – It is bad enough to tell a lie, but he who loves a lie shall lie lower in hell. MS p. 95

Malice – The body may as soon thrive while it has the plague as a soul can that is infected with malice. While Christians are debating, grace is abating. As the spleen grows, health decays. As hatred increases, holiness declines. GMP p. 144

Marriage – Love is the best diamond in the wedding ring. GMP p.155

Marriage – The husband should show his love to his wife by covering infirmities; by avoiding occasions of strife; by sweet, endearing expressions; by pious counsel; by love tokens; by encouraging what he sees amiable and virtuous in her; by mutual prayer; by associating with her, unless detained by urgency of business. The pilot who leaves his ship and abandons it entirely to the merciless waves, declares that he does not value it or reckon there is any treasure in it. GMP p. 156

Memory – The memory must be a table book where the Word is written. BD p. 34

Memory – The *memory* is diseased. The memory at first was like a golden cabinet in which divine truths were locked up safe, but now it is like a colander or leaking vessel, which lets all that is good run out. The memory is like a sifter, which sifts out the flour, but keeps the bran. So the memory lets saving truths go, and holds nothing but froth and vanity. HD p. 122

Mercy – Nothing is sweeter than mercy, when it is improved; nothing fiercer, when it is abused; as nothing is colder than lead when taken out of the mine, and nothing more scalding when it is heated. Nothing is blunter than iron, yet nothing is sharper when it is whetted. 'The mercy of the Lord is upon them that fear Him' (Ps. 103:17). Mercy is not for them that sin and fear not, but for them that fear and sin not. God's mercy is a holy mercy; where it pardons it heals. BD p. 97

Mercy – God pours the golden oil of mercy into empty vessels. BD p. 97

Mercy – It is dreadful to have mercy as a witness against any one. It was said with Haman when the queen herself accused him (Esth. 7:6). So will it be when this queen mercy shall stand up against a person and accuse him. It is only mercy that saves a sinner; how sad then to have mercy become an enemy! If mercy be an accuser, who shall be our advocate? The sinner never escapes hell when mercy draws up the indictment. BD p. 95

Mercy – God keeps the best wine until last. Here He gives us mercies only in small quantities; the greatest things are laid up. Here there are some honey drops and foretastes of God's love; the rivers of pleasure are reserved for paradise. Well may we take the harp and violin and triumph in God's praise. Who can tread upon these hot coals of God's love and his heart not burn in thankfulness? GMP p. 136

Mercy – God is more willing to pardon than to punish. Mercy does more multiply in Him than sin in us. Mercy is His nature. The bee naturally gives honey; it stings only when it is provoked. ATFG p. 15

Mercy – If mercy is not a magnet to draw us nearer to God, it will be a millstone to sink us deeper to hell. Nothing so cold as lead, yet nothing more scalding when it is melted. Nothing so sweet as mercy, yet nothing so terrible when it is abused. Sinners never escape when mercy draws up the indictment. MS p. 67

Mercy – Mercy is not like the sun to the fire, to dull it, but like the oil to the wheel, to make it run faster. GMP p. 133

Mercy – As the sea covers great rocks, so God's covenant mercy covers great sins. Some of the Jews that crucified Christ had their sins washed away in His blood. BD p. 158

Morality – Civility is but nature refined; there is nothing of Christ there, and the heart may be foul and impure. Under these fair leaves of civility the worm of unbelief may be hid. A moral person has a secret antipathy against grace: he hates vice and he hates grace as much as vice. The snake has a fine color, but a sting. A person adorned and cultivated with moral virtue has a secret spleen against sanctity. The Stoics who were the chief of the moralized heathens, were the bitterest enemies Paul had (Acts 17:18). BD p. 43

Mortality – Death cannot be resisted. Take a man in his best estate. Let him be dignified with honor like Solomon, armed with strength like Samson. Were his flesh as firm as the leviathan, yet the bullet of death would soon shoot through him. How easily can God look us into our grave! MS p. 85

Obedience – Oh, what a shame it is that the wicked should be fixed in evil and we unfixed in good, that they should be more constant in the devil's service than we are in Christ's! GMP p. 216

Obedience – A gracious heart is like a piece of good ground that, having received the seed of mercy, produces a crop of obedience. GMP p. 133

Obedience – To sweat in some duties of religion and freeze in others is the symptom of a disordered Christian. Jehu was zealous in destroying the idolatry of Baal, but let the golden calves of Jeroboam stand (2 Kings 10:29). This shows that men are not good in truth when they are good by halves. GMP p. 167

Obedience – If a man wants to have the wheels of his watch move regularly, he must mend the spring. Christian, if you want to move more spiritually in duty, get the spring of your heart mended. GMP p. 166

Obedience – It is fitting that the child should obey the parent in all just and sober commands. God's laws are like the curtains of the tabernacle which were looped together. They are like a chain of gold where all the links are coupled. A conscientious man will not willingly break one link of this chain. If one command is violated, the whole chain is broken: 'whosoever shall keep the whole law, yet offend in one point, he is guilty of all' (Jas. 2:10). GMP p. 167

Obedience – Do we think walking with God can do us any hurt? Did we ever hear any cry out on their deathbed that they have been too holy, that they have prayed too much, or walked with God too much? No, that which has cut them to the heart has been this, that they have not walked more closely with God; they have wrung their hand and torn their hair to think that they have been so bewitched with the pleasures of the world. Close walking with God will make our enemy (death) be at peace with us. GMP p. 181

Obedience – Get off the old road of sin. He that would walk in a pleasant meadow must turn off the road. The way of sin is full of travelers. There are so many travelers on this road that hell, though it is of a great circumference, would gladly enlarge itself and make room for them (Isa. 5:14). This way of sin seems pleasant but the end is damnable. GMP p. 182

Obedience – A good Christian is like the sun, which not only sends forth heat, but goes its circuit round the world. Thus, he who glorifies God, has not only his affections heated with love to God, but he goes his circuit too; he moves vigorously in the sphere of obedience. BD p. 9

Obedience – We glorify God when we are devoted to His service; our head studies for Him, our tongue pleads for Him, and our hands relieve His members. The wise men that came to Christ did not only bow the knee to Him, but presented Him with gold and myrrh (Matt. 2:11). So we must not only bow the knee, give God worship, but bring presents of golden obedience. BD p. 8

Obedience – The true obedience of faith is a cheerful obedience. God's commands do not seem grievous. Have you obedience, and obey cheerfully? Do you look upon God's command as your burden, or privilege; as an iron fetter about your leg, or as a gold chain about your neck? BD p. 219

Omnipresence of God – If a man owes a debt to another he may make his escape, and flee into another land, where the creditor cannot find him. 'But whither shall I flee from Thy presence?' God is infinite, He is in all places; so that He will find out His enemies and punish them. BD p. 53

Omniscience of God – Would men go after strange flesh if they believe God was spectator of their wickedness, and would make them do penance in hell for it? Would they defraud in their dealings, and use false weights, if they thought God saw them, and for making their weights lighter would make their damnation heavier. Viewing ourselves as under the eye of God's omniscience, would cause reverence in the worship of God. God sees the frame and carriage of our hearts when we come before Him. How would this call in our straggling thoughts? How would it animate and spirit duty? It would make us put fire to the incense. 'The tribes instantly served God day and night' (Acts 26:7), with utmost zeal and intenseness of spirit. To think God is in this place would add wings to prayer, and oil to the flame of our devotion. BD pp. 58-9

Parenting – Correction is a hedge of thorns to stop children in their full career to hell. GMP p. 157

Parenting – A parent must give his children discipline: 'Withhold not correction from the child; for if thou beatest him with the rod, he shall not die' (Prov. 23:13). The rod beats out the dust and moth of sin. A child indulged and humored in wickedness will prove a burden instead of a blessing. GMP p. 157

Parenting – A good piece of ground bears not only a fore-crop but an after crop. He who is godly does not only bear God a good crop of obedience himself while he lives, but by training his child in the principles of religion, he bears God an after-crop when he is dead. GMP p. 187

Parenting – The time of childhood is the fittest time to be sowing seed of religion in our children. 'Whom shall he make to understand doctrine? Them that are weaned from the milk, and drawn from the breasts' (Isa. 28:9). The wax, while it is soft and tender, will take any impression. Children, while they are young, will fear a reproof; when they are old, they will hate it. GMP p. 186

Parenting – The soul of your child is in a snare and will you not pray that it may 'recover out of the snare of the devil' (2 Tim. 2:26)? Many parents are careful to lay up portions for their children, but they do not lay up prayers for them. GMP pp. 156-7

Parenting – Children are young plants which must be watered with good education, so that they may, with Obadiah, fear the Lord 'from their youth up' (1 Kings 18:12). Plato said, 'In vain does he expect a harvest who has been negligent in sowing.' Nor can a parent expect to reap any good from a child, where he has not sown the seed of wholesome instruction. And though, notwithstanding all counsel and admonition, the child should die in sin, yet is it a comfort to a godly parent to think that before his child died, he gave it a spiritual medicine. GMP p. 156

Parenting – Masters of families must glorify God, must season their children and servants with the knowledge of the Lord; their houses should be little churches. 'I know that Abraham will command his children, that they may keep the way of the Lord' (Gen. 18:19). You that are masters have a charge of souls. For want of the bridle of family discipline youth runs wild. BD p. 20

Parenting – Another makes a god of his child, sets his child in God's room, and so provokes God to take it away. If you lean too hard upon glass it will break, so many break their children by leaning too hard upon them. BD pp. 106-7

Patience of God – If God lets men prosper awhile in their sin, His vial of wrath is all this while filling; His sword is all this time whetting: and though God may forbear men a while, yet long forbearance is no forgiveness. The longer God is in taking His blow, the heavier it will be at last. BD p. 90

Patience – Patience is a star which shines in a dark night. GMP p.118

Patience – By faith a man possesses God and by patience he possesses himself. GMP p. 123

Patience – Faith argues the soul into patience. Faith is like that town clerk in Ephesus who allayed the contention of the multitude and argued them soberly into peace (Acts 19:35, 36). So when impatience begins to clamor and make a hubbub in the soul, faith appeases the tumult and argues the soul into holy patience. GMP p. 127

Peace – Peace is the nurse of plenty. 'He maketh peace in thy boarders, and filleth thee with the finest of the wheat' (Ps. 147:14). How pleasant it is when the waters of blood begin to recede and we can see the windows of our ark open, and the dove returning with an olive branch of peace! BD p. 261

Peace – God pours the golden oil of peace into broken hearts. BD p. 263

Peace – When Christians abate their fervency, God abates their peace. If you slacken the strings of the violin, the music is spoiled; so, if Christians slack in duty, they spoil the sweet music of peace in their souls. As the fire decays, the cold increases; so, as fervency in duty abates, our peace cools. BD p. 264

Peace – Through the fury of temptation, though the devil cannot destroy us, he will disturb us. He disputes against our adoption; he would make us question the work of grace in our hearts, and so disturb the waters of our peace. He is like a subtle cheater, who, if he cannot make a man's title to his land void, yet will put him to many troublesome suits in law. If Satan cannot make us ungodly, he will make us unquiet. Violent winds make the sea rough and stormy; so the winds of temptation blowing disturb peace of spirit, and put the soul into a commotion. BD pp. 263-4

Peace – If you would have peace, make war with sin. Sin is the Achan that troubles us, the Trojan horse. 'When Joram saw Jehu, he said, Is it peace, Jehu? And he answered, What peace, so long as the whoredoms of your mother Jezebel and her witchcrafts are so many' (2 Kings 9:22)? What peace, so long as sin remains unmortified? If you would have peace with God, break the league with sin; give battle to sin, for it is a most just war. BD p. 266

Persecution – God works sometimes by contraries. He raises His church by bringing it low. The blood of the martyrs has watered the church, and made it more fruitful. BD p. 126

Persecution – The gospel is a rose that cannot be plucked without prickles. The legacy Christ has bequeathed is the Cross. While there is a devil and a wicked man in the world, never expect a charter of exemption from trouble. BD p. 3

Persecution – Though there may be a private grudge between such as are wicked, yet they will all agree and unite against the saints. If two greyhounds are snarling at a bone and you put a hare between them, they will leave the bone and chase the hare. So if wicked men have private differences amongst themselves, and the godly are near them, they will leave snarling at one another and chase the godly. GMP p. 143

Perseverance – Though grace lives with so much difficulty, like the infant that struggles for breath, yet being born of God, it is immortal. Grace conflicting with corruption is like a ship tossed and beaten by the waves, yet it weathers the storm and at last gets to the desired haven. GMP p. 234

Perseverance – A godly man will follow Christ though it is death every step. He will keep his goodness when others are bad. As all the water in the salt sea cannot make the fish salt, but they retain their freshness, so all the wickedness in the world cannot make a godly man wicked, but he still retains his piety. He will follow Christ in the worst of times. GMP p. 39

Perseverance – It is not our holding to God, but His holding to us that preserves us. A little boat tied fast to a rock is safe, and so are we, when we are tied to the 'rock of ages'. GMP p. 215

Perseverance – Gold, though cast into the fire, retains its purity. Acts 20:23-24, 'Bonds and afflictions abide me, but none of these things move me, neither do I count my life dear.' Though the archers shoot at a godly man, yet the bow of his faith abides in strength. Whatever he loses, he holds fast the jewel of a good conscience. He knows the crown of religion is constancy. And though persecution brings death in one hand, it brings life in the other. Though religion may have thorns strewn in the way, the thorns cannot be as sharp as the crown is sweet. MS p. 62

Pleasure – Pleasure is a silken halter, a flattering devil, which kills with embracing. HD p. 115

Politics – God loves to counterplot politicians; He makes use of their own wit to undo them, and hangs Haman upon his own gallows. BD p. 75

Power of God – He has salvation and damnation in His power. He has the key of justice in His hand, to lock up whom He will in the fiery prison of hell; and He has the key of mercy in His hand, to open heaven's gate to whom He pleases. The name engraven upon His vesture is, 'King of kings, and Lord of lords' (Rev. 19:16). BD p. 77

Praise to God – We glorify God, when we sacrifice the praise and glory of all to God. 'I labored more abundantly than they all' (1 Cor. 15:10), a speech, one would think, savored of pride; but the apostle pulls the crown from his own head, and sets it upon the head of free grace: 'yet not I, but the grace of God which was with me'. As Joab, when he fought against Rabbah, sent for King David, that he might carry away the crown of the victory (2 Sam. 12:28-30), so a Christian, when he has gotten power over any corruption or temptation, sends for Christ, that he may carry away the crown of the victory. As the silkworm, when she weaves her curious work, hides herself under the silk, and is not seen; so when we have done anything praiseworthy, we must hide ourselves under the veil of humility, and transfer the glory of all we have done to God. As Constantine used to write the name of Christ over his door, so should we write the name of Christ over our duties. Let Him wear the garland of praise. BD p. 17

Praise to God – When we praise God, we spread His fame and renown, we display the trophies of His excellency. BD p. 15

Praise to God – Praise is the quiet rent we pay God: While God renews our lease, we must renew our rent. BD p. 15

Praise to God – Praise is not comely for any but the godly: 'praise is comely for the upright' (Ps. 33:1). A profane man stuck with God's praises is like a dunghill stuck with flowers. Praise in the mouth of a sinner is like an oracle in the mouth of a fool. How uncomely it is for anyone to praise God if his whole life dishonors God! It is as indecent for a wicked man to praise God as it is for a usurer to talk of living by faith, or for the devil to quote Scripture. GMP p. 129

Praise to God – Musicians love to play on their music where there is the loudest sound; and God loves to bestow His mercies where there is the loudest praises. You that have angels' reward, do angels' work. Begin that work of praise here, which you hope to be always doing in heaven. BD p. 161

Prayer – Let us, then, close ranks and with our Savior pray yet more earnestly (Luke 22:44). Let us be importunate suitors, and resolve with St. Bernard that we will not come away from God without God. Prayer is a bomb which will make heaven's gates fly open. GMP p. 96

Prayer – Jacob never prayed so fervently as when he was in fear of his life. He oiled the key of prayers with tears. MS p. 43

Prayer – Many pray, 'Let this cup pass away,' but few, 'Thy will be done.' BD p. 17

Prayer – A godly man is on the mount of prayer every day; he begins the day with prayer; before he opens his shop, he opens his heart to God. We burn sweet perfumes in our houses; a godly man's house is 'a house of perfume'; he airs it with the incense of prayer; he engages in no business without seeking God. GMP p. 88

Prayer – The devil, if he cannot hinder us *from* duty, will hinder us *in* duty. When we come before the Lord, he is at our right hand to resist us (Zech. 3:1). Like when a man is going to write, and another stands at his elbow and jogs him, so that he cannot write evenly. Satan will set vain objects before the fancy to cause a diversion. The devil does not oppose formality but fervency. If he sees that we are setting ourselves in good earnest to seek God, he will be whispering things in our ears, so that we can scarcely attend to what we are doing. GMP pp. 162-3

Prayer – When the fire of fervency is put to the incense of prayer, then it ascends as a sweet odor. BD p. 49

Prayer – What would become of our duties without a high priest? Christ's intercession is to our prayers, as the fan to the chaff. It winnows it from the corn; so Christ winnows out the chaff which intermixes with our prayers. BD p. 182

Prayer – See the reason why men's prayers are not heard. It is because they sin still. Sin clips the wings of prayer so that it will not fly to the throne of grace. MS p. 58

Prayer – The reason why so many prayers suffer shipwreck is because they split against the rock of unbelief. Praying without faith is shooting without bullets. When faith takes prayer in hand, then we draw near to God. GMP p. 90

Prayer – Prayer is a sovereign plaster for a wounded soul, but sin pulls off the plaster so that it will not heal. MS p. 59

Prayer – Prayer is delightful to God when it ascends from the altar of a broken heart. DR p. 77

Prayer – A godly man cannot live without prayer. A man cannot live unless he takes his breath, nor can the soul, unless it breaths forth its desire to God. As soon as the babe of grace is born, it cries; no sooner was Paul converted than 'behold, he prayeth' (Acts 9:11). GMP p. 88

Prayer – Sin lived in makes the heart hard and God's ear deaf. Sin stops the mouth of prayer. It does what the thief does to the traveler – puts a gag in his mouth so that he cannot speak. Sin poisons and infests prayer. A wicked man's prayer is sick of the plague, and will God come near him? GMP pp. 90-1

Prayer – These wandering thoughts [in prayer] arise from the world. These vermin are bred out of the earth. Worldly business often crowds into our duties, and while we are speaking to God, our hearts are talking with the world: 'They sit before me as my people, but their heart goeth after their covetousness' (Ezek. 33:31). GMP p. 163

Prayer – Incense without fire makes no sweet smell. Prayer without fervency is like incense without fire. Christ prayed with 'strong crying and tears' (Heb. 5:7); crying prayer prevails. When the heart is inflamed in prayer, a Christian is carried as it were in a fiery chariot up to heaven. GMP pp. 89-90

Prayer – A spiritual prayer is a fervent prayer: 'The effectual fervent prayer ... availeth much' (Jas. 5:16). The heart, like the mainspring, should carry the affections in a most zealous and rapid manner; fervency is the wing of prayer by which it ascends to heaven. GMP p. 89

Prayer – Patience is a flower of God's planting. Pray that it may grow in your heart, and send forth its sweet perfume. Prayer is a holy charm, to charm down the evil spirit. Prayer composes the heart and puts it in tune, when impatience has broken the strings and put everything into confusion. Oh, go to God. Prayer delights God's ear; it melts His heart; it opens His hand. GMP p. 127

Prayer – Hot passions make cold payers. Where animosities and contentions prevail, instead of praying for one another, Christians will be ready to pray against one another, like the disciples who prayed for fire from heaven on the Samaritans (Luke 9:54). And will God, do you think, hear such prayers as come from a wrathful heart? Will He eat our leavened bread? Will He accept those duties which are soured with bitterness of spirit? Shall that prayer which is offered with strange fire of our sinful passions ever go up as incense? GMP p. 144

Prayer – Prayer is the Christian's gun, which he discharges against his enemies. Prayer is the sovereign medicine for the soul. ATFG p. 20

Prayer – Prayer sanctifies your mercies (1 Tim. 4:5). Prayer weeds our sin and waters grace. GMP p. 94

Preacher – Under the law, before the priests served at the altar, they washed in the laver. Such as serve in the Lord's house must first be washed from gross sin in the laver of repentance. The life of a minister should be a walking Bible. Basil said of Gregory Nazianzene that he thundered in his doctrine and lightened in his conduct. A minister must imitate John the Baptist, who was not only 'a voice crying', but 'a light shining' (Jn. 5:35). They who live in contradiction to what they preach disgrace this excellent calling. They turn their books into cups. And though they are angels by office, yet they are devils in their lives (Jer. 23:15). GMP p. 155

Preaching – Ministers are physicians under God to cure sick souls; God has set in His church pastors and teachers (Eph. 4:11). The ministers are a college of physicians, their work is to find out disease and apply medicines; it is a hard work, while ministers are curing others they themselves are nigh unto death (Phil. 2:30). They find their people sick of several diseases; some have poisoned themselves with error, some are surfeited with the love of the creature, some have stabbed themselves at the heart with gross sin. O how hard is it to heal all these sick gangrened souls! Many ministers do sooner kill themselves by preaching than cure their patients; but though the work of the ministry be a laborious work, it is a needful work; while there are sick souls, there will be need of spiritual physicians. HD pp. 127-8

Preaching – The ministry of the word is the pipe or organ; the Spirit of God blowing in it, effectually changes men's hearts. 'While Peter spoke, the Holy Ghost fell on all them that heard the word of God' (Acts 10:44). Ministers knock at the door of men's hearts, the Spirit comes with a key and opens the door. 'A certain woman named Lydia, whose heart the Lord opened' (Acts 16:14). BD p. 221

Preaching – Inward grace is wrought by outward means; the preaching of the Word is God's engine that He uses for working grace; it is called 'the rod of His strength' (Ps. 110:2), and 'the breath of His lips' (Isa. 11:4). By this He causes breath to enter; out of this golden pipe of the sanctuary, God empties the golden oil of grace into the soul; the ministry of the gospel is called 'the ministry of the Spirit' in 2 Corinthians 3:8, because the Spirit of God ordinarily makes use of this to work grace; this ministry of the Spirit is to be preferred before the ministry of angels. HD p. 170

Preaching – The Word preached will not only make us knowing Christians, but growing Christians. Ministers are compared to clouds (Isa. 5:6); their doctrine drops as the rain, and makes the trees of God fruitful. I wonder not that they are barren trees and nigh unto cursing, that are not under the droppings of the sanctuary. A Christian can no more be fruitful without ordinances, than a tree without showers. HD p. 188

Preaching – Many have enjoyed the prayers, tears, and studies of God's choicest ministers. They have been put in the fattest pastures of ordinances, but yet they may say with the Prophet, 'My leanness, my leanness,' (Isa. 24:16). They have had warm preaching but they freeze in the sun. They can hear ministers preach the most startling doctrine and see them throw the flashes of hellfire about in the congregation, but their consciences are no more stirred than the pillars in the church. Proud they were and they are proud still. Profane they were and they are profane still. All the sermons they have heard are like showers falling on a rock which is never made softer or more fruitful. MS pp. 97-8

Preaching – God's watchmen have been sent to warn men of their evil ways. They have told them how damnable a thing it is to persist in sin. The judgments of God, like arrows, have been shot at them for sin. Yet, for all this, they sin still. This is worse than to be Balaam the Sorcerer. For when he saw the angel before him with the naked sword, he dared not ride on. But these desperate, heaven-daring sinners, though they see the flaming sword of God's justice before them, resolvedly venture on in sin. MS pp. 70-1

Preaching – St. Paul's preaching was not with enticing words of wisdom but in the demonstration of the Spirit and power, (1 Cor. 2:4). Plainness is ever best in beating down sin. When a wound festers, it is fitter to lance it than to embroider it with silk or lay vermilion upon it. MS p. x

Preaching – Some will fall a-weeping at a sermon, but it is like an April shower, soon over, or like a vein opened and presently stopped again. True sorrow must be habitual. DR p. 25

Preaching – In the law, the lips of the leper were to be covered; that minister who is by office an angel, but by his life a leper, ought to have his lips covered, he deserves silencing. A good preacher but a bad liver is like a physician that has the plague; though his advise and receipts which he gives may be good, yet his plague infects the patient: so though ministers may have good words, and give good receipts in the pulpit, yet the plague of their lives infects their people. If you find Hophni and Phinehas among the sons of Levi, whose unholy carriage make the offering of God to be abhorred, you will save God a labor in ejecting them. HD pp. 113-14

Preaching – Zeal in a minister is as proper as fire on the altar. Some are afraid to reprove, like the swordfish which has a sword in his head but is without a heart. So they carry the sword of the Spirit about them, but have no heart to draw it out in reproof against sin. How many have sown pillows under their people (Ezek. 13:18), making them sleep so securely that they never woke till they were in hell! GMP pp. 154-5

Preaching – Samuel thought it had been the voice of Eli only that called him; but it was God's voice (1 Sam. 3:6). So, perhaps, you think it is only the minister that speaks to you in the word, but it is God Himself who speaks. Therefore Christ is said to speak to us from heaven (Heb. 12:25). How does He speak but by His ministers? As a king speaks by his ambassadors. Know, that in every sermon preached, God calls to you; and to refuse the message we bring, is to refuse God Himself. BD p. 221

Preaching – There is little hope of the metal which has lain long in the fire but is not melted and refined. When God has sent his ministers one after another, exhorting and persuading men to leave their sins, but they settle upon the lees of formality and can sit and sleep under a sermon, it will be hard for these ever to be brought to repentance. DR p. 61

Preaching – Some at a sermon are like Jonah: their heart is tender and they let fall tears. Others are no more affected with it than a deaf man with music. Some grow better by the word, others worse. The same earth which causes sweetness in the grape causes bitterness in the wormwood. What is the reason the Word works so differently? It is because the Spirit of God carries the Word to the conscience of one and not another. One has received the divine unction and not the other (1 Jn. 2:20). O pray that the dew may fall with the manna, that the Spirit may go along with the Word. The chariot of ordinances will not carry us to heaven unless the Spirit of God join Himself to this chariot (Acts 8:29). DR p. 14

Preaching – The Word preached is the engine God uses to effect repentance. It is compared to a hammer and to a fire (Jer. 23:29), the one to break, the other to melt the heart. How great a blessing it is to have the Word, which is of such virtue, dispensed! And how hard they who put out the lights of heaven will find it to escape hell. DR p. 14

Preaching – The Word written is a repository in which God has laid up sovereign oils and balsams to recover sick souls; and the word preached is the pouring out of these oils, and applying them to the sick patient. HD p. 138

Preaching – Many love the Word preached only for its eloquence and notion. They come to a sermon as to a music lecture (Ezek. 33:31-32) or as to a garden to pick flowers, but not to have their lusts subdued or their hearts bettered. These are like a foolish woman who paints her face but neglects her health. GMP p. 66

Preaching – 'Preach the word; be instant in season, out of season' (2 Tim. 4:2). The minister must not be idle. Sloth is as inexcusable in a minister as sleeping in a sentry. John the Baptist was a 'voice crying' (Matt. 3:3). A dumb minister is of no more use than a dead physician. A man of God must work in the Lord's vineyard. GMP p. 154

Preaching – A godly man loves the Word preached, which is a commentary upon the Word written. The Scriptures are the sovereign oils and balsams; the preaching of the Word is the pouring of them out. The Scriptures are the precious spices; the preaching of the Word is the beating of these spices, which causes a wonderful fragrance and delight. GMP p. 64

Preaching – [The minister must be] a plain preacher, suiting his matter and style to the capacity of his audience (1 Cor. 14:19). Some ministers, like eagles, love to soar aloft in abstruse metaphysical notions, thinking they are most admired when they are least understood. They who preach in the clouds, instead of hitting their people's conscience, shoot over their heads. GMP p. 154

Preaching – Suppose a man were in the mouth of a lion, and another should shoot the lion and save the man, would he not be thankful? So, when we are in the mouth of sin, as of a lion, and the minister by a reproof shoots this sin to death, shall we not be thankful? A gracious soul rejoices when the sharp lance of the Word has pierced his abscess. He wears a reproof like a jewel on his ear: 'As an earring of gold, so is a wise reprover upon an obedient ear' (Prov. 25:12). GMP p. 67

Preaching – The ship of ordinances will not carry us to heaven, though an angel is pilot, unless the wind of God's Spirit blows. The Spirit is the soul of the Word without which it is but a dead letter. Ministers may prescribe medicine, but it is God's Spirit who must make it work. GMP p. 76

Preaching – The patient is thankful to the physician that tells him of his disease, and uses means to recover him. When ministers tell you, in love, of your sins, and would reclaim you, take it in good part; the worst they intend is to cure you of your sickness. HD p. 130

Preaching – The word is a hammer (Jer. 23:29). Every blow of the hammer is to fasten the nails to the building; so the preacher's words are to fasten you the more to Christ; they weaken themselves to strengthen and settle you. This is the grand design of preaching, not only for the enlightening, but for the establishing of souls; not only to guide them in the right way, but to keep them in it. BD p. 2

Preaching – Such as hinder preaching, as the Philistines that stopped the wells, stop the well of the water of life. They take away the physicians that should heal sin-sick souls. Ministers are lights (Matt. 5:14), and who but thieves hate the light? BD p. 19

Presumption – To sin willfully accents and enhances the sin. It is like dye to the wool or like a weight put in the scale which makes it weigh heavier. This leaves men without excuse, Jn. 15:22. If a sea mark is set up to give notice that there are shelves or rocks, the mariner still will sail there. If he splits his ship, no one will pity him because he had warning given. MS p. 71

Presumption – To sin still is to dare God's justice; 'tis to affront Him to His face, and an affront will make God draw His sword. MS p. 63

Pride – Proud nominal Christians, who do not lay the whole stress of their salvation upon Christ, but would mingle their dross with His gold, their duties, with His merits. This is to steal a jewel from Christ's crown and implicitly to deny Him to be a perfect Savior. GMP p. 49

Pride – You that do set up your shield, and blaze your coat of arms, behold your pedigree; you are but walking ashes: and will you be proud? What is Adam? The son of dust. And what is dust? The son of nothing. BD p. 201

Pride – 'The doves', says Pliny, 'take pride in their feathers, and in their flying high; at last they fly so high that they are prey to the hawk.' Men fly so high in pride that at last they are prey to the devil, the prince of the air. GMP pp. 85-6

Pride – The proud man is the mark which God shoots at, and He never misses the mark. He threw proud Lucifer out of heaven; He thrust proud Nebuchadnezzar out of his throne, and turned him to eat grass (Dan. 4:25). BD p. 201

Pride – They who stand upon the pinnacle of pride look upon other men as no bigger than crows. GMP p. 83

Pride – Many dress themselves in such fashions as to make the devil fall in love with them. Black spots, gaudy attire, naked breasts, what are these but the flags and banners which pride displays? GMP p. 82

Pride – There is no idol like self; the proud man bows down to this idol. GMP p. 83

Pride – Oh, let us search if there is none of this leaven of pride in us. Man is naturally a proud piece of flesh; this sin runs in the blood. Our first parents fell by their pride. They aspired to deity. There are the seeds of this in the best, but the godly do not allow themselves in it. They strive to kill this weed by mortification. GMP p. 84

Profession – If we are the prizers of Christ, we cannot live without Him; things which we value we know not how to be without. A man may live without music, but not without food. A child of God can lack health and friends, but cannot lack Christ. GMP pp. 50-1

Promises of God – God's truth, which is the brightest pearl in His crown, is pawned in a promise. The promises are suitable, like a medical garden, in which there is no disease but there is some herb to cure it. In the dark night of desertion God has promised to be a sun; in temptation, to tread down Satan (Rom. 16:20). BD p. 240

Promises of God – The promises [of God] are as cork to the net, to bear up the heart from sinking in the deep waters of distress. ATFG p. 17

Providence – If in covenant with God all things shall co-operate for your good. Not only golden paths, but his bloody paths are for good. Every wind of Providence shall blow them nearer heaven. Affliction shall humble and purify (Heb. 12:10). Out of the bitterest drug God distills your salvation. Afflictions add to the saints' glory. The more the diamond is cut, the more it sparkles; the heavier the saints' cross is, the heavier shall be their crown. BD p. 160

Providence – The wheels in a watch move cross one to another, but they all carry on the motion of the watch; so the wheels of Providence often move cross to our desires, but still they carry on God's unchangeable decree. BD p. 70

Providence – As the elements, though of contrary qualities, yet God has so tempered them, that they all work in a harmonious manner for the good of the universe. Or as in a watch, the wheels seem to move contrary one to another, but all carry on the motions of the watch: so things that seem to move cross to the godly, yet by the wonderful providence of God work for their good. ATFG p. 25

Providence – Several poisonous ingredients put together, being tempered by the skill of the pharmacist, make a sovereign medicine, and work together for the good of the patient. So all God's providences, being divinely tempered and sanctified, work together for the best to the saints. He who loves God and is called according to His purpose, may rest assured that every thing in the world shall be for his good. ATFG p. 11

Providence – The most dark, cloudy providences of God have some sunshine in them. What a blessed condition is a true believer in! When he dies, he goes to God; and while he lives, everything shall do him good. Affliction is for his good. ATFG p. 56

Providence – Jacob wrestled with the angel, and the hollow of Jacob's thigh was out of joint. This was sad; but God turned it to good, for there he saw God's face, and there the Lord blessed him. 'Jacob called the name of the place Peniel, for I have seen God face to face' (Gen. 32:30). Who would not be willing to have a bone out of joint, so that he might have sight of God? ATFG p. 26

Providence – 'It is good for me that I have been afflicted' (Ps. 119:71). This text, like Moses' tree cast into the bitter waters of affliction, may make them sweet and wholesome to drink. Afflictions to the godly are medicinal. Out of the most poisonous drugs God extracts our salvation. Afflictions are as needful as ordinances (1 Pet. 1:6). No vessel can be made of gold without fire; so it is impossible that we should be made vessels of honor, unless we are melted and refined in the furnace of affliction. 'All the paths of the Lord are mercy and truth' (Ps. 25:10). As the painter intermixes bright colors with dark shadows, so the wise God mixes mercy with judgment. AFTG p. 26

Providence – Spiritual good things work for hurt to the wicked. From the flower of heavenly blessings they suck poison. The ministers of God work for their hurt. The same wind that blows one ship to heaven blows another ship upon a rock. The same breath in the ministry that blows a godly man to heaven, blows a profane sinner to hell. They who come with the word of life in their mouths, yet to many are a savor of death. ATFG p. 58

Providence – We are fed every day out of the alms-basket of God's providence. BD p. 126

Providence – The providences of God are sometimes dark, and our eyes dim, and we can hardly tell what to make of them; but when we cannot unriddle providence, let us believe that it will work together for the good of the elect (Rom. 8:28). The wheels in a clock seem to move contrary one to the other, but they help forward the motion of the clock, and make the larum strike; so the providences of God seem to be cross wheels; but for all that, they shall carry on the good of the elect. BD p. 125

Providence – All things work together for good to them that love God. To know that nothing hurts the godly, is a matter of comfort; but to be assured that ALL things which fall out shall co-operate for their good, that their crosses shall be turned into blessings, that showers of affliction water the withering root of their grace and make it flourish more; this may fill their hearts with joy till they run over. ATFG p. 8

Providence – Providence is the queen and governess of the world; it is the hand that turns the wheel of the whole creation; it sets the sun its race, the sea its bounds. If God did not guide the world, things would run into disorder and confusion. When one looks on a clock, and sees the motion of the wheels, the striking of the hammer, the hanging of the plummets, he would say, some artificer made it; so, when we see the excellent order and harmony in the universe, the sun, that great luminary, dispensing its light and heat to the world, without which the world were by a grave or a prison; the rivers sending forth their silver streams to refresh the bodies of men, and prevent a drought; and every creature acting within its sphere, and keeping its due bounds; we must needs acknowledge there is a God, who wisely orders and governs all these things. BD p. 40

Providence – Afflictions are the medicine which God uses to carry off our spiritual diseases; they cure the tumor of pride, the fever of lust, the dropsy of covetousness. Do they not work for good? ATFG p. 29

Providence – The most dark, cloudy providences of God have some sunshine in them. What a blessed condition is a true believer in! When he dies, he goes to God; and while he lives everything shall do him good. Affliction is for his good. What hurt does the fire to the gold? It only purifies it. ATFG p. 56

Providence – The evil of affliction works for good to the godly. It is one heart-quieting consideration in all the afflictions that befall us, that God has a special hand in them: 'The Almighty hath afflicted me' (Ruth 1:21). Instruments can no more stir till God gives them a commission, than the axe can cut of itself without a hand. Job eyed God in his affliction: therefore, as Augustine observes, he does not say, 'The Lord gave, and the devil took away,' but, 'The Lord hath taken away.' Whoever brings an affliction to us, it is God that sends it. ATFG p. 25

Providence – See here the wisdom of God, who can make the worst things imaginable turn to the good of the saints. He can by a divine chemistry extract gold out of dross. 'Oh the depth of the wisdom of God!' (Rom. 11:33). It is God's great design to set forth the wonder of His wisdom. The Lord made Joseph's prison a step to preferment. There was no way for Jonah to be saved, but by being swallowed up. God suffered the Egyptians to hate Israel (Ps. 106:41). God enriches by impoverishing; He causes the augmentation of Grace by the diminution of an estate. When the creature goes further from us, it is that Christ may come nearer to us. God works strangely. He brings order out of confusion, harmony out of discord. He frequently makes use of unjust men to do that which is just. He is wise in heart (Job 9:4). He can reap His glory out of men's fury (Ps. 76:10). Either the wicked shall not do the hurt that they intend, or they shall do the good which they do not intend. God often helps when there is least hope, and saves His people in that way which they think will destroy. He made use of the high-priest's malice and Judas' treason to redeem the world. ATFG p. 60

Providence – Suppose you were in a smith's shop, and should see there several sorts of tools, some crooked, some bowed, others hooked, would you condemn all these things, because they do not look handsome? The smith makes use of them all for doing his work. Thus it is with the providences of God; they seem to us to be very crooked and strange, yet they all carry on God's work. BD p. 121

Providence – It is a sin as much to quarrel with God's providence as to deny His providence. If men do not act as we would have them, they shall act as God would have them. His providence is His master-wheel that turns these lesser wheels, and God will bring His glory out of all at last. BD p. 125

Providence – All winds of providence shall blow you to heaven. Romans 8:28, 'All things work together for good.' You shall be a gainer by your losses. Your crosses shall be turned into blessings. Poverty shall starve your lusts. Sickness shall refine your grace. Persecution shall bring you nearer to God. All the stones the Jews threw at Stephen knocked him faster to Christ the cornerstone, Isa. 28:16. Every cut of God's spiritual diamonds makes them sparkle the more. MS p. 76

Reason – Some speak of the light of reason improved: alas! the plumb-line of reason is too short to fathom the deep things of God; the light of reason will no more help a man to believe, than the light of a candle will help him to understand. A man can no more by the power of nature reach Christ, than an infant can reach the top of the pyramids, or the ostrich fly up to the stars. BD p. 170

Reason – Some speak of how far reason will go if put to good use; but alas! the plumb-line of reason is too short to fathom the deep things of God. A man can no more reach the saving knowledge of God by the power of reason, than a pygmy can reach the pyramids. The light of nature will no more help us to see Christ, than the light of a candle will help us to understand. GMP p. 27

Redemption – The doctrine of redemption by Jesus Christ is a glorious doctrine; it is the marrow and quintessence of the gospel, in which all a Christian's comfort lies. Great was the work of creation, but greater the work of redemption; it cost more to redeem us than to make us; in the one there was but the speaking of a word, in the other the shedding of blood. BD p. 209

Remembering – Our sins and God's kindnesses are apt quickly to slip out of our memory. We deal with God's mercies as with flowers. When they are fresh, we smell them and put them in our bosom. But within awhile, we throw them away and mind them no more. MS p. 2

Repentance – A medicine, though it be ever so sovereign, if not applied, will do no good; though the plaster be made of Christ's own blood, it will not heal, unless applied by faith; the blood of God, without faith in God, will not save. This applying of Christ is called receiving Him (Jn. 1:12). The hand receiving gold, enriches; so the hand of faith, receiving Christ's golden merits with salvation enriches us. BD p. 216

Repentance – A man has gone on long in sin. At last God arrests him, shows him what desperate hazard he has run, and he is filled with anguish. Within a while the tempest of conscience is blown over, and he is quiet. Then he concludes that he is a true penitent because he has felt some bitterness in sin. Do not be deceived: this is not repentance. Ahab and Judas had some trouble of mind. It is one thing to be a terrified sinner and another to be a repenting sinner. DR p. 15

Repentance – It is dangerous to procrastinate repentance because the longer any go on in sin the harder they will find the work of repentance. Delay strengthens sin and hardens the heart and gives the devil fuller possession. A plant at first may be easily plucked up, but when it has spread its roots deep in the earth, a whole team cannot remove it. It is hard to remove sin when once it comes to be rooted. The longer ice freezes the harder it is to be broken. The longer a man freezes in security, the harder it will be to have his heart broken. When sin has got a haunt it is not easily shaken off. DR pp. 88-9

Repentance – What will not a sinner do, what vows will he not make, when he knows he must die and stand before the judgment seat? Self-love raises a sickbed vow, and love of sin will prevail against it. Trust not to a passionate resolution; it is raised in a storm and will die in a calm. DR p. 16

Repentance – O blessed repentance, that has such a light side with the dark, and has so much sugar at the bottom of the bitter cup! DR p. 83

Repentance – Repentance and faith are both humbling graces; by repentance a man abhors himself; by faith he goes out of himself. As Israel in their wilderness march, behind them saw Pharaoh and his chariots pursuing, before them the Red Sea ready to devour; so the sinner behind sees God's justice pursuing him for sin, before, hell ready to devour him; and in this forlorn condition, he sees nothing in himself to help, but he must perish unless he can find help in another. BD p. 216

Repentance – A broken heart and a broken Christ do well agree. The more bitterness we taste in sin, the more sweetness we shall taste in Christ. DR p. 27

Repentance – Knowledge without repentance will be but a torch to light men to hell. DR p. 77

Repentance – It should be our grief on our death-bed that our lives have had so many blanks and blots in them, that our duties have been so fly-blown with sin, that our obedience has been so imperfect, and we have gone so lame in the ways of God. When the soul is going out of the body, it should swim to heaven in a sea of tears. DR p. 28

Repentance – Wax that melts is fit for the seal. A melting soul is fit to take the stamp of all heavenly blessing. Let us give Christ the water of our tears and He will give us the wine of His blood. GMP p. 60

Repentance – This is the emblem of a moral man, who is swept by civility and garnished with common gifts, but is not washed by true repentance. The unclean spirit enters into such a one. If civility were sufficient to salvation, Christ need not have died. The civilian has a fair lamp, but it lacks the oil of grace. DR pp. 67-8

Repentance – 'Happy is the man that feareth alway' (Prov. 28:14). A sinner is like the leviathan who is made without fear (Job 41:33).

A repenting person fears and sins not; a graceless person sins and fears not. DR p. 94

Repentance – After Paul's shipwreck he swam to shore on planks and broken pieces of the ship (Acts 27:44). In Adam we all suffered shipwreck, and repentance is the only plank left us after shipwreck to swim to heaven. DR p. 13

Repentance – The penitent has a wet seed-time but a delicious harvest. Repentance breaks the abscess of sin, and then the soul is at ease. DR p. 20

Repentance – Those who are not bruised penitentially shall be broken judicially. Those whose hearts would not break for sin shall break with despair. In hell there is nothing to be seen but a heap of stones and a hammer. A heap of stones – that is hard hearts; a hammer – that is God's power and justice, breaking them in pieces. GMP p. 224

Repentance – Do not say then that there is no hope. Disband the army of your sins, and God will sound a retreat to His judgments. Remember, great sins have been swallowed up in the sea of God's infinite compassions. Manasseh made the streets run with blood, yet when his head was a fountain of tears, God grew propitious. DR p. 103

Repentance – How happy it would be if we were more deeply affected with sin, and our eyes did swim in their orb. We may clearly see the Sprit of God moving in the waters of repentance, which though troubled, are yet pure. Moist tears dry up sin and quench the wrath of God. Repentance is the cherisher of piety, the procurer of mercy. The more regret and trouble of spirit we have first at our conversion, the less we shall feel afterwards. DR p. 7

Repentance – The very day a Christian turns from sin he must enjoin himself a perpetual fast. The eye must fast from impure glances. The ear must fast from hearing slanders. The tongue must fast from oaths. The hands must fast from bribes. The feet must fast from the path of the harlot. And the soul must fast from the love of wickedness. DR p. 52

Repentance – Judge not holy weeping superfluous. Tertullian thought he was born for no other end but to repent. Either sin must drown or the soul burn. Let it not be said that repentance is difficult. Things that are excellent deserve labor. Will not a man dig for gold in the ore though it makes him sweat? It is better to go with difficulty to heaven than with ease to hell. What would the damned give that they might have a herald sent to them from God to proclaim mercy upon their repentance? What volleys of sighs and groans would they send up to heaven? What floods of tears would their eyes pour forth? But it is now too late. They may keep their tears to lament their folly sooner than to procure pity. O that we would therefore, while we are on this side of the grave, make our peace with God! Tomorrow may be our dying day; let this be our repenting day. DR p. 8

Repentance – Turning from sin is like pulling the arrow out of the wound; turning to God is like pouring in the balm. DR p. 55

Repentance – Sorrow is good for nothing but sin. If you shed tears for outward losses, it will not advantage you. Water for the garden, if poured in the sink, does no good. Powder for the eye, if applied to the arm, is of no benefit. Sorrow is medicinal for the soul, but if you apply it to worldly things it does not good. Oh that our tears may run in the right channel and our hearts burst with sorrow for sin. DR p. 63

Repentance – In true repentance the heart points directly to God as the needle to the North Pole. DR p. 55

Repentance – A real penitent turns out of the road of sin. Every sin is abandoned: as Jehu would have all the priests of Baal slain (2 Kings 10:24) – not one must escape – so a true convert seeks the destruction of every lust. He knows how dangerous it is to entertain any one sin. He that hides one rebel in his house is a traitor to the Crown, and he that indulges one sin is a traitorous hypocrite. DR p.54

Repentance – There is no rowing to paradise except upon the stream of repenting tears. Repentance is required as a qualification.

It is not so much to endear us to Christ as to endear Christ to us. Till sin be bitter, Christ will not be sweet. DR p. 63

Repentance – Turning to God makes for our profit. Our repentance is of no benefit to God, but to ourselves. If a man drinks of the fountain he benefits himself, not the fountain. If he beholds the light of the sun, he himself is refreshed by it, not the sun. If we turn from our sins to God, God is not advantaged by it. It is only we ourselves who reap the benefit. DR p. 58

Reproof – Reproof is a duty; when we see others walk irregularly, like soldiers that march out of rank and file, we ought mildly, yet gravely, to tell them of their sin (Lev. 19:17). HD p. 175

Resurrection – God can more easily raise the body out of the grave, than we can wake a man out of sleep. BD p. 307

Resurrection – When the archangel's trumpet sounds, the bodies of believers shall come out of the grave to be made happy, as the chief butler came out of the prison, and was restored to all his dignity at the court; but the bodies of the wicked shall come out of the grave, as the chief baker out of prison, to be executed (Gen. 40:21-22). BD p. 307

Salvation – To be able to say, God is mine, is more than to have all mines of gold and silver. BD p. 45

Salvation – If a man were poisoned, what a comfort would it be to him to hear that there was an herb in the garden that could heal him! If he had a gangrene in his body, and were given over by all his friends, how glad would he be to hear of a surgeon that could cure him! O sinner, you are full of sinful diseases, you have a gangrened soul; but there is a physician that can recover you. 'There is hope in Israel concerning this'; though there be an old serpent to sting us with his temptations, yet there is a brazen serpent to heal us with his blood. HD pp. 146-7

Salvation – You that have neglected a physician all this while, now when the sun of the gospel, and the sun of your life is even setting, bring your sick souls to Christ to be cured. Christ complains that though men are sick even to death, yet they will not come or send to the physician: 'Ye will not come to Me that you might have life' (Jn. 5:40). In bodily diseases the physician is the first that is sent to; in soul diseases the Physician is the last that is sent to. HD p. 147

Salvation – If we could weep rivers of tears, out-fast Moses on the mount, if we were exact moralists, touching the law blameless, if we could arrive at the highest degree of sanctification in this life, all this would not save us, without looking to the merits of Him who is God. BD p. 165

Salvation – You are happy, the lot of free grace has fallen upon you; you were once in the devil's prison, but have broken from that prison; you were once bound in the chains of sin, but God has begun to beat off your chains, and has freed you from the power of sin, and the curse due it. BD p. 213

Salvation – The will is like a garrison which holds out against God: the Spirit with sweet violence conquers, or rather changes it; making the sinner willing to have Christ upon any terms; to be ruled by Him as well as saved by Him. BD p. 217

Sanctification – It is better to be a pattern of holiness, than a partner in wickedness. It is better to go to heaven with a few, than to hell in the crowd. We must walk in an opposite course to the men of the world. ATFG p. 121

Sanctification – The Spirit of God works progressively, He carries it on from one degree to another. Pelagians hold that the beginning of grace is from God; but the progress of grace is from ourselves; so God shall be the author of our faith, and we the finishers. God shall lay the first stone, and we the superstructure. But alas, there needs the continual influence of the Spirit to the carrying on the work of grace in our hearts. Should God withdraw His Spirit from the most holy men, their grace might fail and annihilate; if the sun withdraw its light, though ever so little, there follows darkness in the air; we need not only habitual grace, but assisting, exciting, subsequent grace. The ship needs not only the sails of our abilities and endeavors, but the wind of the Spirit to blow us to the heavenly port. HD p. 158

Sanctification – It is with graces as it is with fire; if it be not blown up and increased, it will soon decay. Such as thrive not in their spiritual estate, we may perceive sadly to decline. Though a Christian cannot lose the seed of grace, yet he may lose the actings of grace and the comfort of grace. Therefore bring forth more fruit: no sooner does a Christian begin to stand still, but you may perceive him going backward. HD pp. 185-6

Sanctification – Our bodies are the temples of the Holy Ghost, our tongues must be the organs in these temples. BD p. 208

Sanctification – Dew wets the leaf, the sap is hid in the root; so the religion of some consists only in externals, but sanctification is deeply rooted in the soul. 'In the hidden part thou shalt make me to know wisdom' (Ps. 51:6). BD p. 241

Sanctification – Christian, you could defile yourself, but not sanctify yourself; but God has done it, He has not only chained up sin, but changed your nature, and made you as a king's daughter, all glorious within. He has put upon you a breastplate of holiness, which, though it may be shot at, can never be shot through. BD p.250

Sanctification – The Spirit stamps the impression of its own sanctity upon the heart, as the seal prints its likeness upon the wax. The Spirit of God in a man perfumes him with holiness, and makes his heart a map of heaven. BD p. 249

Sanctification – A hypocrite may leave sin, yet love it; as a serpent casts its coat, but keeps its sting; but a sanctified person can say he not only leaves sin, but loathes it. BD p. 246

Sanctification – Weeds grow of themselves. Flowers are planted. Sanctification is a flower of the Spirit's planting, therefore it is called, 'The sanctification of the Spirit' (1 Pet. 1:2). BD p. 241

Satan – Satan does value souls, he knows their worth; he says as the king of Sodom did to Abraham, 'Give me the persons, and take the goods to thyself.' So saith Satan, 'Give me the persons.' He cares not how rich you are, he doth not strive to take away your estates, but your souls. Give me the persons, saith he, take you the goods; whence are all his *noemata*, his warlike stratagems, his subtle snares, but to catch souls? Why does this lion so roar but for his prey? He envies the soul its happiness, he lays the whole train of temptation to blow up the whole fort-royal of the soul. Why does he lay such suitable baits? He allures the ambitious many with a crown; the covetous man with a golden apple; the sanguine man with beauty. Why does he tempt to Delilah's lap, but to keep you from Abraham's bosom? The devil is angling for the precious soul; to undo souls is his pride; he glories in the damnation of souls; it is next to victory to die revenged. If Samson must die, it is some comfort that he shall make more die with him; if Satan, that lion, must be kept in his hellish den, it is all the heaven he expects, to reach forth his paw, and pull others into the den with him. HD p.111

Scoffing – The tongue of the scoffer is the devil's gun out of which he shoots his bullets against religion. MS p. 99

Self control – Too much oil chokes the lamp, whereas a smaller quantity makes it burn more brightly. A godly man holds the golden bridle of temperance, and will not allow his table to be a snare. GMP p. 170

Self control – A godly man will not go as far as he may, lest he go further than he should; he will not swallow all that others (bribed with promotion) may plead for. It is easy to put a golden color on rotten material. GMP p. 33

Self deception – A sinner is well-conceited of himself while he dresses himself by the flattering mirror of presumption. But if he knew how loathsome and disfigured he was in God's eye, he would abhor himself in the dust. MS p. 5

Self deception – He who takes copper instead of gold, wrongs himself; the most counterfeit saint deceives others while he lives, but deceives himself when he dies. To pretend to holiness when there is none is a vain thing. What were the foolish virgins better for their blazing lamps, when they wanted oil? What is the lamp of profession without the oil of saving grace? What comfort will a show of holiness yield at last? Will painted gold enrich? painted wine refresh him that is thirsty? or painted holiness be a cordial at the hour of death? A pretense of sanctification is not to be rested in. Many ships, that have had the name of Hope, the Safeguard, the Triumph, have been cast away upon the rocks; so, many who have had the name saints, have been cast into hell. BD pp. 243-4

Self examination – A gracious soul searches whether there is any duty omitted, any sin cherished. He examines his evidences for heaven. As he will not take his gold on trust, so neither will he take his grace. He is a spiritual merchant; he casts up the estate of his soul to see what he is worth. He *'sets his house in order'*. Frequent reckonings keep God and conscience friends. A carnal person cannot abide this heart-work; he is ignorant how the affairs go in his soul. He is like a man who is well acquainted with foreign parts but a stranger in his own country. GMP p. 168

Serving – It is not enough for the servant of the vineyard that he does no hurt in the vineyard, that he does not break the trees, or destroy the hedges; if he does not do service in the vineyard, he loses his pay; so, if you do not good in your place, do not glorify God, you will lose your pay, you will miss of salvation. Oh, think of this, all you that live unserviceably! Christ cursed the barren fig tree. BD p. 8

Sin – Sin gratifies Satan. When lust or anger burn in the soul, Satan warms himself at the fire. Men's sins feast the devil. Samson was called out to make the Lords of the Philistines sport (Judg. 16:25). Likewise the sinner makes the devil sport. It is meat and drink to him to see men sin. How he laughs to see them venturing their souls for the world, as if one should venture diamonds for straws, or should fish for gudgeons with golden hooks. Every wicked man shall be indicted for a fool at the day of judgment. DR p. 112

Sin – If, then, you would show yourself godly, give a certificate of divorce to every sin. Kill the Goliath sin: 'Let not sin reign' (Rom. 6:12). GMP p. 153

Sin – We are apt to plead for sin, 'Is it not a little one?' Who would plead for the one who seeks his life? We are ready to say to the minister concerning sin, as David said to Joab concerning Absalom, 2 Sam. 18:5, 'Deal gently with the young man.' So we are ready to say, 'Sir, deal gently with my sins. Oh, do not be too sharp in your reproofs!' MS p. 50

Sin – Sin first tempts and then damns. It is first a fox and then a lion. Sin does to a man as Jael did to Sisera. She gave him milk, but then she brought him low. Judges 5:26-27, 'She put her hand to the nail, and with the hammer she smote Sisera, she smote off his head; when she had pierced and stricken through his temples, at her feet he bowed.' Sin first brings us pleasures which delight and charm the senses, and then comes with its nail and hammer. Sin does to the sinner as Absalom did to Amnon. When his heart was merry with wine, then he killed him, (2 Sam. 13:28). Sin's last act is always tragic. MS p. 20

Sin – He who hides one rebel in his house is a traitor to the crown. The person who indulges one sin is a traitorous hypocrite. GMP p. 151

Sin – Sin is such a trade that whoever follows is sure to break. What did Achan get by his wedge of gold? It was a wedge to cleave asunder his soul from God. What did Judas get by his treason? He purchased a hangman's noose. What did King Ahaz get by worshipping the gods of Damascus? They were the ruin of him and all Israel, 2 Chronicles 28:23. Sin is first comical then tragical. I may fitly apply those words of Solomon to sin, Proverbs 7:26. 'She hath cast down many wounded.' O what harvest of souls is the devil likely to have! Isaiah 5:14, 'Hell hath enlarged itself.' It is fain to make room for guests. 'Tis a matter of grief to think that the dragon should have so many followers and the lamb so few. MS pp. viii-ix

Sin – Some of the Jews would not be seen openly bowing to an idol, but they would put it in their closet or some other place and there worship it. There are many in like manner who will not sin on the balcony, or be like Absalom and sin in the sight of all Israel, 2 Samuel 16:22 (that would be to call the devil 'Father' out loud), but they shut up their shop windows and follow their trade within doors. They carry their sins cunningly. They have a private back door to hell which nobody knows of. Perhaps they live in secret adultery or secret envy and malice or secret neglect of duty. God and men's consciences know whether they are guilty of living in secret sins. MS p. 70

Sin – Sin has turned beauty into deformity; as some faces by sickness are so disfigured, and look so ghastly, they can hardly be known: so the soul of man is by sin so sadly metamorphosed (having lost the image of God) that it can hardly be known. HD pp. 124-5

Sin – Pride is the swelling of the soul, lust is the fever, error the gangrene, unbelief the plague of the heart, hypocrisy the scurvy, hardness of heart the stone, anger the frenzy, malice the wolf in the breast, covetousness the dropsy, spiritual sloth the green sickness, apostasy the epilepsy; here are eleven soul-diseases and when they come to the full height they are dangerous, and most frequently prove mortal. HD pp. 125-6

Sin – Sins against illumination and conviction make deep wounds in the soul. Other sins fetch blood; these are a stab in the heart. Every little hole in the roof lets in rain, but a crack in the foundation endangers the fall of the house. Every sin of weakness is prejudicial, but sins against illumination crack the conscience and threaten the ruin of the soul. To sin in this matter makes sin the heavier and hell the hotter. MS p. 94

Sin – Adam's leprosy cleaves to us, as Naaman's leprosy did to Gehazi (2 Kings 5:27).

Sin – Some sin out of ignorance, yet even the blind can find the way to hell. MS p. ix

Sin – Sin is the womb of sorrow and the grave of comfort. Sin turns the body into a hospital. It causes fevers, ulcers, and strokes. MS p. 6

Sin – Thus sinners walk according to the flesh. If a drunken or unclean lust calls, they gratify it. They brand as cowards all who dare not sin at the same rate as they do. These, instead of walking with God, walk contrary to Him. Lust is the compass they sail by. Satan is their pilot and hell the port they are bound for. GMP pp. 177-8

Sin – He that feeds a disease, feeds an enemy. Some diseases are starved. Starve your sins by fasting and humiliation. Either kill your sin, or your sin will kill you. HD p. 131

Sin – The sins of the wicked pierce Christ's side. The sins of the godly go to his heart. DR p. 72

Sin – It cannot but grieve the regenerate person to think he should be so foolish as, after he has felt the smart of sin, still to put this fire in his bosom again. GMP p. 57

Sin – The longer God's arrow is drawing, the deeper it will wound. Sins against patience will make a man's hell so much the hotter. DR p. 104

Sin – As in one volume there may be many works bound up, so there may be many sins in one sin. BD p. 142

Sin – A spot on the face may easily be wiped off, but to have the liver and lungs tainted is far worse. Such a pollution is sin, it has gotten into the mind and conscience (Tit. 1:15). It is compared to a menstrous cloth (Isa. 30:22), the most unclean thing under the law. A sinner's heart is like a field spread with dung. Some think sin an ornament; it is rather an excrement. Sin so besmears a person with filth that God cannot abide the sight of him: 'my soul loathed them' (Zech. 11:8). DR p. 108

Sin – The disease of sin, though it be most damnable, yet is least discernible; many a man is sin-sick, but the devil has given him such a stupefying physic that he sleeps the sleep of death, and all the thunders of the world cannot awaken him. But the Lord Jesus, this blessed physician, awakes the soul out of its lethargy, and then it is in a hopeful way of recovery. The jailer was never so near a cure, as when he cried out, 'Sirs, what must I do to be saved?' (Acts 16:30). HD p. 142

Sin – Sin is a mere cheat. While it pretends to please us, it beguiles us! Sin does as Jael did. First she brought the milk and butter to Sisera, then she struck the nail through his temples so that he died (Judg. 5:26). Sin first courts, and then kills. It is first a fox and then a lion. Whoever sin kills it betrays. DR p. 110

Sin – Sin is like the usurer who feeds a man with money and then makes him mortgage his land. Sin feeds the sinner with delightful objects and then makes him mortgage his soul. Judas pleased himself with thirty pieces of silver, but they proved deceitful riches. Ask him now how he likes his bargain. DR p. 110

Sin – Sin is like the Egyptian reed – too feeble to support us but sharp enough to wound us. MS p. 6

Sin – Sin is not only a defection, but a pollution. It is to the soul as rust is to gold, as a stain to beauty. It makes the soul red with guilt, and black with filth. BD p. 133

Sin – Sin is the devil's first-born. BD p. 133

Sin – Sin drops poison on our holy things, it infects our prayers. BD p. 133

Sin – Sin stamps the devil's image on a man. BD p. 133

Sin – The sins of the godly go nearest to God's heart. Others' sins anger God; these grieve him. The sins of the wicked pierce Christ's sides, the sins of the godly wound His heart. The unkindness of a spouse goes nearest to the heart of her husband. GMP p. 58

Sin – Sin is a coal, that not only blacks, but burns. Sin creates all our troubles; it puts gravel into our bread, wormwood in our cup. Sin rots the name, consumes the estate, buries relations. Sin shoots the flying roll of God's curses into a family and kingdom (Zech. 5:4). BD p. 136

Sin – One sin lived in will be a cankerworm to eat out the peace of conscience. It takes away the manna from the ark and leaves only a rod. 'Alas! What a scorpion lies within!' (Seneca). One sin is a pirate to rob a Christian of his comfort. One jarring string puts all the music out of tune. One sin countenanced will spoil the music of conscience. GMP p. 152

Sin – Walking in the ways of sin is like walking on the banks of a river. The sinner treads on the banks of the bottomless pit, and if death gives him a jog, he tumbles in. GMP p. 180

Sin – Sin is an enemy. It is compared to a 'serpent' (Prov. 23:32). It has four stings – shame, guilt, horror, and death. Will a man love that which seeks his death? Surely then it is better to love God than sin. God will save you, sin will damn you; is he not become foolish who loves damnation? ATFG p. 95

Sin – We are ready to charge many of our first sins to Satan's temptations, but this sin of our nature is wholly from ourselves; we cannot shift it off to Satan. We have a root within that bears gall and wormwood (Deut. 29:18). Our nature is an abyss and seminary of all evil, from whence come those scandals that infest the world. DR pp. 30-1

Sin – The besetting sin is of all others most dangerous. As Samson's strength lay in his hair, so the strength of sin lies in this beloved sin. This is like a poison striking the heart, which brings death. A godly man will lay the axe of repentance to this sin and hew it down. He sets this sin, like Uriah, in the forefront of battle, so that it may be slain. He will sacrifice this Isaac, he will pluck out this right eye, so that he may see better to go to heaven. GMP p. 150

Sin – The sin which a man does not love to have reproved is the darling sin. Herod could not endure having his incest spoken against. If the prophet meddles with that sin, it shall cost him his head. Men can be content to have other sins declaimed against, but if the minister puts his finger on the sore, and touches this sin, their hearts begin to burn in malice against him. GMP p. 148

Sin – There is usually one sin that is the favorite, the sin which the heart is most fond of. A beloved sin lies in a man's bosom as the disciple whom Jesus loved leaned on His bosom. GMP p. 148

Sin – All will not sin on a balcony but perhaps they will sin behind the curtain. Rachel did not carry her father's images like a saddle cloth to be exposed to public view, but she put them under her and sat on them (Gen. 31:34). Many carry their sins secretly like a candle in a dark lantern. GMP p. 147

Sin – One sin will make way for more, as a little thief can open the door to more. Sins are linked and chained together. One sin will draw on more. David's adultery made way for murder. One sin never goes alone. If there is only one nest egg, the devil can brood on it. GMP pp. 151-2

Sin – Not only the plowing but the praying of the wicked is sin: 'The sacrifice of the wicked is an abomination to the Lord' (Prov. 15:8; 21:4). If the water is foul in the well, it cannot be clean in the bucket. If the heart is full of sin, the duties cannot be pure. GMP p. 192

Sin – Sinners have no sense of god in them: 'who being past feeling' (Eph. 4:19). All their moral endowments are only flowers strewn on a dead corpse, and what is hell but a sepulcher to bury the dead in? GMP p. 192

Sin – Sin is the Trojan horse out of which comes a whole army of troubles. I need not name them because almost everyone feels them. While we suck the honey we are pricked with the briar. Sin gives a dash in the wine of our comforts; it digs our grave (Rom. 5:12). DR p. 51

Sin – If only one sin is allowed in the soul, you leave open a gap for the devil to enter. It is a simile of Chrysostom that a soldier may have his helmet and his breastplate on, but if only one place has no armor, the bullet may enter there and he may as well be shot as if he had no armor on. So if you favor only one sin, you leave a part of your soul unprotected and the bullet of God's wrath may enter there and shoot you. One sin may shut you out of heaven. And as Jerome says, what difference is there between being shut out for more sins and for one? Therefore, beware of cherishing one sin. One millstone will sink a man into the sea as well as a hundred. GMP pp. 152-3

Sincerity – Sincerity is a Christian's ensign of glory; it is both his breastplate to defend him and his crown to adorn him. GMP p. 101

Sincerity – Sincerity is what the devil attacks most. Satan's spite was not so much at Job's estate, as his integrity; he would have wrested the shield of sincerity from him, but Job held that fast (Job 27:6). A thief does not fight for an empty purse but for money. The devil would have robbed Job of the jewel of a good conscience, and then he would have been poor Job indeed. Satan does not oppose profession, but sincerity. Let men go to church and make glorious pretences of holiness. Satan does not oppose this; this does him no hurt and them no good; but if men want to be sincerely pious, then Satan musters up all his forces against them. Now what the devil most assaults, we must strive most to maintain. Sincerity is our fort royal, where our chief treasure lies. This fort is most shot at, therefore let us be more careful to preserve it. While a man keeps his castle, his castle will keep him. While we keep sincerity, sincerity will keep us. GMP pp. 100-1

Slander – The scorpion carries its poison in its tail, the slanderer in his tongue. His words pierce deep like the quills of the porcupine. DR p. 37

Slothfulness – Some boast of their high calling, but they lie idly at anchor. Religion does not seal warrants to idleness. Christians must not be slothful. Idleness is the devil's bath; a slothful person becomes a prey to every temptation. Grace while it cures the heart, does not make the hand lame. He who is called of God, as he works for heaven, so he works in his trade. ATFG p. 118

Sorrow for the lost – Sinners in scarlet are not the objects of envy, but pity; they are under 'the power of Satan' (Acts 26:18). They tread every day on the brink of the bottomless pit; and what death should cast them in! O pity unconverted sinners! If you pity an ox or an ass going astray, will you not pity a soul going astray from God, who has lost his way and his wits, and is upon the precipice of damnation. ATFG pp. 119-20

Sorrow – Spiritual sorrow will sink the heart if the pulley of faith does not raise it. As our sin is ever before us, so God's promise must be ever before us. As we much feel our sting, so we must look up to Christ our brazen serpent. Some have faces so swollen with worldly grief that they can hardly look out of their eyes. That weeping is not good which blinds the eye of faith. If there are not some dawnings of faith in the soul, it is not the sorrow of humiliation but of despair. DR p. 22

Soul – The soul is a sparkling diamond set in a ring of clay. The soul is the bird of paradise that soars aloft; it may be compared to the wings of the cherubim, it has a winged swiftness to fly to heaven. The soul is capable of communion with God and angels. The soul is God's house He has made to dwell in. The understanding, will and affections are the three stories in this house. What pity is it that this goodly building should be let out, and the devil become tenant in it. HD p. 108

Soul – How sad it is that the soul, that princely thing, which is made for communion with God and angels, should be put to the mill to grind, and made a slave to the earth! How like the prodigal the soul has become, choosing rather to converse with swine and feed upon husks than to aspire after communion with the blessed Deity! Thus does Satan befool men, and keep them from heaven by making them seek a heaven here. GMP p. 107

Soul – The soul is a glass wherein some rays of divine glory shine, and much of God is to be seen in it. Though this glass be cracked by the fall, yet it shall one day be perfect; we read of spirits of just men made perfect (Heb. 12:23). The soul since the fall of Adam, may be compared to the moon in its conjunction, very much obscured by sin; but when it is sanctified by the Spirit, and translated from there, it shall be as the moon in the full, shining forth in its perfect glory. HD p. 112

Soul – There are four sorts of persons that abuse souls. Firstly, they degrade their souls that set the world above their souls; 'Who pant after the dust of the earth' (Amos 2:7). As if a man's house were on fire, and he should take care to preserve the lumber, but let his child be burnt in the fire.... Secondly, they abuse their souls that sell their souls. The covetous person sells his soul for money. As it is said of the lawyer, he hath a tongue that will be sold for a fee, so the

covetous man has a soul that he is to be set for money. Achan did
sell his soul for a wedge of gold. Judas did sell his soul for silver;
Judas sold cheap pennyworths; for thirty pieces of silver he did sell
Christ, who was more worth than heaven and his own soul which
was more worth than a world! How many have damned their souls
with money? (1 Tim. 6:9-10). HD p. 115

Soul – The soul is the glory of the creation; the soul is a beam of
God; it is a sparkle of celestial brightness, as Demascen called it; it
is, according to Plato, a glass of the Trinity. HD p. 107

Soul – The soul moves to God, as to its rest: 'Return to thy rest, O
my soul' (Ps. 116:7). He is the ark to which this dove flies; nothing
but God can fill a heaven-born soul; if the earth were turned into a
globe of gold, it could not fill the heart, it would still cry, Give, give.
The soul being spiritual, God only can be the adequate object of it.
HD p. 109

Sovereignty of Christ – He rules by love. He is a king full of mercy
and clemency; as He has a scepter in His hand, so an olive branch
of peace in His mouth. Though He be the Lion of the tribe of Judah
for majesty, yet He is the Lamb of God for meekness. His regal rod
has honey at the end of it. He sheds abroad His love into the heart
of His subjects; He rules them with promises as well as precepts.
This makes all His subjects become volunteers; they are willing to
pay their allegiance to Him. 'Thy people shall be a willing people'
(Ps. 110:3). BD p. 188

Speaking – God has given us two ears, but one tongue, to show that
we should be swift to hear, but slow to speak. God has set a double
fence before the tongue, the teeth, and the lips, to teach us to be
wary that we offend not with our tongue. BD p. 115

Spiritual blindness – In the dark the greatest beauty is hid. Let there
be rare flowers in the garden, and pictures in the room, in the dark
their beauty is veiled over; so, though there be such transcendent
beauty in Christ as amazes the angels, man in the state of nature
sees none of this beauty. BD p. 169

Spiritual blindness – [Satan] rules the understanding. He blinds men with ignorance, and then rules them; as the Philistines first put out Samson's eyes, and then bound him. Satan can do what he will with the ignorant man; because he does not see the error of his way, the devil can lead him into any sin. BD p. 149

Spiritual blindness – We pity blind men. How is every graceless man to be pitied whom the god of this world has blinded, 2 Corinthians 4:4? The devil carries a wicked man as the falconer does the hawk, hoodwinked to hell. But he does not see the danger he is in. He is like a bird that hastens to the snare and does not see the snare. MS p. 55

Stewardship – The Lord has sent us into the world, as a merchant sends his factor beyond the seas to trade for him. We live to God when we trade for his interest, and propagate His gospel. God has given every man a talent; and when a man does not hide it in a napkin, but improves it for God, he lives to God. BD p. 14

Study – David valued the Word more than gold. What would the martyrs have given for a leaf of the Bible! The Word is the field where Christ the pearl of price is hid. In this sacred mine we dig, not for a wedge of gold, but for a weight of glory. The Scripture is a sacred eye-salve to illuminate us. 'The commandment is a lamp, and the law is light' (Prov. 6:23). The Scripture is the chart and compass by which we sail to the new Jerusalem. It is a sovereign cordial in all distresses. What are the promises but the water of life to renew fainting spirits? BD pp. 35-6

Study – Oh how many can be looking at their faces in a glass all the morning, but their eyes begin to be sore when they look upon a Bible! Heathens die for want of Scripture, and these in contempt of it. They surely must needs go wrong who slight their guide. Such as lay the reigns upon the neck of their lusts, and never use the curbing bit of Scripture to check them, are carried to hell, and never stop. BD p. 33

Suffering – To bless God in heaven when He is crowning us with glory is no wonder, but to bless God when He is correcting us, to bless Him in a prison, to give thanks on a sickbed, not only to kiss the rod but to bless that hand that holds it, here is the sun in its zenith. This speaks a very high degree of grace, indeed, and very much adorns our sufferings. MS p. 49

Suffering – If Jesus Christ should have said to us, 'I love you well, you are dear to me, but I cannot suffer, I cannot lay down my life for you,' we should have questioned His love very much; and may not Christ suspect us, when we pretend to love Him, and yet will endure nothing for Him? ATFG pp. 85-6

Suffering – Has Christ waded through a sea of blood and wrath, to purchase my peace? Has He not only made peace, but spoken peace to me? How should my heart ascend in a fiery chariot of love! How willingly should I be to do and suffer for Christ! BD p. 265

Sufficiency of God – We can think, what if all the dust were turned to silver, if every flower were a ruby, every sand in the sea a diamond; yet God can give more than we can think, because He is infinite. BD p. 53

Superstition – The snake has a fine color, but it has a sting. So outwardly men may look zealous and devout, but retain a sting of hatred in their hearts against goodness. Hence it is that they who have been most hot on superstition have been most hot on persecution. GMP pp. 36-7

Temptation – [The godly] have good foresight. They foresee the evil of a temptation: 'we are not ignorant of his devices' (2 Cor. 2:11). The wicked swallow temptation like pills, and when it is too late, feel these pills afflict their conscience. But the godly foresee a temptation and will not come near. They see a snake under the grass; they know Satan's kindness is craftiness. He does what Jephthah's daughter did: he brings out the tambourine and dances before men with a temptation and then brings them very low (Judg. 11:35). GMP p. 199

Temptation of Christ – Temptation to Christ was like a spark of fire upon a marble pillar, which glides off. BD p. 202

Temptation – Satan will be sure to besiege the weakest Christian; all his darts fly that way, and a strong temptation may overcome a weak faith. But a flourishing faith stands like a cedar, and it is not blown down by the wind of temptation. A strong faith can stop the mouth of the devil, that roaring lion (1 Pet. 5:8). HD p. 184

Thankfulness – You who are enriched with treasures of godliness, bless God for it. This flower does not grow in nature's garden. You had enlisted yourselves under the devil and taken pay on his side, fighting against your own happiness, and then God came with converting grace and put for a loving and gentle violence, causing you to espouse his quarrel against Satan! You had lain many years soaking in wickedness, as if you had been parboiled for hell, and then God laid you steeping in Christ's blood and breathed holiness into your heart! Oh, what cause you have to write yourselves as eternal debtors to free grace! He who does not give God the praise for His grace denies that God is its author. GMP pp. 220-1

Thankfulness – An unthankful person is a monster in nature, a paradox in Christianity. He is the scorn of heaven and the plague of earth. An ungrateful man never does well except in one thing – that is, when he dies. GMP p. 137

Threatening of God – God's threats are like the buoy, which shows the rocks in the sea and threatens death to such as come near. The threat is a curbing bit to check us, so that we may not run in full career to hell. There is mercy in every threat. GMP p. 61

Time – Make spending your time a matter of conscience: 'redeeming the time' (Eph. 5:16). Many people fool away their time, some in idle visits, others in recreations and pleasures which secretly bewitch the heart and take it away from better things. What are our golden hours for but to attend to our souls? Time misspent is not time lived but time lost. Time is a precious commodity. A piece of wax in itself is not worth much, but when it is affixed to the label of a will and conveys an estate, it is of great value. Thus, time simply in itself is not so considerable, but as salvation is to be worked out in it, and a conveyance of heaven depends on using it well, it is of infinite concern. GMP p. 207

Transformation – As a painter looking at a face draws a face like it in the picture, so looking at Christ in the mirror of the gospel, we are changed into His similitude. GMP p. 23

Trials – When we are brought low, let our faith be high. Let us believe that God intends us no harm. Though He casts us into the deep, He will not drown us. Believe that He is still a Father. He afflicts us in as much mercy as He gives Christ to us. By His rod of discipline, He fits us for the inheritance, Col. 1:12. Oh, let this star of faith appear in the dark night of affliction. Jonah's faith was never more in heaven than when he lay in the belly of hell, (Jon. 2:4). MS pp. 43-4

Trinity – The Trinity is purely an object of faith; the plumb line of reason is too short to fathom this mystery; but where reason cannot wade, there faith may swim. BD p. 112

Trinity – Our narrow thoughts can no more comprehend the Trinity in Unity, than a nut-shell will hold all the water in the sea. BD p. 109

Truth – Truth is the most orient pearl in Christ's crown. Let us contend for the truth, as one would for a large sum of money, that it should not be wrested out of his hand. BD p. 208

Truth – A godly man holds no more than he will die for. The martyrs were so confirmed in the knowledge of the truth that they would seal it with their blood. GMP p. 21

Truth – We have not a richer jewel to trust God with than our souls, nor has God a richer jewel to trust us with than His truth. Truth is a beam that shines from God. Much of His glory lies in His truth. BD p. 15

Unbelief – 'He that believeth not, the wrath of God abideth on him' (Jn. 3:36). Whoever lacks grace is like someone who lacks pardon; every hour he is in fear of execution. How can a wicked man rejoice? Over his head hangs the sword of God's justice and under him hell-fire burns. GMP p. 195

Unbeliever – If the devil bids a man lie or steal, he does not refuse; and, what is worse, he willingly obeys this tyrant. Other slaves are forced against their will: 'Israel sighed by reason of their bondage' (Exod. 2:23); but sinners are willing to be slaves, they will not take their freedom; they kiss their fetters. BD p. 150

Unbeliever – By sin we are enslaved to Satan, who is a hater of mankind, and writes all his laws in blood. Sinners before conversion are under Satan's command; as the ass at the command of the driver, so he does all the devils' drudgery. No sooner Satan tempts but he obeys. As the ship is at the command of the pilot, who steers it which way he will, so is the sinner at the command of Satan; and he ever steers the ship into hell's mouth. The devil rules all the powers and faculties of a sinner. BD p. 149

Unbeliever – Nothing of God can be seen in an unsanctified man, but you may see Satan's picture in him. Envy is the devil's eye, hypocrisy his cloven foot; but nothing of God's image can be seen in him. BD p. 248

Unbeliever – Sad, if all a man eats should turn to poison; yet the sinner eats and drinks his own damnation at God's table. Thus it is before conversion. As the love of God makes every bitter thing sweet, so the curse of God makes every sweet thing bitter. BD p. 151

Understanding – Sin does corrupt the *understanding*. Gregory Nazianzene calls the understanding the lamp of reason. This lamp burns dim: 'Having their understanding darkened' (Eph. 4:18); sin has drawn a veil over the understanding, it has cast a mist before our eyes, that we neither know God nor ourselves. Naturally we are only wise to do evil (Jer. 4:22). Witty at sin, wise to damn ourselves; the understanding becomes defiled. We can no more judge of spiritual objects till the Spirit of God anoint our eyes, than a blind man can judge of colors; our understandings are subject to mistakes; 'we call evil good, and good evil; we put bitter for sweet and sweet for bitter' (Isa. 5:20). A straight stick under water seems crooked; so to a natural understanding the straight line of truth seems crooked. HD p. 122

Unfruitfulness – O how many unfruitful hearers are there, who evaporate into nothing but froth and fume, being like those ears which run out all into straw! They give God neither the early fruit nor the latter. There are many Christians like arbors, covered only with the leaves of profession, they may be compared to the wood of the vine, which is good for nothing (Ezek. 15:2-5). HD p. 179

Unfruitfulness – They that do not bring forth good fruit shall never taste of the fruits that grow in heaven. Heaven is the garden of God, the paradise of pleasure, where the most rare delicious fruits grow; there are fruits that the angels themselves delight to feed on. If you do not bring God your fruit, you shall never taste His fruit: you that do not bring forth the fruits of righteousness shall never taste the fruits of paradise. HD p. 180

Unrepentance – Sin unrepented of brings final damnation. The canker that breeds in the rose is the cause of its perishing; and the corruptions that breed in men's souls are the cause of their damning. Sin, without repentance, brings the 'second death', that is, Bernard, 'a death always dying', (Rev. 20:14). Sin's pleasure will turn to sorrow at last; like the book the prophet did eat, sweet in the mouth, but bitter in the belly (Ezek. 3:3; Rev. 10:9). Sin brings the wrath of God, and what bucket or engines can quench that fire? 'Where the worm never dies, and the fire is not quenched' (Mk. 9:44). BD p. 36

Vainglory – They rob God, who take the glory due to God to themselves. 1. If they set the crown upon their own head, not considering that, 'Thou shalt remember the Lord thy God, for it is He that gives you power to get wealth' (Deut. 8:18). 2. If they do any duty of religion, they look to their own glory, 'That they may be seen of men' (Matt. 6:5); that they may be set upon a theater for others to admire and canonize them. The oil of vainglory feeds their lamp. How many by the wind of popular breath have been blown to hell! Whom the devil cannot destroy by intemperance, he does by vainglory. BD p. 19

Watchfulness – When you have prayed against sin, watch against temptation. Most wickedness in the world is committed for want of watchfulness. Watchfulness maintains godliness. It is the edging which keeps religion from fraying. GMP p. 207

Will – The *will* is diseased. The will is the soul's commander-in-chief, it is the master-wheel; but how irregular and eccentric is it! The will in the creation was like that golden bridle which Minerva was said to put upon Pegasus to guide and rule him; it did answer to God's will. This was the language of the will in innocency, 'I delight to do thy will, O God' (Ps. 40:8). But now it is distempered, like an iron sinew that refuses to yield and bend to God (Isa. 48:4); 'Ye will not come to Me, that you might have life' (Jn. 5:40). Men will rather die than come to their physician. HD pp. 122-3

Wisdom of God – The wisdom of God is seen in making the most desperate evils turn to the good of His children. As several poison ingredients, wisely tempered by the skill of the artist make a sovereign medicine, so God makes the most deadly afflictions co-operate for the good of His children. He purifies them, and prepares them for heaven (2 Cor. 4:17). These hard frosts hasten the spring flowers of glory. The wise God, by a divine chemistry, turns afflictions into cordials. He makes His people gainers by losses, and turns their crosses into blessings. BD p. 75

Wisdom of God – We must not ask a reason of God's will; it is dangerous to pry into God's ark; we are not to dispute but adore. BD p. 192

Witnessing – If Christ appears for us in heaven, then we must appear for Him upon earth. Christ is not ashamed to carry our names on His breast, and shall we be ashamed of His truth? Does He plead our cause, and shall we not stand up in His cause? What a might argument is this to stand up for the honor of Christ in times of apostasy! Christ is interceding for us. Does He present our names in heaven, and shall not we profess His name on earth? BD p. 185

Witnessing – A Christian should be both a magnet and a diamond; a magnet, in drawing others to Christ: a diamond, in casting a sparkling luster of holiness in his life. Oh let us be so just in our dealings, so true in our promises, so devout in our worship, so unblamable in our lives, that we may be the walking pictures of Christ. BD p. 202

Word of God – The motions of the Spirit are always consonant with the Word. The Word is the chariot in which the Spirit of God rides; whichever way the tide of the Word runs, that way the wind of the Spirit blows. GMP p. 68

Word of God – The Word shows what is truth and what is error. It is the field where the pearl of price is hidden. How we should dig for this pearl! A godly man's heart is the library to hold the Word of God; it dwells richly in him (Col. 3:16). GMP p. 61

Word of God – Chrysostom compares the Scripture to a garden set with knots and flowers. A godly man delights to walk in this garden and sweetly solace himself. He loves every branch and part of the Word. GMP p. 60

Word of God – The Word written is our pillar of fire to guide us. It shows us what rocks we are to avoid; it is the map by which we sail to the new Jerusalem. GMP p. 63

Word of God – The Book of God has no errata in it; it is a beam of the Sun of Righteousness, a crystal stream flowing from the fountain of life. All laws and edicts of men have had their corruption but the Word of God has not the least tincture, it is of meridian splendor. 'Thy word is very pure' (Ps. 119:140), like wine that comes from the grape, which is not mixed nor adulterated. It is so pure that it purifies everything else. BD p. 28

Word of God – But alas, how can they who are seldom conversant with the Scriptures say they love them? Their eyes begin to be sore when they look at a Bible. The two testaments are hung up like rusty armor which is seldom or never made use of. The Lord wrote the law with His own finger, but though God took pains to write, men will not take pains to read. They would rather look at a pair of cards than at a Bible. GMP p. 65

Word of God – The Scripture is like the garden of Eden: as it has a tree of life in it, so it has a flaming sword at its gates. This is the threatening of the Word. It flashes fire in the face of every person who goes on obstinately in wickedness. GMP p. 60

Word of God – The Scripture is profitable for all things. If we are deserted, here is spiced wine that cheers the heavy heart; if we are pursued by Satan, here is the sword of the Spirit to resist him; if we are diseased with sin's leprosy, here are the waters of the sanctuary, both to cleanse and cure. Oh, then, search the Scriptures! There is no danger in tasting this tree of knowledge. BD p. 35

Word of God – The Word is a jewel; the heart is the cabinet where it must be locked up. Many hide the Word in their memory, but not in their heart. And why would David enclose the Word in his heart? 'That I might be kept from sinning against Thee.' As a man would carry an antidote about him when he comes near an infected place, so a godly man carries the Word in his heart as a spiritual antidote to preserve him from the infection of sin. Why have so many been poisoned with error, others with moral vice, but because they have not hidden the Word as a holy antidote in their heart? GMP p. 62

Word of God – A pious soul meditates on the truth and holiness of the Word. He not only has a few transient thoughts, but leaves his mind steeping in the Scripture. By meditation, he sucks from this sweet flower and ruminates on holy truths in his mind. GMP p. 62

Word of God – This sword of the Spirit cuts down vice (Eph. 6:17). Out of this tower of Scripture is thrown a millstone upon the head of sin. The Scripture is the royal law which commands not only the actions, but affections; it binds the heart to good behavior. Where is there such holiness to be found, as is dug out of this sacred mine? Who could be the author of such a book but God Himself? BD p. 28

Word of God – The Word of God has never wanted enemies to oppose, and, if possible, to extirpate it. They have given out a law concerning Scripture, as Pharaoh did the midwives, concerning the Hebrew women's children, to strangle it in the birth; but God has preserved this blessed Book inviolable to this day. The devil and his agents have been blowing at Scripture light, but could never blow it out; a clear sign that it was lighted from heaven. BD p. 27

Word of God – How sweetly does this harp of Scripture sound, what heavenly music does it make in the ears of the distressed sinner, especially when the finger of God's Spirit touches this instrument! There is divinity in Scripture. It contains the marrow and quintessence of religion. It is a rock of diamonds, a mystery of piety. The lips of Scripture have grace poured into them. The Scripture speaks of faith, self denial, and all the graces which as a chain of pearls, adorns a Christian. BD p. 34

Word of God – The design of the Word is to be a test whereby our grace is to be tried; a sea-mark to show us what rocks are to be avoided. BD p. 31

Word of God – It is true, the church is a pillar of truth; but it does not therefore follow that the Scripture has its authority from the church. The king's proclamation is fixed on the pillar, the pillar holds it out, that all may read, but the proclamation does not receive its authority from the pillar, but from the king; so the church holds forth the Scriptures, but they do not receive their authority from the church, but from God. BD p. 30

Word of God – As the spirits are conveyed through the arteries of the body, so divine comforts are conveyed through the promises of the Word. BD p. 29

Works – Works are not required for the justification of our persons, but as an attestation of our love to God; not as the cause of our salvation, but as an evidence of our adoption. Works are required in the covenant of grace, not so much in our own strength as in the strength of another. 'It is God which worketh in you' (Phil. 2:13). As a teacher guides a child's hand, and helps him to form his letters, so that it is not so much the child's writing as the master's, so our obedience is not so much our working as the Spirit's co-working. BD p. 129

Works – In the first covenant, works were required as the condition of life; in the second, they are required only as the signs of life. In the first covenant, works were required as grounds of salvation; in the new covenant, they are required as evidences of our love to God. In the first, they were required to the justification of our persons; in the new, to the manifestation of our grace. BD p. 156

Works – We must not only cast ourselves into Christ's arms to be saved by Him, but we must cast ourselves at His feet to serve Him. BD p. 204

Works – Good works are not an usher to go before justification but a handmaid to follow it. BD p. 230

World – As birds that light upon the ground to pick up a little seed, immediately fly up to heaven again; so the redeemed of the Lord use the world, and take the lawful comforts of it, but their hearts are presently off these things and then ascend to heaven. They live here, and trade above. BD p. 213

World – The Arabic proverb is, 'The world is a carcass, and they who hunt after it are dogs.' MS p. 46

World – The world is but a great inn where we are to stay a night or two and be gone. What madness it is so to set our heart upon our inn as to forget our home! GMP p. 109

World – The world is only a passage-room to eternity; the world is to us as the wilderness was to Israel, not to rest in, but to travel through to the glorious Canaan. The world is a dressing-room to dress our souls in, not a place where we are to stay for ever. The apostle tells us of the world's funeral. 'The elements shall melt with fervent heat, the earth also and the works that are therein shall be burnt up' (2 Pet. 3:10). BD pp. 115-6

Worldliness – Take heed of the world. It is hard for a clod of dust to become a star. 'Love not the world' (1 Jn. 2:15). Many would like to be godly, but the honors and profits of the world divert them. Where the world fills the heart, there is no room for Christ. GMP p. 206

Worldliness – The world eats the heart out of godliness, as the ivy eats the heart out of the oak. The world kills with her silver darts. GMP p. 206

Worldliness – The world thinks that religion to be best which, like gold-leaf, is spread very thin. GMP p. 177

Worldly pleasures – Pride and luxury are the two worms that are bred of worldly pleasures. BD p. 269

Worldly pleasures – All worldly delights have a death's-head set on them. They are only shadows and they are fleeting. Earthly comforts are like Paul's friends, who took him to the ship and left him there (Acts 20:38). So these will bring a man to his grave and then take their farewell. GMP pp. 203-4

Worship – It is the same with us as it was with Abraham when he was going to worship – the birds came down on the sacrifice (Gen. 15:11). GMP p. 163

Worship – Whatever is not of God's own appointment in His worship He looks upon as 'strange fire'. And no wonder He is so highly incensed at it, for it is as if God were not wise enough to appoint the manner in which He will be served. Men will try to direct Him, and as if the rules for His worship were defective, they will attempt to correct the copy, and superadd their inventions. GMP p. 35

Worship – This divine worship God is very jealous of; it is the apple of His eye, the pearl of His crown; which He guards, as He did the tree of life, with cherubims and flaming sword, that no man may come near it to violate it. Divine worship must be such as God Himself has appointed, else it is offering strange fire (Lev. 10:1). BD p. 8

Wrath – As guilt increases so does wrath. Every sin committed is a stick to heat hell and make it hotter. It is a thing to be lamented that men should live in the world only to increase their torments in hell. MS p. 68

Wrath – Oh, sinner, who still wallows in your swinish filthiness, do you know what an enemy you have in the field? It is He who stretches out the heavens and laid the foundations of the earth, Isa. 51:13, who rebukes the wind and bridles the sea. It is He who can look you into your grave, who can bind you in chains above the devils; and will you go on to provoke Him? MS p. 74

Wrath – God is the best friend but the worst enemy. If He can look men into their grave, how far can He throw them? 'Who knows the power of His wrath' (Ps. 90:11)? What fools are they, who, for a drop of pleasure, drink a sea of wrath! BD p. 44

Zeal – When we are zealous in devotion, and our heart waxes hot within us, here is a fire from heaven kindling our sacrifice. How odious it is for a man to be all fire when he is sinning, and all ice when he is praying! A pious heart, like water seething hot, boils over in holy affections. GMP p. 115

Zeal – The Jews did not spare any cost in their idolatrous worship. No, they 'cause their sons and daughters to pass through the fire to Molech' (Jer. 32:35). They were so zealous in their idol worship that they would sacrifice their sons and daughters to their false gods. How far the purblind heathen went in their false zeal! When the tribunes of Rome complained that they wanted gold in their treasuries to offer to Apollo, the Roman matrons plucked off their chains of gold and rings and bracelets and gave them to the priests to offer up sacrifice. Were these so zealous in their sinful worship, and will you not be zealous in the worship of the true God? GMP pp. 117-8

Zeal – Christ's zeal was hotter than the fire, and His holiness purer than the sun. GMP p. 114

Zeal – In this let us be like Christ, zealous for God's truth and glory, which are the two orient pearls of the crown of heaven. Zeal is as needful for a Christian as salt for the sacrifice, or fire on the altar. Zeal without prudence is rashness; prudence without zeal is cowardliness. Without zeal, our duties are not acceptable to God. Zeal is like rosin to the bow-strings, without which the lute makes no music. BD p. 201

Zeal – The Pharisees were more zealous about washing their cups than their hearts. GMP p. 113

Zeal – Zeal is a mixed affection, a compound of love and anger. GMP p. 112

SELECT BIBLIOGRAPHY

Adams, Jay E. *Sense Appeal in the Sermons of Charles Haddon Spurgeon.* Grand Rapids: Baker Book House, 1975.

_____. *Truth Apparent: Essays on Biblical Preaching.* Phillipsburg: Presbyterian and Reformed, 1982.

_____. *Preaching With Purpose: The Urgent Task of Homiletics.* Grand Rapids: Zondervan Publishing House, 1982.

Barstow, Lewis O. *Representative Modern Preachers.* New York: The MacMillan Co., 1904.

Baxter, Batsell Barrett. *The Heart of the Yale Lectures.* New York: The MacMillan Co., 1947.

Baumann, J. Daniel. *An Introduction to Contemporary Preaching.* Grand Rapids: Baker Book House, 1972.

Baxter, Richard. *The Reformed Pastor.* First published in 1656; abridged edition 1829; Fifth edition abridgement 1862; reprinted Carlisle: The Banner of Truth Trust, 1974.

Beecher, Henry Ward. *Yale Lectures on Preaching.* Boston: The Pilgrims Press, 1902.

Blackwood, Andrew W. *Preaching from the Bible.* New York: Abingdon–Cokesbury Press, 1941.

_____. *The Preparation of Sermons.* New York: Abingdon Press, 1948.

_____. *Expository Preaching For Today.* Grand Rapids: Baker Book House, 1975.

Blaiklock, E. *Word Pictures from the Bible.* Grand Rapids: Zondervan Publishing House, 1969.

Bolton, Samuel, Nathaniel Vincent and Thomas Watson. *The Puritans on Conversion.* Morgan: Soli Deo Gloria, 1990.

Breed, David R. *Preparing to Preach.* New York: George H. Doran, 1911.

Bridges, Charles. *The Christian Ministry.* First published in 1830; reprinted, Carlisle: The Banner of Truth Trust, 1991.

Broadus, John A. *On the Preparation and Delivery of Sermons.* New York: Harper & Brothers, 1944.

Brown, Charles Reynolds. *The Art of Preaching.* New York: MacMillan, 1922.

Bryan, Dawson C. *The Art of Illustrating Sermons.* New York: Abingdon – Cokesbury Press, 1938.

Bull, Paul B. *Lectures on Preaching and Sermon Construction.* New York: The MacMillan Co., 1932.

Bullinger, E. W. *Figures of Speech Used in the Bible.* Grand Rapids: Baker Book House, 1968.

Burrell, David James. *The Sermon: Its Construction and Delivery.* Chicago: Fleming H. Revell, 1913.

Buttrick, David. *Homiletic Moves and Structures.* Philadelphia: Fortress Press, 1987.

Byington, Edwin H. *Pulpit Mirrors.* New York: George H. Doran, 1927.

Caird, G. B. *Language and Imagery of the Bible.* Philadelphia: The Westminster Press, 1980.

Calamy, Edmond. *The Nonconformists Memorial.* Volumes 1–3. London: J. Cundree, 1802.

Cox, James W. *Preaching.* San Francisco: Harper & Row, 1985.

Davies, Horton. *The Worship of the English Puritans.* First printed by Dacre Press, 1948; reprinted, Morgan: Soli Deo Gloria, 1997.

Davis, Henry Grady. *Design for Preaching.* Philadelphia: Fortress Press, 1958.

Demaray, Donald E. *An Introduction to Homiletics.* Grand Rapids: Baker Book House, 1990.

_____. *Pulpit Giants: What Made Them Great.* Chicago: Moody Press, 1973.

Doughty, W. L. *John Wesley Preacher.* London: Epworth Press, 1955.

Duduit, Michael. *Communicate With Power.* Grand Rapids: Baker Book House, 1996.

Edwards, John. *A Primer of Homiletics.* London: The Epworth Press, 1932.

Elbow, Peter. *Writing with Power: Techniques for Mastering the Writing Process.* New York: Oxford University Press, 1981.

Elliot, Emory. *Power and the Pulpit in Puritan New England.* Princeton: Princeton University Press, 1975.

Erickson, Millard J. and James L. Heflin. *Old Wine in New Wineskins.* Grand Rapids: Baker Book House, 1997.

Etter, John W. *The Preacher and His Sermon.* Dayton: United Brethren Publishing House, 1988.

Evans, William. *How to Prepare Sermons and Gospel Address.* Chicago: The Bible Institute Colportage Association, 1913.

Fabun, Don. *Communications: The Transfer of Meaning.* Beverly Hills: Glencoe Press, 1974.

Fant, Clyde E. *Preaching for Today.* San Francisco: Harper & Row, 1987.

Freeman, Harold. *Variety in Biblical Preaching.* Waco: Word Books.

Fritz, John H. C. *The Essentials of Preaching.* St. Louis: Concordia Publishing House, 1948.

Garrison, Webb B. *Creative Imagination in Preaching.* New York: Abingdon Press, 1960.

_____. *The Preacher and His Audience.* Los Angeles: Fleming H. Revell, 1954.

Garvie, Alford Ernest. *A Guide to Preachers.* New York: George H. Doran, 1906.

_____. *The Christian Preacher.* Charles Scribner's Sons, 1921.

Greidanus, Sidney. *Preaching Christ from the Old Testament.* Grand Rapids: William B. Eerdmans, 1999.

Henry, Hugh T. *Hints to Preachers.* New York: Benzinger Brothers, 1924.

Hoyt, Arthur S. *The Work of Preaching.* New York: MacMillan, 1925.

Jones, Winston E. *Preaching and the Dramatic Arts.* New York: The MacMillan Co., 1948.

Jordan, Ray G. *You Can Preach.* New York: Fleming H. Revell, 1951.

Kidder, Daniel P. *A Treatise on Homiletics.* New York: Carlton & Porter, 1866.

Levy, Babette May. *Preaching in the First Half Century of New England History.* New York: Russel & Russel, 1945.

Lloyd-Jones, D. Martyn. *Preachers and Preaching.* Grand Rapids: Zondervan Publishing House, 1971.

Logan, Samuel T., Jr. ed. *The Preacher and Preaching.* Phillipsburg: Presbyterian and Reformed, 1986.

Long, Thomas G. *Preaching and the Literary Forms of the Bible.* Philadelphia: Fortress Press, 1989.

Luccock, Halford E. *The Minister's Workshop.* New York: Abingdon–Cokesbury Press, 1944.

MacArthur, John F. and The Master's Seminary Faculty. *Rediscovering Expository Preaching.* Dallas: Word Publishing, 1992.

Macky, Peter W. *The Centrality of Metaphors to Biblical Thought: A Method for Interpreting the Bible.* New York: The Edwin Mellen Press, 1990.

Markquart, Edward F. *Quest for Better Preaching.* Minneapolis: Augsburg Publishing House, 1985.

McCracken, Robert J. *The Making of the Sermon.* New York: Harper & Brothers, 1956.

Otto Via, Dan. *The Parables*. Philadelphia: Fortress Press, 1967.

Packer, J. I. *A Quest For Godliness*. Wheaton: Crossway Books, 1990.

Pattison, T. Harwood. *The Making of the Sermon*. Chicago: American Baptist Publication Society, 1968.

Perkins, William. *The Art of Prophesying*. First printed in 1592; reprinted, Carlisle: The Banner of Truth Trust, 1996.

Reierson, Gary B. *The Art in Preaching: The Intersection of Theology, worship, and Preaching with the Arts*. New York: University Press of America, 1988.

Rhoades, Ezra. *Case Work in Preaching*. New York: Fleming H. Revell, 1952.

Riley, W. B. *The Preacher and His Preaching*. Wheaton: Sword of the Lord Publishers, 1948.

Robinson, Haddon W. *Biblical Preaching*. Grand Rapids: Baker Book House, 1980.

Ryken, Leland. *Worldly Saints*. Grand Rapids: Zondervan Publishing House, 1986.

Spurgeon, C. H. *Lectures to My Students*. Grand Rapids: Zondervan Publishing House, 1970.

Stanfield, Vernon L. *Homiletics*. Grand Rapids: Baker Book House, 1974.

Stott, John R. W. *Between Two Worlds: The Art of Preaching in the Twentieth Century*. Grand Rapids: William Eerdmans Publishing Company, 1982.

_____. *The Preacher's Portrait*. Grand Rapids: William B. Eerdmans, 1961.

Stowe, Everet M. *Communicating Reality Through Symbols*. Philadelphia: Westminster Press, 1966.

Vanderwell, Howard D. *Preaching that Connects*. Fullerton: R. C. Law & Co. Inc., 1989.

Watson, Thomas. *A Body of Divinity*. First published as part of *A Body of Practical Divinity*. 1692; reprinted 1890; reprinted

Carlisle: The Banner of Truth Trust, 1958; revised edition 1965.

_____. *All Things for Good.* First edition 1663; reprint, Carlisle: The Banner of Truth Trust, 1986.

_____. *Gleanings from Thomas Watson.* First edition, *Gleanings from the Past: Extracts from the writings of Thomas Watson.* London: Central Bible Truth Depot, 1915; reprinted, Morgan, Soli Deo Gloria, 1995.

_____. *Harmless as Doves.* Reprint, Geanies House, Fearn, Ross-shire: Christian Focus Publications, 1993.

_____. *Heaven Taken By Storm.* First edition, New York: E. Low, 1810; reprinted, Ligonier: Soli Deo Gloria, 1992.

_____. *Plea for the Godly and other sermons by Thomas Watson.* Pittsburgh: Soli Deo Gloria, 1993.

_____. *Religion Our True Interest.* First edition, 1682; reprinted, Edinburgh: Blue Banner Productions, 1992.

_____. *The Doctrine of Repentance.* First edition 1668; reprinted, Carlisle: The Banner of Truth Trust, 1987.

_____. *The Duty of Self Denial and Ten Other Sermons by Thomas Watson.* Its most recent edition is a collection of sermons taken from three separate works. *The Duty of Self Denial. 1675; Sermons on Several Subjects Preached by Mr. Thomas Watson (sometime minister of the gospel at St. Stephen's, Walbrook, London). 1689;* James Nichols, ed. *The Morning Exercises at Cripplegate.* London: 1844; reprinted Morgan: Soli Deo Gloria, (no date).

_____. *The Fight of Faith Crowned: The Remaining Sermons of Thomas Watson.* Morgan: Soli Deo Gloria, 1996.

_____. *The Godly Man's Picture.* First edition 1666; reprinted, Carlisle: The Banner of Truth Trust, 1992.

_____. *The Lord's Prayer.* First published as part of *A Body of Practical Divinity. 1692;* reprinted 1890; reprinted Carlisle: The Banner of Truth Trust, 1960; revised edition 1965.

_____. *The Mischief of Sin.* First edition, Thomas Parkhurst, 1671; reprinted, Soli Deo Gloria, 1994.

_____. *The Sermons of Thomas Watson.* First edition, Glasgow: 1829; reprinted Ligonier: Soli Deo Gloria, 1990.

_____. *The Ten Commandments.* First published as part of *A Body of Practical Divinity.* 1692; reprinted 1890; reprinted Carlisle: The Banner of Truth Trust, 1959, revised edition 1965.

Whitesell, Faris D. and Lloyd M. Perry. *Variety in Your Preaching.* New York: Fleming H. Revell, 1954.

_____. *Power in Expository Preaching.* New York: Fleming H. Revell, 1963.

Wiersbe, Warren W. *Preaching and Teaching with Imagination: The Quest for Biblical Ministry.* Grand Rapids: Baker Book House, 1994.

_____. *Listening to Giants.* Grand Rapids: Baker Book House, 1880.

SUBJECT AND PERSON INDEX

SCRIPTURE INDEX

Dr. Jack Hughes is pastor-teacher of Calvary Bible Church in Burbank, California where he lives with his wife Lisa and three children Leah, Nate and Mark. Jack received his Master's of Divinity degree from The Master's Seminary, Sun Valley, California and his Doctorate of Ministry degree from Westminster Theological Seminary in Escondido, California.